CAO-DAI GREAT WAY:

THE GRAND CYCLE

OF ESOTERIC TEACHING

Translated by
Anh-Tuyet Tran, Ph.D.
Cao-Dai Temple Overseas
2015

Editor: Ann Hedrick, Ph.D.
Cover designer: Bri Bruce Productions

Copyright © 2015 Cao-Dai Temple Overseas

ISBN-10: 0997136707

ISBN-13: 978-0997136708

Foreword

Caodaism is a new religion founded in Vietnam by the Supreme God early in the 20th century. One of the outstanding characteristics of this religion is its disclosure of the esoteric teaching. As evidence, the sacred scripture Đại Thừa Chơn Giáo (translated as The Grand Cycle of Esoteric Teaching) is a collection of Cao-Dai Holy Messages to delineate Cao-Dai esoteric teaching. Although the title mentions only the esoteric feature, the book also includes the exoteric section. In fact, it consists of three parts: The Exoteric Teaching, the Esoteric Science, and the Divine Investiture.

Part I, the Exoteric Teaching, discusses the meaning of the words "The Grand Cycle of Esoteric Teaching", the revelation of God's Will, the foundation and sacred goal of Cao-Dai Great Way, the essential virtues or qualities that disciples should acquire to prepare for their esoteric practice, and the method of self-perfection.

Part II, the Esoteric Science, is the core of this scripture in which Cao-Dai Supreme God unravels the secret of the Genesis, the Celestial Law, the evolution of humans and all beings, the universe as the macro-cosmos, humans as micro-cosmos carrying all the corresponding constituents of the macro-cosmos, method to manage them, the stages and levels of spiritual initiation, and the esoteric method of deliverance.

Part III, the Divine Investiture, shows proofs of sanctification of Cao-Dai esoteric disciples who achieved spiritual enlightenment, and manifested in spiritual séances from 1926 to 1950 (as this scripture was published in 1952). Through this part one can realize another outstanding characteristic of Caodaism, which is the promotion and support for male-female equality in spiritual self-perfection and deliverance.

Note: This scripture has been translated in the French language twice (1950s and 2013, in References section) and its Chinese version will also come out very soon.

Acknowledgments

This book is dedicated to Rev. Minh Lý and the author's biological father, Mr. Thanh D. Tran, for their trust in her ability to start and complete this project. She heartily thanks her Cao-Dai fellows in Trùng Dương group for their continuous support and encouragement in the publishing process. She would like to thank religious brother and sister, Drs. Hum D. Bui and Hong Bui, for their invaluable comments and discussions. She also thanks all family members, friends, co-religionists for their care and patience.

About the Author: Born in Vietnam, Anh-Tuyet Tran was raised in Buddhist traditions. Early in the 1980s she had a chance to read the sacred scripture entitled *Đại Thừa Chơn Giáo* (translated as The Grand Cycle of Esoteric Teaching).in which she found the answers for most of her questions on the origin and the meaning of life. Since then she has become a Cao-Dai follower. She immigrated to California, USA in early 1990s, where she received a Master degree from San Jose State University and a Ph.D. in Chemistry from University of California-Davis. Currently she is a Chemistry and Biochemistry Lecturer at San Jose State University, and a member of Cao Dai Temple Overseas. After the busy hours of teaching and interacting with students, she lives quietly with her mother in San Jose, CA. Hoping that everyone could access and benefit from the aforementioned Cao-Dai sacred scripture, she translated and published its English version.

Contents

P A R T I I

THE ABSTRACT PART– THE ESOTERIC SCIENCE

P A R T I I I

THE SUPPLEMENTAL PART - DIVINE NOMINATION

The

Grand Cycle

of

Esoteric Teaching

*I **radiate** the **GRAND CYCLE**
to return your True Nature,*

*And **enlighten** you with the **ESOTERIC TEACHING** to
restore your Divine Origin.*

(Cao Dai Supreme God)

Sacred Preface for the Second Edition

CAO-DAI SUPREME GOD

Your MASTER greets you all.

Poem:

The GRAND CYCLE is founded on the profoundly
 mystic DAO,
Its ESOTERIC TEACHING is the key to avoid errors
and aberration;
Enlightened people study it to augment their wisdom,
Non-awakened ones read it to diminish their ignorance;
Its literature explicitly shows *the simple DAO of man*,
Its context implicitly conceives *the esoteric traditions*.
This Scripture is imparted to the sound and righteous
people,
Who find in it the secret mechanism of ascension.

Lesson in verse:

The book of **GRAND CYCLE** is in its second edition,
To revivify **ESOTERIC TEACHING** and preach
Universal Harmony.
When the day of the Final Judgment comes,
The world will know the name of **CAO-DAI**.
This Scripture is open to everybody;
But only the enlightened seek its implicit Esoteric Teaching,
Which is the method of forging Buddha and Immortals,
And also the way leading to self-deliverance and eternal life.

PREFACE

A PRAISE

According to the Ancient Teachings, only the Supreme Being is absolute. Except for this Spiritual Unity, everything in the Universe is under Relativity. From the infinite beings such as Heaven and Earth, to the infinitesimal creatures such as insects and microbes, none can escape from the Yin-Yang dimorphism. Neither do human beings and other species. Thus, Relativity or Dualism is the universal law, especially in this Visible World.

CAO-DAI GREAT WAY FOR THE THIRD UNIVERSAL SALVATION, revealed to the visible world, is also bound to the law of Dualism by exposing the two formats: CAO DAII GREAT WAY and CAO DAI RELIGION. These two formats are the "**TWO WINGS**" of God-Way to guide humans from the "IGNORANT and GRIEVOUS WORLD" toward the "INFINITE and IMMUTABLE SOJOURN" so as to unite with the SUPREME MASTER of the Universe.

CAO-DAI GREAT WAY, at present, is given privilege to CHIẾU MINH disciples. It specializes in the Esotericism or the Mystic Science of Dematerialization.

CAO DAI RELIGION excels in the universal salvation. At this being time, it comprises Cao Dai Churches and 'TIÊN THIÊN' Sect.

Being 'the Two Wings of God-Way', Cao Dai Esotericism and Cao Dai Exotericism should unite in action, support and complement each other to ensure the perpetuity of the Salvation Ark as well as the fecundity of CAO DAI TREE. The reason for this collaboration is as simple as follows.

Without the ESOTERICISM, the EXOTERICISM cannot lead mankind to the ultimate goal of SELF-PERFECTION. Then, on which foundation would Cao Dai Doctrine be based, for its worldwide propagation in the future?

On the other hand, without the EXOTERICISM, how can the ESOTERICISM recruit selected candidates to serve as vehicles for the transmission of its "MYSTIC TRADITIONS"?

The process of self-perfection is a "STEEPLY UPHILL", comprising two sections along which the two aforementioned formats of CAO DAI WAY play essential roles. The EXOTERICISM participates in the first half, from bottom to midway, and the ESOTERICISM stages in the second half, from midway to top.

These two parts must complement each other for a person to achieve his/her self-perfection from start to end.

In the Ancient Religions, the Esotericism chronologically preceded the Exotericism. In our time, the Exotericism has proceeded quite ahead, such that the Esotericism should be initiated to guide sound and righteous disciples to self-perfection. That is why the Scripture of the GRAND CYCLE of ESOTERIC TEACHING has come in due time.

Indeed, publication of the GRAND CYCLE of ESOTERIC TEACHING is a true bliss and great blessing for mankind. It is so, because although many books and scripts on metaphysics or immortality exist, they are written in cabalistic languages with very hermetic styles. As a result, only several practitioners could penetrate the truth while innumerable others get lost.

The Universe is currently in the Last Era of Cosmic Revolution. "The Universal Renovation" is about to start, transferring mankind to the Supremely Virtuous Age. With Infinite Mercy, GOD Himself commands the Congress of Three Ancient Religions to disclose the GRAND CYCLE of ESOTERIC TEACHING so as to save the currently agonized and impious mankind. The three objectives of this scripture are:

1) To unveil all obscurity that hinders humans from recognizing God-Way, so that they can eagerly step in with faith or certainty.

2) To wake up predestined people and hasten them on the path of Deliverance.

3) To expose to entire mankind the DOCTRINE of CAO DAI GREAT WAY for the THIRD UNIVERSAL SALVATION, and clearly demonstrate that "the mechanism of deliverance is for everyone, with no discrimination on social class, sect, belief, or race".

Therefore, although the GRAND CYCLE of ESOTERIC TEACHING found its nest in TRƯỚC TIẾT TÀNG THƠ of CHIÉU

MINH, it is truly for all Cao Dai Churches, and probably for all social classes, as Truth is ONE.

Found in this precious Teaching are some sections on Humanism. Indeed, they are implicit revelations: Humans should maintain IMPARTIALITY AND TOLERANCE throughout the process toward self-perfection, because the immutable DAO is not established on ABSOLUTISM but instead, it manifests through the MIDDLE WAY.

EXOTERIC SCHOOL should rely on the ESOTERICISM to revive "the blissful and peaceful time under the legendary patriarch of kings Yao and Yu the Great"[1]. In reverse, ESOTERIC SCHOOL should depend on the EXOTERICISM to accomplish the UNIVERSAL SALVATION.

With that in mind, may opportune people, after reading the GRAND CYCLE of ESOTERIC TEACHING, hasten on the abrupt path of ascension, and may all CAO DAI Branches heartily join CHIÊU MINH branch in the effort to revamp the organization so as to preach the God-Way worldwide.

TRẦN-VĂN-QUÉ

Cao Dai Brother of TRƯỚC LÝ MINH ĐÀI
Lauding this Scripture with all his heart
Saigon, November 19th, 1936

---

[1] King NGHIÊU, or YAO (尧), 2356 – 2255 BC, was a legendary Chinese ruler. King THUẤN, or YU THE GREAT (大禹), 2200 - 2100 BC, was a legendary ruler in ancient China, famed for his introduction of flood control, inaugurating dynastic rule in China by founding the Xia Dynasty, and for his upright moral character.

A PLEGDE

In addition to natural calamities, humans throughout the world dread imminent wars. Are they distressed by such a miserable life, which displays all its atrocities and horrors day after day?

Indeed, more and more people are disenchanted. But can they simply quit life by committing suicide with a gun, a rope, or a poison? Brothers! Keep in mind that no one can escape from the Law of Expiation!

There is only one method to get away, an unfailing and straightforward method as one plus one is equal to two. It is nothing else than the single term: "SELF-CULTIVATION".

Let us tell you about ourselves!

Some of us struggled in pursuing vain honors, others were absorbed in lucrative business; some were swamped in the four dungeons,[2] others slackened in their moods and desires.[3] Yet, some of us readily pulled out their swords and fought for justice, others showed their fervor in salvaging the world.

But lately we have renounced all enjoyments of worldly life. Day and night, we diligently focus our efforts on self-purification and self-enlightenment.

Are we foolish? Are we idiots?

No ... We are simply disenchanted of life, like millions of other people in the world! But we are blessed being able to access the perfect and supreme ESOTERIC TEACHING. We are overjoyed because day after day, we see more clearly the word "DELIVERANCE" at the end of our Path. It is so certain, with no doubts or afterthoughts.

Receiving this invaluable treasure of the universe, we heartily express our gratefulness to Divine Beings. And we also want to overly convey our joy to everyone in the Orient, so that the entire mankind could share with us this celestial manna. Unfortunately, the time for the

---

[2] The four dungeons are beauty, riches, alcoholic imbibing, and vanity.
[3] The moods and desires consist of the seven emotions and six passions.

Universal Salvation has not come yet. Thus, we had to hide this gratification.

All of a sudden, in the Inauguration of Thánh Đức Temple in Cần-Thơ last year, GOD announced the parallel verses as follows:

"*I **RADIATE** the **GRAND CYCLE** to return your initial nature,*

*And **ENLIGHTEN** you with **ESOTERIC TEACHING** to restore your divine origin.*"

We were so hopeful because the parallel verses revealed the four words "GRAND CYCLE of ESOTERIC TEACHING", as GOD promised to impart it. Then unexpectedly, HE approved our sincere wish. Late in the spring, GOD once again suddenly announced as follows: Starting from Mid-Autumn Full Moon (the 15th day of the 8th month) of Bính Tý year (1936), the GRAND CYCLE of ESOTERIC TEACHING would be released to the world. Ahah! Our joy was inexpressible! We immediately proceeded the collection, edition and publication of the Holy Scripture.

Of course, everyone is *free to decide* whether to read it or not, whether to follow its teaching or not. In our part, because we have in possession a map in which the Path to Deliverance is traced clearly and precisely, we never want to hoard just for ourselves the favor that GOD intends for everyone. Thus, we are so honored to give out, at no cost or regulation, this truly and invaluable "**COMPASS**" to all people.

We urge you to sincerely make an effort to study, research, and contemplate on the Holy Messages delivered in this precious scripture to discover the implicit Teaching.

Should such humble wish be granted, we would gladly disseminate this Teaching to everyone in the country.

Sincerely,

Disciples of Chiếu-Minh
Autumn of Bính Tý year (1936)

Part I
THE COMMON PART
THE EXOTERIC TEACHING

The 4th day of the 9th month of Bính Tý year (1936).

THE SACRED PREFACE

The Great Immortal at Động-Đình Lake
(LI TAIPEI)
Poem:

Touched by miseries of this world,

Divine Beings manifest many times to save it.

Yet humans are still deeply wallowing in reveries,

The GREAT IMMORTAL descends to teach them Self-Deliverance.

Humble Devout. I greet you all. Receiving Divine Order, I manifest in this séance to expose some saintly words, so as to wake humans up and lead them toward the quest for their Original Nature. Also I congratulate the disclosure of the GRAND CYCLE of ESOTERIC TEACHING to promulgate the mystic Method of Deliverance, so that righteous people can break up the reincarnation cycle and return to their Celestial Origin.

Poem:

GOD preaches the Saintly Doctrine in Vietnam;

HE reveals the mystic science to wake human spirits,

HE shows them the method to return to their spiritual nature,

And teaches them the doctrine to cultivate their mind.

Lesson in verse:

The Spirit of Truth is elucidated in this late Era of Destruction,

To warn the incarnate of the upcoming Judgment;

It preaches the Universal Fraternity,

So that all beings recognize their same GOD THE FATHER.

CAODAISM promulgates the new doctrine,

The true method of self-deliverance to liberate mankind;

It revives this spirit throughout the world,

So that everyone receives the great favor of CAO-DAI,

Near the end of the Cosmic Cycle, GOD THE SON reveals Himself,

To lead humans back to their original nature;

HE points out their Saintly Origin,

Waking them from illusion, focusing them on self-attainment.

The fatal vicissitudes are threatening,

But the profane seems not recognize it!

Then one day the blaze breaks out,

The impious could hardly escape.

The upcoming torment is so dreadful,

In which all beings will be destroyed;

But humans do not foresee this catastrophe,

Which exactly follows the Periodic Cycle of the Universe!

GOD and Buddha anticipate this perilous danger,

They descend into the world to save all wretched souls;

They preach the doctrine of Universal Fraternity,

Converging the Three Ancient Religions to restore the worldly peace.

They also trace the Great Way

To lead humans back to their divine origin;

As the Three Ancient Doctrines were swayed after millennia of preaching,

CAO-DAI Great Way is exposed to restore their original Spirit.

It reveals the infinity,

Since the Esotericism is profoundly mystic.

Successful practitioners will become immortal,

And will leisurely enjoy the Eternal Facility in the Divine Realm.

Profane! The Divine Ark is waiting,

To pick up the sound and righteous spirits;

Repent your sins and expiate your karma,

Valiantly persevere in esoteric exercises to return to your Original Nature.

Poem:

Beyond these perishable worlds extends the Divine Realm,

Where reside the absolutely pure and tranquil beings;

In the immutable Divine Light,

They enjoy the Eternal Facility.

At the end of the Inferior Era, The Great Way is revitalized to bring righteous people back to their divine origin. From the debut of the Primitive Period till the incarnation of the Messiahs, the Esotericism was preached throughout the world to wake and save humans from the worldly illusions, so that they live in accord with the Original Nature, seek the method of Deliverance and the Path of Salvation. Thus, the Three Ancient Doctrines forged innumerable elects at the culmination of the propagation.

After millennia of Evangelization, the Spirit of Truth has no longer been invigorated in these Ancient Doctrines, and their spiritual tradition was interrupted. Disciples are outnumbered, but few or none become Buddha or Immortals. It is because the Esotericism is profoundly mystic. Even Divine Beings dare not unduly reveal it, and only transmit it orally. Humans tried to describe and save it in "Manuals for achieving the Immortality. But the languages used in these scripts were undecipherable and absolutely hermetic. Each Master added his own ideas, expressed them with myriad abstract words, to confuse even the most clairvoyant researchers in later times.

I ascend.

The 30th day of the 7th month of Bính Tý year (1936).

PRELUDE

GIÁC MINH KIM TIÊN

Greeting all devotees of both sexes.

Listen with peace in mind and quietude in the séance:

Poem:

> Wake up and receive esoteric teaching to liberate yourself,
>
> Research to elucidate it thoroughly;
>
> Shine up your Spark of Divine Light to penetrate the Mechanism of Creation,
>
> Study the Holy Messages transmitted by Buddha and Immortals.

At this time, JADE EMPEROR SUPREME GOD ordains the overture of the GRAND CYCLE of ESOTERIC TEACHING. With all your heart and mind, pray GOD to bless all beings so that everyone can be liberated from this world of suffering and ignorance. Check your protocol and rites. I would like to announce the coming of the GREAT ETERNAL INSTRUCTOR, and the FOUNDING MASTERS of the THREE ANCIENT RELIGIONS, to approve the GRAND CYCLE of ESOTERIC TEACHING.

Upon the manifestation of Divine Beings, you should venerate with your deepest sincerity. Execute my commands. I leave the séance.

THỈ TỔ ĐẠI TÔN SƯ
THE GREAT ETERNAL INSTRUCTOR HỒNG-QUÂN

From the Primordial Chaos, the pure and the impure separate,

The wise learn this secret to attain spiritual enlightenment.

I purify the ethereal body until it illuminates,

And transmit this Esoteric Tradition so that you can forge yourself.

Your TEACHER. I greet and bless you all.

This time being, with Love and Mercy, I drag my feet to this séance to expose the source of Wisdom to you.

Poem:

The **GREAT WAY** liberates humans from this ocean of suffering,

With the Aura of Light they will ascend to the spiritual realm,

And with the immaculate spirit they return to the Origin;

Practice **ESOTERIC TEACHING** to extract the pure from the impure.

I congratulate all humans on receiving this Sacred Torch to illumine the entire world in this era of darkness. I am so glad, so blissful, so honored for you, children! I bless each of you so that you strive to cultivate and purify your mind, and to perform your work of piety and fraternity.

YOUR TEACHER ascends.

TAM THANH THƯỢNG GIÁO
THE SUPERIOR DOCTRINES OF THE THREE PURITIES

000
THÁI THƯỢNG ĐẠO TỔ
THE SUPREME MASTER OF DAO

Poem:

The Imponderable Supreme is the infinite Unity,

It centers the pure and centrifuges the impure.

Esoteric method forges humans into Immortals and Buddha,

It teaches them the secret of dematerialization.

I congratulate the disciples and all beings. I am glad to see the blissful day for the entire mankind. With Infinite Mercy, SUPREME GOD ordained the overture of the GRAND CYCLE of ESOTERIC TEACHING to bring the predestined people back to their divine origin.

Poem:

The GRAND CYCLE of ESOTERIC TEACHING manifests the third time,

To lead humans to the Celestial Realm;

Freed from ignorance and darkness, they enjoy the enchantment,

And prepare for the Final Judgment.[4]

I bless the disciples and congratulate all beings. I ascend.

---

[4] Original Vietnamese term 'Hội Long Hoa' literally means the Contest of Flowery Dragons.

NGUƠN THỈ THIÊN TÔN,[5]
MINISTER OF GOD

Poem:

In order for the Original Spirit to emanate an Aura of Light,

First, purify it to return to the PURITIES symbolized by QIAN (☰) cycle,

In the Yellow River chart,[6] QIAN (☰) is the Master,

It is known as DAO that few people comprehend.

Your TEACHER. I greet all disciples.

Long Poem:

Seated at my post, I look out on the court,

Suddenly comes a Divine Order.

Hurrying up I descend in this séance,

To approve the ESOTERIC TEACHING for its Universal Salvation.

The GRAND CYCLE that GOD gracefully blesses,

Transforms human nature and leads them onto the radiant path.

Deities, Saints, Immortals, and Buddha frown

On the inexorable Karma of this miserable mankind.

Yet incarnates still wallow in worldly lives,

And ignorantly wander in the pitfalls leading to the dark paths.

Profanes! Why are you so careless and unconscientious

In generating such suffering and calamities?

---

[5] Original Vietnamese term 'NGUƠN-THỈ' literally means the FIRST CAUSE.

[6] the Pre-Genesis Cosmic Plan

Of the three times I manifest in this world, (*I'm smiling…*).

This time the GRAND CYCLE of ESOTERIC TEACHING enlightens mankind.

Dignified men! Find your way back to the Origin,

End up all Karmic links to elevate toward the Jade Palace;

Conserve and sublime your Quintessence,

Unite it with Energy and Spirit to recover the Original Nature.

Practice esoteric method to create the Sacred Body,

To forge yourself into Immortals.

Once detoxifying from worldly passions,

You escalate effortlessly the Celestial Hierarchy.

Poor profanes! Hurry up to perfect yourself!!!

Penetrate the Secret of Creation by persevering in esoteric exercises.

Do not pointlessly discuss about the ranking of this teaching.

Without practicing its method, you tumble again in the corporal world!!!

Poem:

Vices such as talkativeness should be banned,

And worldly vanities should not be cherished.

Appreciating vain honors and wealth means anchoring in the Hell.

Concentrating in the diligent quest for Wisdom leads to enlightenment.

I bless all disciples. I ascend.

LINH BỬU THIÊN TÔN,[7]
MINISTER OF GOD

Poem:

The Saint-Esprit radiates in the union of Divine Beings,

To impart the precious and miraculous Esotericism;

When the Cosmic Revolution returns to its debut,

The Yin and Yang reunite into the Primordial Origin.

Humble Devout. I greet all disciples. At this time being, upon receiving GOD'S Order, I hastily descend in the séance to approve the Sacred Preface of this publication.

Poem:

The Infinite Unity is the Creator of the Universe,

It is the imponderable and immutable DAO,

It reveals the ESOTERICISM to illumine mankind,

To teach them the method of enlightenment.

(I'm smiling, smiling ...) As the Inferior Era of Annihilation is ending, and as the Cosmic Revolution is about to come back to its debut, the GREAT WAY is revivified and the ESOTERICISM of DEMATERIALIZATION is revealed. But the corporal world is a free-for-all bedlam where pearl is silted with sand, gold is mingled with brass, good and evil rise side-by-side, mortals and saints are undistinguishable. Buddha and Immortals manifest along with evils and demons. God saves all beings while Satan attempts to capture them. It is the period of competition; Heaven selects the pious and the Hell robs the impious.

Nowadays, with Infinite Love, GOD imparts THE GRAND CYCLE OF ESOTERIC TEACHING, in which the truth and untruth are clearly exposed, to help humans distinguish the radiant from the

---

[7] Original Vietnamese term 'LINH-BỬU' literally means the DIVINE TREASURE.

dark paths so as to avoid the ultimate catastrophe of this world. This Scripture is the ringing bell and the beating drum to awake and gather all beings. It is the brilliant torch that lights up the entire Universe day and night like the Sun and Moon.

Ascension.

The 15th day of the 8th month of Bính Tý year (1936)

THE FOUNDERS OF THE THREE ANCIENT RELIGIONS
000

KHỔNG PHU TỬ
CONFUCIUS

Poem:

CONFUCIUS teaches the Man-Way,

A method of self-attainment to liberate from this world;

HE is enjoying the Eternal Facility in the Purple Cave.

His last incarnation was in Châu Empire, under the Reign of Linh-Vương.

Humble Devout. I exempt everyone from ceremonials, and greet all disciples.

I am very glad to see the Revivification of DAO, during which Buddha and Immortals manifest and impart Holy Teachings. This is a blessing for all beings. I urge you all to persevere in esoteric exercises to discover the marvelous Secret of Genesis and the mystic Nature of the Universe. With such enlightenment, you will be able to revive and save all peoples and profanes from their dark paths.

Poem:

I am always aspiring towards Universal Fraternity,

In which the spiritual union is developed,

When all people practice God-Way,

Together they establish the Neo-Humanism.

Long Poem:

Sitting alone in front of the Peach Cave,

I anxiously foresee the upcoming Cosmic Revolution.

With sad lamentations and deep sighs, I watch this world

Filled with people passionate in beauty, wealth, glory, and vanity!

Suddenly, an Order comes from the THREE PURITIES,

Announcing that "TÀNG THƠ TRƯỚC TIẾT"[8] complete the edition,

And inviting me to radiate the Divine Emission,

To approve and elucidate this Esoteric Teaching.

I hastily descend,

Riding on clouds to come to this séance.

Having mercy for this world, I cannot turn my back to its cruel destiny,

So, I deliver this Esoteric Teaching,

With the hope that it would be useful

In waking humans to return to their origin.

Recall the preaching of Confucianism in the past,

Which opened an era of peace with good customs and traditions.

Following the natural laws of the Providence,

This Humanism established moral relationships and social

---

[8] The ARCHIVES and COPYRIGHT of CHIEU-MINH

duties,

So as to save people from errors and ordeals,

And liberate them from the world of fatal calamities.

Depending on circumstances from past till present,

It crystallizes the spiritual and temporal values around the National Spirit.

It demonstrates the model of *Impartiality and Harmony,*

And shows the method to attain enlightenment and deliverance.

Unfortunately, humans are so greedy,

They prefer illusions and cherish incredible vanities.

In such moral corruption Confucianism falls in ruin,

I bitterly regret for the disintegration of such a beautiful edifice.

Confucianism is human wisdom in practical life,

Where the Three Duties and the Five Virtues form the basic rules.

It teaches Impartiality and Harmony,

So deeply that no one has touched its enigma.

Its Forest of Wisdom and Ocean of Virtues[9] are also immense,

As it is one of the Three Ancient Doctrines, originating from the same root.

Mankind departs farther and farther from Wisdom,

Altruism diminishes while egoism prevails.

The world cynically spreads its atrocities and brutalities,

As humans are deprived of love and abandon justice.

Such impiety upsets Divine Beings and Devil Spirits,

---

[9]'the Forest of Sages and the Ocean of Saints' implicitly means all Confucian Scriptures and Teachings.

Leading to further anomalies in the universe.

Troubles overflow everywhere in the world,

Celestial calamities and earthly scourges do not spare anyone.

Up in the Heaven, God holds the Divine Balance,

To reward the pious and punish the immoral.

Deeply touched by the sadness and grief of this world,

Deities, Saints, Immortals, and Buddha silently sigh.

With Infinite Mercy, GOD the SON

Abandons His Throne and once again carries His Cross.

HE manifests in this world to found Caodaism,

And imparts the Esotericism to regenerate the Universe.

His Ark of Love salvages the predestined,

As well as those who drown in the ocean of Karma.

HE revivifies CAO-DAI GREAT WAY,

To restore peace in this world for the third time.

In the past, the Three Doctrines were in three separate Temples,

Now they are under the same roof of CAO-DAI,

To preach the Universal Fraternity,

And assure the Hồng-Lạc[10] a glorious bloom.

It restores the era of Five Emperors and Three Messiahs,

Bringing peace, prosperity, and happiness to all Peoples.

No one really penetrates the Secret of Genesis,

Yet they frequently discuss and criticize it.

Caodaism is well organized in cycles and levels,

Along with different classes to facilitate human access.

GOD-WAY is infinite, immutable, and eternal,

---

[10] 'Hồng-Lạc' is the Vietnamese Race.

Any imbalance, leap or gap, is normally excluded.

Poem:

Absolute Infinity is the method of liberation.

Day and night forge your Aura of Light;

Absolute Emptiness is the mechanism of self-dematerialization,

Maintain peace and serenity in mind to sublime your divine light.

Verse:

You should sincerely revere CAO-DAI Immortal,

I return to the West Kingdom, the home of Saints.

Ascension.

LÝ LÃO TỬ
LAO-TZU

Poem:

With prune and peach buds symbolizing dragon and unicorn,[11]

LAO-TZU succeeded in creating the double body[12].

Sitting in the Blue Cave, HE concentrates in meditation.

He incarnated in the Thượng Empire under the name of Võ Đinh Quân.

Humble Devout. I greet all disciples.

---

[11] dragon and unicorn symbolize for fire and water elements

[12] spiritual body

000

This Holy Scripture implicitly contains a profound Esotericism,

And is commanded by God Himself!

The GRAND CYCLE OF ESOTERIC TEACHING reveals the God-Way,

To liberate mankind from the ocean of Karma.

Long Poem:

Sitting in the Blue Cave, I prepare the magic pill,

And build the Eight-Trigram furnace[13] to harmonize the Yin-Yang.

This miraculous remedy is for gaining immortality,

Which can be formed only with a lot of effort and hard work.

Suddenly I look out of the Cave,

And receive the Order to approve the publication of this Scripture.

Hastily I fly with the wind to come to this séance,

To elucidate the Esotericism so as to wake humans,

To help them understand in depth this teaching,

So as not to consider it a superstition.

In the past, Taoism founded on a solid background,

But its inaccessible criteria discouraged a lot of seekers.

The Secret of Genesis cannot be exposed at first view,

Only persistent researchers could grasp it.

Very rare devotees succeeded in penetrating this secret,

Due to the innumerable latches that protect it.

---

[13]alluding to the Pre-Genesis Cosmic Plan

Hidden in the Eight-Trigram plan[14]

Is the Omniscient Key to the Celestial Door.

This imminent Wisdom is impregnable,

Like a precious pearl on the ocean floor.

Esoteric disciples should have an unshakeable faith,

Their serene mind is the base for their interior Temple.

The spiritual tradition is profoundly mystic,

It teaches the method to evade from the ocean of Karma.

To taste the sweetness of the DAO of Saints,

Cultivate body and mind to clear up passive karma.

Persevere until you can penetrate the origin,

Look inward to achieve peace of mind.

Principles of DAO were found in ancient books,

But now they are adulterated and no longer conserved.

As vicissitudes happen so frequently in this world,

The human body touches its last stages of degradation.

No matter how good the ancient remedy is,

It cannot cure the contemporary malady!

As this peril is due to climate changes,

Newly expressed remedy should be made.

Certainly these pills can cure current problems,

Devotees learn this lesson to choose appropriate method.

Poem:

Strictly observe the esoteric method to initiate your nine spiritual senses,

Persistently maintain a calm and pure mind to shine up your

---

[14] the Pre-Genesis Cosmic Plan

original nature,

Harmoniously unite energy and spirit by following the rhyme of your breath,

Constantly turn your interior Cosmic Wheel to fraternize dragon and tiger.[15]

I am now departing you, disciples. I leave.

Ascension.

SĨ ĐẠT TA
SIDDHARTA

Poem:

SIDDHARTA has deep pity for this world of reincarnation;

After penetrating DAO to guide mankind back to the Divine Origin,

HE decided to break up the devilish cycle of the four sufferings,

And incarnated under the reign of Chiêu-Vương to found Buddhism.

Humble Devout of Mercy. I greet all disciples.

Poem:

The GRAND CYCLE of ESOTERIC TEACHING is condensed in this book,

Seekers should make effort to discover in it the principles of DAO.

This Holy Scripture is imparted to liberate humans from sufferings,

---

[15] the union of dragon and tiger means the union of fire (the LI trigram) and water (the K'AN trigram).

Predestined people should hurry to rally it.

000

Rally to be secure in the coming torment,

Grip the Esotericism to protect you from being lost.

Take Divine Order to practice the true DAO,

Do not tie yourself to the worldly links.

000

Buddhism teaches the only word "EMPTINESS",

The infinite and immutable Nirvana is the Sojourn of Immortals,

Where pure spirits leisurely enjoy the Eternal Facility,

As regaining spiritual origin means penetrating DAO.

Disciples! Persevere in esoteric exercises. I bless you all. I leave.

Ascension.

The 15th day of the 8th month of Bính Tý year (1936)

COMMENCEMENT OF CAODAISM – REVIVIFICATION OF THE GREAT WAY

Poem:

CAO-DAI manifests in this world to save the predestined,

His Jade Palace welcomes the disincarnated.

His teaching transforms the ignorant to the wise,

Who are able to purify and enlighten their minds.

Your MASTER. I greet all children.

Disciples of both sexes! Listen in quietude.

Poem:

This Bible is transmitted to clear up the Karma of this world,

It implicitly conveys the Saintly Doctrine;

It contains the most complete Esotericism of Deliverance,

In which the opportune can find the words of Truth.

Lesson in verse:

In this world of dust, people frantically compete with each other;

They jostle, squabble, and compete,

So as to ignorantly dash into the abyss of depravity.

Alas! They are like miserable fireflies, attracted to the lamp light!

People in this world hardly have a chance,

As it takes three lifetimes with much blessing to contact Saints and Buddha.

Catching this unprecedented period of revivifying DAO

Is an immeasurable bliss for mankind!

Look up in the annals of past and present times,

To learn about Sages and heroes.

To acquire the Esotericism of Deliverance,

They persisted day and night in researching, trying, and praying.

They overcame mountains of obstacles,

Hard work and austere asceticism further sharpened their will.

They observed strict codes of the ancient doctrines,

And were indifferent to beauty, wealth, alcoholic drinking, and honor.

They purified their bodies and souls by observing
vegetarianism,

And took control of their desires under the scraped Buddhist
gown.

Ascetics should pretend idiot and dumb,

Pretend blind and deaf while seeking the miraculous DAO.

Preserve dignity by fulfilling secular duties,

Overcome challenges with unshakeable faith and strong will.

Ward off all legions of demon and crowds of evil,

Shun away the seven emotions and six passions.

Put out the malignant fire of desire in your heart,

Do not surrender to the exigencies of the inferior self.

Incarnated in a heavy and treacherous body,

The soul has to bear and fight all obstacles.

Who dare to say he never commits errors or makes mistakes,

As the body likes to satisfy its demands!

Ban sexual instincts and sensual love,

Renounce even the most benign desires.

Maintain tranquility and harmony in the mind,

Unify the Three Treasures and the Five Primordial
Elements.

Grasping the deep sense of DAO and its foretaste,

Why do you still hesitate and what else do you wait for?

Do not neglect the integrity of conscience,

As flickering faith is good bait for devils.

Guard up the eyes, ears, nose, mouth, and thoughts,

Keep them always under control.

Limited in a heavy body,

It is not easy to go a long way.

Even galloping on a horseback,

Never can you reach the destination throughout your lifetime!!!

Only when you listen piously to ME,

I will teach you the esoteric method.

I will forge you into Buddha and Immortals,

By turning the mystic wheel to activate the mechanism of DAO.

You will be able to leave your physical body,

To travel the universe and penetrate the Divine Realm.

Assimilating your soul with the ethereal void,

You comprehend all Heaven and Earth just in a wink.

You can freely wander throughout the universe,

Leaving your body means breaking all fetters and yokes.

DAO of Immortals means preserving "**EMPTINESS**" of mind,

To break up all cages or traps of this sentient world.

Stop embracing the worldly attractions,

Keep your mind pure and quiet to unite with Divine Beings.

Poem:

Immortals and Buddha use the same method,

To enlighten and dissipate the foggy veil of their mind.

Mankind! Do not content to bury your divine light,

Without trying to evade from the cage of your body.

***

Blessing is imparted in Mid-Autumn,

While the full moon witnesses the worldly calamities.

Who knows the Autumn comes and leaves?

Autumn comes to recruit the devotees!!

I bless you all. I ascend.

The 24th day of the 9th month of Bính Tý year (1936)

MEANING OF THE FOUR WORDS
"ĐẠI THỪA CHƠN GIÁO"
(i.e., the "GRAND CYCLE of ESOTERIC TEACHING")

LÝ THÁI BẠCH ĐẠI TIÊN TRƯỞNG
GREAT SENIOR IMMORTAL LI TAI-PEI

Humble Devout greets all disciples of both sexes.

The four words ĐẠI THỪA CHƠN GIÁO (i.e., the GRAND CYCLE of ESOTERIC TEACHING) imply a profoundly mystic meaning.

The word **ĐẠI (GRAND)** means Infinite. Nothing is larger than Infinity. It includes the entire universe; it is supreme and invisible, yet nothing can escape from it.

Also, this word conveys the esoteric meaning as follows:

The word **ĐẠI (大)**[16] is the combination of the words MAN (人) and ONE (一). The word MAN means human; the two strokes in this word symbolize the Yin-Yang union, which is the origin of the Universal Genesis.

Moreover, the word MAN signifies human. If a man practices spiritual exercises and succeeds in conquering the Secret Mechanism of Creation, he attains ONENESS.[17] As the word MAN

---

[16] written in demoted scripts using Sino characters
[17] The Saintly Trinity One and Indivisible

combines with the word ONE (MAN plus ONE is equal to GRAND) (大), he becomes everlasting and immortal.

What is the meaning of ATTAINING ONENESS?

It means identifying oneself with ONENESS. This integral Self is the unique and miraculous method that Immortals and Buddha only transmit from heart to heart, from mouth to ears to initiate the dematerialization and elevate to the Divine Realm. There is a saying: the Heaven is SERENE when attaining Oneness; the Earth is FIRM when attaining Oneness; the Man is PERFECT and EVERLASTING when attaining Oneness.

The word **THỪA (CYCLE)** designates Levels. The high grade is infinitely elevated while the low grade is infinitely sunken to the bottom. It has no limit, and encompasses the entire universe. From the tiny grain of sand to the Great Mountain, none is beyond it. GOD MASTER imparts this Sacred Doctrine at the appropriate level of human evolution. Clairvoyant or ignorant, everyone can understand and practice it.

The word **CHƠN (ESOTERIC)** refers to the Truth, i.e., Wisdom of God. Everybody in the universe has to conform to it. Those who obey it enjoy the comfort and peace; those who are against it live in trouble and ignorance.

Also, it carries another meaning as follows: CHƠN signifies **True**. It means transmitting the Spirit of Truth in a straightforward and transparent manner, without any mystic or hermetic shade that can make the Doctrine inaccessible to profane humans and lead to its decadence.

The word **GIÁO (TEACHING)** means instructing humans about their Celestial Origin, so that they can restore their Divine Nature. The word GIÁO refers to teaching humans on how to dissipate bad karma, which is the result of serious sins committed in previous lives. Thank to this TEACHING, humans can unceasingly escalate the ladder of moral, ethical, and spiritual evolution from life to life without respite.

In summary, the four words ĐẠI THỪA CHƠN GIÁO mean:

ĐẠI THỪA or the GRAND CYCLE is the cultivation method much superior to those of the Small Cycle. It is for those who are disenchanted with this world, and who look for the method of deliverance or spiritual ascension. Such method of the Grand Cycle belongs to the profoundly mystic method of heart, the esoteric vestiges that Saints transmitted orally or intuitively to those who aspire toward the complete deliverance or immortality.

CHƠN GIÁO or the ESOTERIC TEACHING is the metaphysics that explains and reveals the imponderable DAO; it exposes the Natural Principles that humans should follow so as not to be against the Celestial Codes, nor err into the dark and sinful paths. Emergence of this Esotericism is justified by the decadence of the Three Ancient Doctrines. Nowadays, the Great DAO should be revivified to teach humans the true and mystic mechanism of deliverance, without which they can never evade from this world of calamities and suffering, nor break up the Karmic cycle to leave the ocean of fatal vicissitudes.

These aforementioned explanations delineate the meanings of the four words: ĐẠI THỪA CHƠN GIÁO, i.e., the GRAND CYCLE of ESOTERIC TEACHING.

The Humble Devout ascends.

The 25th day of the 9th month of Bính Tý year (1936)

REVELATION OF GOD'S WILL

CAO-DAI FOUNDER

Poem:

The SUPREME DAO has rooted in your deep sincerity,

It opens up the Nirvana to the pious,

It teaches the Truth and transmits the esoteric method.

Practice it with all your heart.

Your MASTER. I greet and exempt you from ceremonials.

Verse:

In the last term of the Universal Cycle, Buddha and Immortals manifest to impart DAO everywhere throughout the world.

At the end of the Inferior Era when the Cosmic Revolution returns to its debut, annihilation and calamities are unavoidable.

Such tribulation is predestined. Alas! This world is so ignorant! People are not awakened!

Morals are corrupt, customs and traditions that constitute the saintly affections are neglected.

Why do humans not make any effort in seeking the celestial mechanism through which they can return to the original nature?

Why do they keep enduring the endless cycle of reincarnation? I am profoundly annoyed in perceiving such disaster.

Thus, in front of the Tribunal of the Three Doctrines, I solemnly swore to impart the miraculous DAO to salvage entire mankind.

Should you not self-correct, nor leave the dark paths and return to the radiant one, the DAO would fail and I swear not to get back to my Throne!

I teach you till losing my voice, but you do not pay attention, nor open your mind to receive the advices from the MERCIFUL FATHER!

I hold the eternal sovereignty to straighten all misshaped;

yet, due to Love and Piety, I humble myself to save you.

Children! You are like a brood of chicken anxiously chirping in the absence of mother hen,

Innumerable horrors and catastrophes occur in this world, as expiation displays in variant forms.

Vicissitudes expose under your eyes but you do not awake; the saintly doctrine is imparted but you receive it with indifference; indeed, your impiety deserves severe punishment!

It is because I love you, I have to wipe my tears and swallow thousands of prickly disappointments; to initiate the universal salvation, I have to humble Myself and endure all atrocities of this world.

As the Grand Amnesty forgives your anterior sins, you should thoroughly purify your soul and apply the saintly remedy to uproot the evils of your flesh and bones.

Listen, children! Wake up and cultivate your mind! Practice the DAO to forge your souls, so that I can deliver you from this material world and bring you back to the Nirvana.

Serenity in mind progresses the spirit; with such noble natures you can discover the Celestial Mechanism.

Why are you still dazed, vague, and foolish?

My Saintly Words are absolutely honest and universal. But you do not put them into practice; instead, you denature them.

Having pity on you, I have to be merciful and hold back My Omnipotence; otherwise, nothing can prevent ME from punishing you.

Why were you so ungrateful in handing ME over to Satan and letting ME endure such bloody abuse?

Yet, driven by the Universal Mercy, I brave again in this world to found the Supreme Doctrine.

I am profoundly grieved in perceiving that the intellectual tend to exploit and oppress the virtuous and the weak.

If so, this world must be degraded; humans are miring in the materialism, and imprisoned in the devilish dungeons of beauty, wealth, vanity, and binge drinking.

Those who repent should self-correct so as to hastily return to the divine origin and reunite with GOD, which are the main goal of the wise.

In front of you is an inextricable lattice of paths. Select the right one that leads straight to your celestial home, so as not to be trapped in devilish religions.

You are imprisoned in multiple compartments of prejudice. These innumerable veils of ignorance prevent you from penetrating the marvelous mechanism of Genesis.

Your spirit, enslaved by the seven emotions and the six passions, loses its equilibrium and thus falls into the vicious cycle of reincarnation.

Wake up, children! I call you with the most intense voice! I am the SUPREME GOD who abandons My Throne and descends to this world to save you.

I do not mind the hard work and can swallow the humiliation, as long as you realize that this world is unreal, illusionary, and perishable; and as long as you diligently follow My instructions to self-cultivate until enlightenment, so as to penetrate the Nirvana.

This inferior world is heavily corporal and perishable; it can disappear all at once, like a floating cloud in the sky.

Your carnal body is a temporary envelope; it can also disappear like a gown that you take off. Children! Release your body as it causes myriad troubles.

Poem:

You have been erred in innumerable lives,

I am deeply moved in witnessing such miseries;

In front of Buddha and Immortals, I solemnly swore,

If the DAO fails this time, I will be responsible for it.

000

HOW DID YOUR MASTER FOUND CAO-DAI GREAT WAY?

I notice the decadence of this world is due to natural discord as humans aspire towards materialism, deny spiritual values, and head to erroneous ways. They jostle, squabble, compete with each other in the aggressive pursuit of profane values, and disregard their noble characters.

The three Doctrines of Truth (CONFUCIANISM, TAOISM, BUDDHISM) were in decrepitude. Without norms, humans prefer materialism from the profound and abstract spiritualism.

Now, as the Universal Genesis is about to recycle, DAO of GOD is founded to salvage all beings.

In the past, the Three Doctrines commenced by preaching the esotericism, gradually going from the mystically oral traditions to the apparent formalities of exotericism. It is when the spiritual traditions are adulterated that the Three Ancient Doctrines come to their end.

I found the DAO this time totally in reverse to those of the Three Ancient Religions. It starts with the exotericism, employing forms and sounds, visible verities, palpable materials, so as to quickly attract and convince humans. Then the temporal practices of this GOD WAY are gradually reduced and replaced by spiritual exercises which constitute the intuitive method of dematerialization, i.e., the ascension to the Nirvana. In other words, it would be best to preach the exotericism first, in order to facilitate the propagation of the religion. Once getting in this door, disciples can allegedly progress toward the esotericism that leads them up until the complete enlightenment and sanctification. Following such strategy, this GOD WAY is hardly degenerated. It cannot be denatured because it begins with the temporal and elevates until the spiritual. In contrast, the Three Ancient Doctrines went from the spiritual and gradually sank into the temporal, degrading the spiritual traditions to superstitious cults.

The evangelization this time is also strikingly different from those of the Ancient Religions. I only use mystic mechanisms to promulgate DAO to the general public. I transmit the profoundly mystic esoteric method to willful people, so that they can practice and attain the complete dematerialization, regaining their original nature. I employ spiritism to develop and promulgate the esotericism of DAI DAO[18]. I decide never to confide this Saintly Doctrine to profane humans. The Three Ancient Religions lost their spiritual traditions because their disciples reformed and denatured them. Thus, as written in Celestial Book, I found the God-Way as follows:

1) Up in the Heaven, Divine Beings utilize spiritual energy to assure the perpetuity of the Doctrine.

2) Down on the Earth, only I have the omnipotence to regenerate human conscience and the omniscience to preach the Doctrine of Truth. Should I have incarnated in a coarse and heavy body, I could have not employed the omnipresence to universally propagate DAO and salvage all beings at the same time. On the other hand, utilizing spiritism, I can traverse everywhere in a wink. Yet, I still had to descend into this world and employ NGÔ-MINH-CHIÊU'S[19] profane body to transfuse the Esoteric Traditions to you, so that you preserve and transmit it to the sound and righteous elects. By this way, I also demonstrated to you the secret of dematerialization, the miraculous method to form the saintly embryo and to develop the spiritual body in which you will elevate toward the ethereal Primordial to identify with ME in the Eternal Sojourn. Accomplishing it, I re-ascend, and employ omnipotence to regenerate human conscience and propagate the DAO of Truth.

Why did I say that I would not confide this Saintly Doctrine to profanes nor incarnate in the temporal world as the Founders of the Three Ancient Religions had done, but in fact I did incarnate and entrust this Doctrine to you? Let ME clarify this paradox:

---

[18] the Great Way.
[19] NGÔ MINH CHIÊU is GOD's first disciple.

As the Three Ancient Religions were denatured, and as their spiritual traditions were corrupted, numerous disciples have persevered in those Doctrines but none attained complete enlightenment. For this reason I had to descend in this world and penetrate in a profane body to transmit the true esoteric traditions to free humans from the incarnation cycle. Without borrowing a physical body, how can I confide to you the key of enigma? As for the esoteric traditions, they are only transmitted mouth-to-ears or heart-to-heart; neither should they be disclosed to other people, nor be divulged in drawing pictures, nor be described in written scripts, nor be transmitted via spiritism.

Spiritism is a means for the authorized to propagate the Saintly Doctrine to the profane; it is like the radiant torch to guide humans to the original nature, the ultimate goal. In other words, I employ this means to impart noble morality and forge profanes into Saints, Immortals, and Buddha.

Children! Keep in mind that although you receive the secret of deliverance, you are always under the authority of Divine Beings. Never can you deceive ME!

You should know that "*The profoundly mystic DAO is the Sacred Standard to guide your ascension*".

I bless you all. I ascend.

The 2nd day of the 8th month of Bính Tý year (1936)

COMMENTARIES ON THE ESOTERICISM

NHỨT BỬU CHƠN NHƠN

Poem:

Emanated from the Imponderable,

The marvelous DAO creates the Yin-Yang twin;

Penetrating it, enlightened people acquire the Wisdom of

God,

Practicing it, awakened minds attain the Secret of Ascension.

Greetings to all devotees of both sexes.

Upon Divine Order, I am coming to announce that the SUPREME GOD is descending to impart the Sacred Teaching. You should prepare to piously greet HIM. I leave.

JADE EMPEROR SUPREME GOD OF THE IMPONDERABLE, aliasing CAO-DAI SENIOR IMMORTAL MAHABODHISHATTVA MAHATATTVA.

Your MASTER. I greet you all.

Poem:

GOD commands the publication of the Scripture of the GRAND CYCLE

In which the ESOTERIC TEACHING wakes humans up from their reveries;

Wise people should enlighten and purify their souls and bodies,

To reach the ultimate goal of ascension toward Unity.

At this time being, I manifest in this world to bring the antidote that saves humans from the hallucination of this ocean of suffering and ignorance. Keep in mind that I hold Omniscience, Omnipotence, and Omnipresence. None of the Holy Powers is beyond my Sovereignty, should I choose to act ruthlessly against the rebellious children. Yet, with the Infinite Mercy I am willing to integrate and bear with my children the miserable circumstances, so as to liberate them from the world of illusion.

Poem:

The **GREAT WAY** is revivified to assure the Universal Amnesty,

Its **CYCLE** is in accord with the Cosmic Revolution to salvage humans,

Its **ESOTERICISM** is open to forge disciples into Immortals and Buddha,

Its **TEACHING** guides all beings back to their Original Destiny.

What is DAO (i.e., the WAY)?

DAO is the Imponderable. It is very mystic, miraculous, and enigmatic. It exists even before the formation of Heaven and Earth. Thus, DAO gives origin to the Universal Genesis and creates all beings. All living creatures inherit this Imponderable so as to conceive and perpetuate themselves.

Who is the MASTER of DAO?

The Great Ancestor HỒNG-QUÂN LÃO TỔ is the Master of DAO, as HE transforms DAO into the Divine Genesis to create all beings. DAO breeds Heaven and Earth; these spiritual and corporal worlds must evolve accordingly with the Principle of DAO. DAO is infinite, immutable, and everlasting. You should never ever leave it, even instantly. With it you live, without it you die. Children! Listen:

Long Poem:

The mystic DAO breeds the Universe,

This Imponderable is under GOD's Sovereignty.

It creates Buddha, Immortals, Saints, Deities,

And all other beings infinitely reproduce and perpetuate.

DAO is infinite in time and space,

DAO is the common Mother of all beings.

DAO differentiates the Universal Triad,

DAO precedes the formation of the universe and assures its continuity.

DAO exists, all beings are alive and secure,

DAO leaves, the souls quit the bodies at once.

DAO preaches even the ignorant to become enlightened,

DAO manifests essentially for the universal preservation.

DAO is currently revealed in Cao-Dai Faith,

DAO establishes the codes for universal life.

DAO gathers the clairvoyant minds and enlightens them,

DAO unifies the Ancient Doctrines to reveal the Cosmic Genesis.

DAO is currently at the point to get back to its origin,

DAO predestines its return to the Spiritual Unity.

DAO forges humans into Saints and Immortals,

DAO re-establishes the Golden Age for mankind.

DAO includes and animates the Universe,

It revolves the Sun and Moon, as well as the five Spiritual Elements.

DAO manifests the Universal Salvation,

DAO is the Divine Nature that circulates unceasingly day and night.

DAO does not diminish nor augment,

DAO immutably and silently commands all beings.

DAO is imponderable, invisible,

Impalpable, inodorous, unutterable, and immaterial.

DAO is not outside human Conscience,

DAO is up and down, far and close, comes and goes around.

DAO excludes the duality of good-bad, right-wrong,

DAO is neither young or old, nor fast or slow.

DAO of the Impartiality is deeply mystic,

DAO of the "Emptiness" is the return to the Origin.

DAO preserves life, order, and harmony,

DAO vivifies the Esoteric Teaching,

DAO revolts against the bad and favors the good,

DAO defines the eternal rhythm of order and harmony.

DAO manifests the Trinity: Father, Son, and the Saint-Esprit,

It shows the Omnipotence of GOD the FATHER, MASTER of the Universe.

The Yin and Yang unite accordingly with GOD's Will,

To breed all beings which perpetuate themselves infinitely.

What is the nature of that unfathomable Trinity?

It emanates everywhere and yet, converges to the Unity.

DAO of your MASTER, never should you neglect it!

DAO brings all of you back to the unique Divine Origin,

DAO of your MASTER is the precious lamp,

DAO lights everywhere up, like the full moon at night.

DAO is inscribed in everyone's mind.

DAO is not hidden nor found in mountains!

DAO is GOD if you can understand,

DAO teaches you to cease desires and ignorance.

DAO of your MASTER glides like the suave fragrance of incense,

Yet none can escape from its invisible net.

Humans forget DAO, but never does DAO leave them,

To understand the GREAT DAO, keep yourself pure and simple.

Poem:

Incarnating in this world you are burdened with grief,

But this tortuous fate is due to your karma;

Expiate it accordingly to the Law of Creation,

And practice the 'EMPTINESS' to break up the karmic cycle.

Children! Prepare to piously greet THÁI-THƯỢNG SUPREME INSTRUCTOR, who continues the discussion on DAO.

I bless you all. Ascension.

WHY WAS DAO BRANCHING OUT?

THÁI THƯỢNG ĐẠO TỔ
THÁI THƯỢNG SUPREME INSTRUCTOR

Poem:

The Grand Harmony evolves Deities, Saints, and Immortals,

Saints and profanes, all unify in preaching it;

It is predetermined that DAO split into Three Religions,

SUPREME INSTRUCTOR restores them to the primordial Unity.

SUPREME INSTRUCTOR greets His disciples.

Lesson in Verse:

The Doctrine of GOD varies appropriately to every circumstance,

To assure universal peace to all creatures.

This impious world is suffering from myriad vicissitudes,

Because humans are dashing towards the pursuit of illusion.

They deny Wisdom and pious life,

They devour each other and corrupt the world with their

trickeries and violence.

GOD is touched by such miseries;

 Having pity on His rebellious children who violate His Law,

HE abandons His Throne and manifests Himself in the corporal world.

HE assures the Universal Amnesty by teaching the miraculous DAO,

And revealing the mystic Law of Genesis,

To revivify the Three Doctrines and preach the universal Love and Justice.

Confucianism, Buddhism, and Taoism were the three branches of DAO,

Founded by the Messiahs who had discovered the Celestial Mechanism.

They preached these doctrines by utilizing the intuitive method,

Yet, their pure Esotericism was denatured after millennia of evangelization.

BUDDHISM was adulterated by the sect of decadent Zen,

It employed exoteric means to deviate from the original Buddhism;

Its overabundance of sounds, colors, forms and other formalities

Submerged and suffocated the EMPTINESS!

TAOISM was to regenerate body and soul,

In disciplining the five corporal senses to liberate the Three Treasures,

In maintaining the pure and serene mind to prepare the Immortality Pill,

And in following the Universal Rhythm to regain human Conscience.

Such a profound doctrine was hardly penetrated by profanes,

And its Esotericism was gradually hidden in the haziness;

Later Taoists understood it lesser and lesser,

And denatured that Doctrine with ridiculous books of magic spells and pictures.

CONFUCIANISM drifted too far from its origin,

Decadent Confucians[20] had lots of vices;

Just memorizing the scriptures without practicing the teachings,

They wasted their lives in the pursuit of vain honors and personal interests.

These Three Ancient Doctrines were founded in the same epoch,

To preach spiritualism and forge national spirit.

In later generations, when humans sank into a loathsome materialism,

The spiritual traditions of these Doctrines were gradually corrupted.

Nowadays GOD founds the Great Way,

Aliasing CAO-DAI, HE guides pious people back to their spiritual destiny.

His Wisdom illumines the darkness of this Era,

To lead humans on their abrupt path toward the original Unity.

But the Great Way is split into numerous churches,

To accommodate human diversities, while protecting it from being degraded.

DAO comprises two sections: the Spiritual and the Temporal.

The ESOTERICISM of DELIVRANCE is purely intuitive,

Its disciples shun the worldly life to seek Wisdom and Virtue;

Freed from their instincts and passions, they reunite with the

---

[20] later generations of Confucian disciples, alluding to false literates, cracked scholars, fogyish Confucians.

original nature;

Day and night they contemplate and meditate,

To practice the Dematerialization Mechanism and the Spiritual Revivification.

The EXOTERICISM is to improve human conduct,

It teaches the three main duties, the willfulness, and the five essential virtues.

Following piously the religious codes,

Disciples propagate the Exoteric Teaching as the means to save the world.

Poem:

The Temporal and Spiritual Way should complement each other;

A Temporal world without Spirituality certainly suffers from miseries,

As the union of Spiritual and Temporal results in peace and order.

Despite their abruptness, you should escalate the Temporal and Spiritual Way.

I bless you all. I ascend.

The 1st day of the 9th month of Bính Tý year (1936)

THE FOUNDATION OF CAO-DAI GREAT WAY

GIÁC MINH KIM TIÊN

Poem:

WAKE your conscience to find in it the Spirit of Truth,

ENLIGHTEN your mind to prepare the Immortality Pill,

Fabricate your Aura of Light to evade from the three worlds;[21]

IMMORTALS and Buddha bless and accept your sincerity.

Greetings to all devotees of both sexes present in this séance. Upon SUPREME GOD'S Order, I am coming to expose some saintly words. Listen with sincerity in your mind and quietude in the séance.

Long Poem:

Spiritual-Temporal is the bi-directional way of human life,

Devotees should seek the one leading to their divine origin.

This grievous world conceals humans in its hazy smoke,

Where passions embed them in the worldly frame.

This world constantly changes like moving stars,

Flattening mounts, draining seas, in accord with the divine plan.

Profanes endure all those calamities,

Brave a way to escape it!

Vicissitudes are unavoidable in human life,

Embark in the Ark of Virtues to be freed from passions.

Poem:

Passionate in worldly matters, you endure endless grief,

Forever it staggers you on the erroneous paths;

Without escape, it keeps you away from God-Way,

And burns your body and soul with the fire of human desires.

000

---

[21] The three worlds are the formed, the formless or non-formed, and the sensuous worlds.

Desires extricated, willpower is revivified,

Wisdom forges you into Buddha and Immortals,

Embark in the Salvation Ark and head up to the Nirvana,

Where you enjoy the eternal comfort and facility.

Verse:

Lots of people cherish alcoholic imbibing, fame, beauty, and riches,

They are contented to bury body and soul in this dusty world.

Human life is quite brief, it comes and goes instantly;

Attaching to worldly matters, you obscure your mind and conscience.

Enslaving in worldly taste, you degrade your spirit and morals.

Wise people! Virtuous people!

Consider the actual state of this world to be convinced of the moral corruption.

The ardent flame of greed and desires develops unceasingly,

The tidal wave of passions submerges the world and destroys human traditions.

The fume given off by human agony intoxicates and enrages all human beings.

Alas! What a catastrophe! But few people consider it!

Poem:

Consider how horrible such tribulation!

Stop the tidal wave of passion,

Escape from the cycle of incarnation,

Put out the flame of desires to restore Wisdom.

Lesson in Verse:

The torch of Truth illumines everywhere,

Radiating DAO to guide humans to their origin.

Repent and receive the esoteric teaching,

Purify your nature to forge into Buddha and Immortals.

Deviating from God-Way, your divine nature is obscure,

Your spirit degrades and becomes irrational;

Crushed by your unbound desires and greed,

Tied by your conjugal bonds, you can hardly free yourself.

Burying your mind and conscience in this slavery world,

Denying your Divine Origin, you run into scourges.

You live a miserable life without dignity,

Due to your cruel destiny of tanked fish or caged bird!

The chaotic Temporal deprives of good hearts and minds,

The decadent Spiritual attracts the arrogance of Satan;

Together they corrupt the foundation of the Ancient Faiths,

And cause calamities and suffering to mankind.

Nowadays, a Saintly Doctrine is founded,

To wake human spirit and restore worldly peace and joy.

Follow and walk straight on this God-Way,

Back to your ancient post to enjoy the eternal comfort.

Leave the carnivals to those who are still passionate,

Thoroughly cleanse your souls of all desires.

Unite them to form the Quintessence,

Reflect DAO in your calm and honest nature.

Poem:

The miraculous remedy is discovered,

To treat the devilish desires and human ignorance.

Repent your sins and regenerate your soul and body,

To completely cure your serious malady.

With your deepest sincerity, prepare to receive GOD THE FATHER. Goodbye. I leave. Ascension.

Poem:

NGỌC HOÀNG THƯỢNG ĐẾ
JADE EMPEROR SUPREME GOD

Like a brilliant pearl, the Spirit of Truth radiates everywhere,

As GOD THE FATHER imparts the Religious Constitution.

Maintaining tranquil mind, virtuous people gain enlightenment,

Returning to divine origin, they unify with the nature.

Your MASTER. I greet you all.

Poem:

The nature of DAO is always immutable,

It becomes mutable due to your errors;

Should you keep forging it diligently,

It will radiate brilliantly like rubies.

Rubies symbolize your infallible faith,

Follow saintly instructions to live in DAO,

Embark in the Ark of Wisdom to return to the origin,

Hold tightly the true teaching and never loosen your grip.

Loosening your grip, you will go astray in the Hades,

Where you endure grief, suffering, and dangers;

Hardly could you find the returning way,

Innumerable obstacles imprison you and block the God-Way.

God-Way has been opened to you multiple times,

It teaches you to accomplish your meditative tasks,

To diligently practice the esoteric deliverance day and night,

To perform works of piety and gather their fruitful results.

Fruitful results are reserved for you,

To taste the Peach of Immortality,

To wander on the Island of Saints,

To enjoy the taste of DAO on the Mount of Immortals.

Mount of Immortals is for those who nurture their nature,

Who persist in austere life bravely,

Who progress on God-Way steadily,

Who persevere in penetrating the Celestial Mechanism.

Celestial Mechanism is an untraceable enigma,

Discover it to avoid aberration;

Freeing from karmic cycle relies on Wisdom,

Transforming profane to Saint occurs in enlightened mind.

Enlightened mind becomes Buddha, Immortals, and Saints,

Learn this lesson to break your karmic links;

Ignorance leads you to the paths of demons,

To incarnate as animals with your confused soul.

Confused soul puzzles between the Spiritual and Temporal;

The Temporal charms you with its treacheries,

The Spiritual offers enviable promises of becoming Buddha;

But choosing the Spiritual, you yearn for the Temporal.

Yearning for the Temporal, you keep sinking in this muddy world,

As the SAVOR, I come to rescue multiple times;

Yet you are ignorantly fascinated with sensuous matters,

Your corrupted soul is hardly detached from illusion and grief.

Grievous epoch comes with tides of material civilization,

Brutally sweeping out all spiritual values;

Its monstrous idolatry captivates human sensations,

Its substantial temptations are so frightening!

Frightened by an imminent catastrophe,

That swallows all creatures in the abyss of distresses,

Compassionately I cannot keep my hands crossed;

Thus, I found the Saintly Doctrine to salvage you this time.

This time I Myself manifest,

To protect the world from harm and risks,

Trust ME and practice the virtuous exercises of DAO,

I will help deliver you from your Karma.

Your Karma has pulled you toward sins and aberration,

Make a serious effort to regenerate your good nature;

Struggle to escape from the labyrinth of dark paths,

Fight against the demons to step out without delay.

Without delay, embark in the Ark of Salvation!

Otherwise, you have to wait for millennia.

This is the once-in-a-lifetime opportunity,

The siren of depart is waking you.

You now comprehend CAO-DAI precepts,

Fabricate the Aura of Light[22] and enlighten your mind,

Proceed naturally to avoid illusions,

Having imaginary visions is a dangerous error.

I briefly explain "THE FOUNDATION OF CAO-DAI GREAT WAY".

You should strictly observe the laws and rules of this Saintly Doctrine. Should it be reformed or denatured, its spiritual traditions would be contorted.

The esoteric method is a metaphysic science. For your spiritual transformation, you should perform spiritual traditions exactly as they are transmitted to you heart-to-heart and mouth-to-ears. Successful or not, it is intuitively conceived; never could you fathom it using human understanding. Whether you progress or not depends solely on your faithfulness and your diligence in practicing these exercises. In the Invisible, I will guard and help you. As you know nothing about it, mind your own business and do not try to break through this mystery.

DAO develops day after day; so do esoteric disciples. Preparation of the Immortality Pill cannot be achieved in one day or in half a day. You must persistently compose your mind in your meditative and contemplative exercises to conserve Quintessence of your body, nourish Energy, and nurture the Spirit. Gradually they crystallize to form the Ethereal Double-Body. But you should patiently perform these exercises day after day, and do not rush or skip any steps. Analogously, to plant a tree you should sow the seed; later on, it germinates and gives the two young leaves, before gradually ramifying. The tree blossoms and fructifies rhythmically with the seasons according to the laws of nature. It absorbs the yin-yang energy to grow up little by little. No one can force its development nor hasten its fructification! Once upon a time, a Chinese farmer, in Tống dynasty, sowed rice seeds and thought that the rice grew so slowly. He restlessly uprooted the rice plants to

---

[22] Aura of Light is the Double Body or the Spiritual Body

make them grow higher. But contrary to his expectation, the plants perished *en masse*. That is a good lesson for impatient disciples. You should persevere in your meditative task, ban talkativeness, and avoid literature searches for information on alchemy; these may confuse you or cast doubt in your mind. Saints and Sages in the past invented different words, expressions, symbols, formulas, parables, and allegories such as the ascending dragon and the descending tiger, or the harmony of QIAN ($\equiv$) and K'UN ($\equiv\equiv$),[23] and many other names. People of later generations mistakenly focus only on the literal meaning of these beautiful words and thus, denatured the spiritual traditions of DAO.

DAO of your MASTER is nothing strange; it is simply the pair of YIN and YANG, SPIRIT and ENERGY. There is nothing else beyond this principle. To understand DAO, you may start with the YIN-YANG pair as the basis.

Long Poem:

Concerning the foundation of CAO DAI FAITH,

Its evangelization evolves into two branches[24].

If the temporal unites with the spiritual,

The original nature of the miraculous DAO is revealed.

Quieting your mind, you find the brilliant pearl,

That splendidly radiates everywhere in the Universe.

The ESOTERICISM is transmitted from heart to heart,

It teaches the method of deliverance to return to the Peach Cave.[25]

Forge your soul to make it pure and brilliant,

Your Spark of Divine Light will identify with the Divine Origin.

Once you fulfill spiritual tasks and secular duties,

---

[23] the trigrams symbolizing Heaven and Earth

[24] The Esotericism and the Exotericism

[25] the Sojourn of Immortals.

The Sacred Banner will guide you back to the Divine Realm.

DAO liberates you from passions and ignorance,

And brings you closer to Buddha and Immortals;

It instructs you the method of meditation and contemplation,

To discover the key to Genesis and the secret of Deliverance.

Once dissipating the hazy smoke that veils your clairvoyance,

You can penetrate the nine worlds of Heaven.

Your MASTER bequeaths a single word: "EMPTINESS";[26]

Achieving "EMPTINESS", you will gain the six supernatural powers.

Ascetics! Regenerate your spiritual nature,

To set a good example of DAO and to penetrate the Truth.

Pay loyally your debts of piety and fraternity,

Be persistent and tolerant, humble and modest, to love and serve others.

By all means, avoid bad behaviors and wrongdoings,

Always follow the examples of Sages and Saints in the past.

Observe punctually the four daily sessions of meditation,

Do not let your mind ramble, even instantly.

Should you leave DAO,

Devilish Satan immediately interferes.

Trust and pray Immortals and Buddha up above,

To guide and guard you on the abrupt path of deliverance.

Maintain the absolute serenity of your mind,

Combine it with an austere life to forge yourself into Saints and Sages.

---

[26] "NOTHINGNESS" or EMPTINESS" or "NON-BEING".

It is not easy to become Buddha and Immortals!

Only those persevering in esoteric method succeed in forging them.

Otherwise, there is no expectation!

Ascetic life without meditation results in reincarnation.

Even if you earn a lot of credit from your work of piety,

It merely assures you riches and social noblesse in your next life.

It does not grant you access to the Celestial Gate,

Nor could it help you escape from the karmic cycle of incarnation!

Why so? Because you are not extremely sincere,

Without the golden body[27], you cannot elevate to the pure and high worlds.

The corporal body is heavy with sullied and vile materials,

Embedded in it, your soul has no way to evade.

Also your karmic links are intricately intertwined,

Without clues, you cannot break them off.

Stuck to the body and its apparition in and outside,

Your soul is anchored to the bottom of the abyss.

Yet, your soul still conserves its immortality,

Thanks to the omniscience of the supreme authority.

Speaking of the EXOTERICISM,

It propagates the true teaching to achieve the Universal Salvation.

It teaches mankind to be righteous and honest,

By accomplishing loyalty, piety, justice, and kindness.

Practice such simultaneous self-perfection

---

[27] Vietnamese term 'kim thân' literally means 'body made of gold', which is the double-body, the spiritual body, or the Aura of Light.

To establish peace and happiness in families, nations, and societies.

It is also to forge into sound and righteous men,

Who utilize their virtues to serve mankind.

To the Heaven, they do not violate Celestial Codes,

To their conscience, they are shameless and dignified in society.

Assembling together, they maintain stability in society,

To effectively join arms and hearts for mutual assistance;

They are like fish in river and birds in forest,

Swimming in schools and flying in flocks.

The senior preceding the junior,

They head up toward the same direction.

They treat each other in fraternity and affection,

They defend common rights and work for public benefits.

Loyally they sacrifice themselves for their country,

And accomplish their filial piety.

They treat each other with love and justice,

Join and share with each other in all circumstances.

The Spiritual Way relies on the Temporal,

In employing visible verities to wake the world up.

The ESOTERICISM teaches spiritual exercises at diverse levels,

The EXOTERICISM establishes society of righteous people.

Should DAO define the unidirectional way,

It is not the radiant DAO of Buddha and GOD.

DAO is formless in life,

DAO is voiceless, yet it commands all beings.

It transforms constantly beyond human understanding,

It is named based on its revelation to mankind.

When the pious attain the absolute sincerity,

They can circulate the divine nature throughout the world.

In such perfect Man, desires are completely extricated,

And his Aura of Light grants him access to the Nirvana.

Poem:

Humans are born to die. Where do you go after life?

The corporal body decomposes after some time,

While the pure and noble spirit stays in the superior realm.

Why do not you practice DAO to sanctify your miraculous soul?

Miraculous soul creates the Aura of Light,

Which crystallizes into the ethereal double-body;

Acquiring it, you gain the diamond-like Eight Beatitudes[28],

And the ability to voluntarily evade the carnal sheath.

Evading your carnal sheath,

You ride with the wind towards the very high above,

Where you delightfully wander around the universe,

And leisurely enjoy the exploration.

Exploring throughout the world,

I lament on human conditions,

Mankind is caught in the vicious cycle of Karma,

---

[28] According to *Ngọc Lộ Kim Bàn Scripture*, the Divine Mother bestows the Eight Beatitudes to every spirit upon his/her incarnation. They are Piety, Fraternity, Loyalty, Credibility, Courtesy, Righteousness, Uprightness, and Sense of shame. It is very sad that humans coming into this world lose all those treasures for beauty, riches, drinking, smoking, and anger.

These miseries make ME grievously cry.

Grievously crying, I devote Myself to your salvation.

Children! The grand distress is coming soon,

The entire mankind has to share this fatal destiny,

Avoid it by submitting yourself to the DAO of GOD.

GOD and Buddha mercifully drip their blessings,

To protect mankind from calamities;

Disregarding divine counsels, they still dive in reveries,

And infuriate ME with their impiety.

I bless you all. I ascend.

The 1st day of the 9th month of Bính Tý year (1936)

THE SACRED GOALS OF CAO-DAI GREAT WAY

NAM PHƯƠNG GIÁO CHỦ
THE FOUNDER OF CAODAISM IN VIETNAM

Poem:

VIETNAM is blessed to receive DAO of GOD,

It is the method of deliverance from this world of distress;

It teaches humans how to build a saintly world,

And guides them in the quest for Truth.

Your MASTER. I greet you all. I am glad being with you.

Poem:

The Esoteric Teaching reveals its mystic mechanism,

This precious pearl is exposed to unveil all obscurity,

To fill up the ocean of suffering,

To calm down the tide of passion.

Long Poem:

As DAO of GOD propagates further and further,

The alias CAO-DAI radiates brighter and brighter.

The Three Ancient Doctrines are revivified,

To assure happiness to entire mankind.

Do not quit when encountering hardships,

Until your MASTER gives you the Key of Enigma.

Those willful and persistent

Seek the true teaching to avoid the furnace of Creator.[29]

Here I discuss the terms: "MATERIAL and SPIRITUAL".[30]

Poem:

Those who adore MATERIAL and deny SPIRITUAL,

Are still imprisoned in the cage of Satan.

DAO is the imponderable and miraculous Truth,

Introspect to forge your mind and preserve your nature.

DAO of your MASTER is formless and immaterial. But this invisible nature has to rely on the visible part (as in the body-soul union). Therefore, you should not embrace the material and neglect the spiritual, or vice versa, as "MATERIAL" and "SPIRITUAL" must co-exist. It is like rice, the food to nourish your body. You only eat the bare grain of rice, as the rice husk has no nutritional value. But in order to get the grain of rice, you have to cultivate the entire padding of the seed. If you think that the husk has

---

[29] alluding to the perpetual cycle of incarnation and reincarnation.

[30] MATERIAL means palpable, visible; SPIRITUAL means immaterial, formless, invisible.

no use and only sow the bare grain, this sterile seed cannot germinate.

Children! Your self-cultivation is exactly the same way as the rice cultivation.

To nurture your soul, you need your physical body on which you perform esoteric exercises. But the key point is that you should not incline toward material matter. If you still cling to forms and appearance, you cannot grasp the deep sense of DAO.

DAO is the miraculous principle of heart, unique in its nature. Every country, every people, all beings, all have to comply with this unique principle.

DAO of your MASTER is in its debut of the universal salvation to all countries and all peoples, with no discrimination. If DAO is presented in the cult appropriate to your customs and traditions, it cannot be widespread to other peoples and countries. For instance, if you come to a country unaccustomed to your cult, would you insist on them adapting your veneration style upon receiving DAO? If your cult offends their customs and traditions, they would not satisfy your request. Then would you deny their inquiries of DAO? Would you let them endure endless karmic expiation? Alas! What naivety! Moreover, as the scriptures and prayers you use are in the Vietnamese language, would you force other peoples to chant prayers in your language and perform the rites in your style in order for them to receive DAO?

DAO of your MASTER is not as such.

You still compete and squabble with each other for belts, caps and gowns.[31] Can those belts, caps and gowns dispense you the Wisdom of Buddha and Immortals? Or do they lead you into sinful aberrations?

You should compete for wisdom and virtues, but not for formalism, so that the Saintly Doctrine can be globally widespread.

I insist that you acquire the virtues to be deserved as GOD's disciples. What you should worry about are hundreds of thousand eyes watching on you, and thousand fingers pointing at you. If they

---

[31] belts, caps, and gowns allude to the ecclesiastic ranking and titles.

find your Doctrine adorable, they would certainly urge you to preach it. Yet, DAO of your MASTER is so "imponderable, profound, and miraculous" that you can hardly grasp its full sense. Therefore, rest assured and steadily persevere in your self-correction and self-cultivation; do not rush nor linger. Once upon a time, a man thought that the Sun moved so slowly, even slower than the crawling ant. He believed that he could walk a hundred times faster than the movement of the Sun. Thus, he engaged in a cross-country race with the Sun. But when the Sun already set down, this foolish man was still on his way, dying of thirst, hunger, and exhaustion in a desolated forest. Similarly, a farmer in Tống territory thought that his rice plants were growing too slowly. He uprooted the plants to make them higher. Ironically, his rice plants perished *en masse*. Children! Learn this lesson!

Self-cultivation is like sowing a seed and knowing that one day it certainly germinates. Once it germinates, you should fertilize and water the plant day after day. Little by little, the plant grows, blossoms, and fructifies. The plant develops following "the Principle of Nature"; by no means could you intervene with it.

Children! Listen:

Long Poem:

Self-cultivation means living a simple life,

Do not seek sophistication to become ridiculous. (*I'm smiling..., smiling...*)

As you know DAO of your MASTER,

It is not something to show off.

Maintain your secular activities as normal as possible,

Meanwhile, diligently purify your body and souls.

Do not insist on wearing clothes dyed in brown,[32]

Nor on shaving your head and leaving your family.

When your parents are alive,

You should fulfill your filial piety.

---

[32] the Buddhist robes

Husband-wife is an indissoluble union,

Keep it as pure as lotus in stinky mud.

Pretend to be idiot and ignorant,

Let no one know the DAO in your heart!

I bless you all. I ascend.

The 2nd day of the 9th month of Bính Tý year (1936)

DIGNIFIED MAN AND VULGAR MAN[33]

NGỌC HOÀNG THƯỢNG ĐẾ
JADE EMPEROR SUPREME GOD

Poem:

The precious JADE radiates throughout the four oceans;

With Universal Love, the EMPEROR convenes all Divine Beings

To approve the SUPREME Cycle of Initiation to the virtuous

And lead them back to GOD'S Kingdom in Jade Palace.

Your MASTER. I greet you all.

Children! The river of ignorance is racing its impetuous flow, while the ocean of suffering is roaring under its furious tide; you live in the world full of fatal vicissitudes and are incessantly plagued with myriads of grief and suffering. Incarnated in a body of Post-Genesis elements, you are so enslaved by the brutal instincts and blind passions that you get lost and err in innumerable ways.

---

[33] Dignified man from Vietnamese term 'Quân tử' literally means children of the Emperor, the Supreme Being or God the Father, and Vulgar man from Vietnamese term 'Tiểu nhơn' literally means man with petty or mean characters.

But in the past, you could falsely blame your ignorance and aberrations on the decadence of the Ancient Doctrines. Nowadays, I have taken all the trouble in granting the miraculous DAO and propagating the Universal Salvation throughout the world, so as to dissipate the veil of ignorance and to liberate you from the ocean of suffering and grief. If you do not wake up and come back, if you still dive in illusion and attach to desires, dare you blame ME on not teaching you? Children, be vigilant! On the day of Universal Judgment I cannot ignore the Law, regardless of my infinite love and mercy.

Humans in this world are generally classified into two categories: Dignified Man and Vulgar Man. You should follow examples of the former and do not imitate the latter.

What does "Dignified Man" mean? What does "Vulgar Man" mean?

Dignified man is an elite who surpasses ordinary people by his exemplary conducts and noble characters. Dignified man always remains calm and cool in all circumstances. He inclines to good deeds and strictly observes the Order and Harmony of Nature; he preaches the Saintly Doctrine, advising humans to give up wrong ways and return to the right one. He is always tolerant and generous, calm and pure; he is not impetuous or impatient. Consequently, desires and passions can no longer enslave, bend, or mislead him into erroneous paths. He thoroughly considers and anticipates everything; he cherishes and serves other beings; he favors loyalty, love, justice, and righteousness. He conforms wisely to all situations and human will, preserving "impartiality and harmony", and never leaning toward any extremes. Even in adversity, he stoically conserves peace of mind, because never does dignified man "care about eating exotic food or living in a comfortable lodge"!

Characters of dignified man are like water circulating everywhere and adopting all forms of receptacles: round, contorted, long, or square. In addition, water always flows down from higher to lower positions. Similarly, dignified man is content to humiliate himself to please other people. Nevertheless, though water seeks the low places, adopts the shape of all receptacles, gives in to everyone, none of the powers in the world could ever trim, chip, destroy, or modify its intrinsic nature. Dignified man tolerates the world but does not attach to it; he pleases everyone but does not flatter anyone;

he conforms to the secular activities but does not submerge in them. He maintains his pure, calm, and noble nature; nothing can sully or wear him out. Thus, never can vanity and riches lure him.

On the other hand, vulgar man abandons his conscience to pursue interests; he compromises himself to gain vain honor; his spirit is impure, nasty, haughty, and vile. To summarize, the characters of vulgar man are completely opposite to those of dignified man, like black and white, sky and abyss.

Ironically, the more dignified man avoids glory, the more the world highly praises him; the more he humiliates himself, the more the world adores him. Regarding vulgar man, the more he runs for glory, the more the world ignores him; the more he swells up with pride, the more the world disdains him.

But if it is so, why do only few people seek to follow examples of dignified man and a lot of others learn to become vulgar man? Alas! What a deep sorrow for mankind!

Long Poem:

How to wake up this dozing mankind?

They seek the evil and deny the good.

This spectacle is so discouraging!

Viewing such impiety I am so worried.

The world is filled with inconceivable superstitions

That entice humans in their illusionary reveries.

The universal catastrophe surpasses all foresights,

Perceiving it, I cry in hot tears for my children;

Most of them exhaust their body and soul,

And put out the light of their conscience.

They leave a bad example to posterity.

What a shame for such corrupt practices!

Children! Advance toward civilization,

Develop your spirit and intelligence;

Shine up the Ten Graces[34],

Serve your people and nation.

Stop coveting vanity and profits,

Ennoble your mind and shut off carnal exigencies.

In all times, favoritism engenders anarchy,

Avoid it and choose the justice, instead.

Unite the South, North, West, and East,

Gather them all in the Universal Fraternity.

Propagate the Saintly Doctrine,

Make its constitution firm and lasting.

Persevere in overcoming challenges,

Maintain high spirit and strong will to succeed.

Those of retarding spirits

Are indifferent to love and justice.

Eminent people in this world

Hold up their will before being blessed.

Should they not willfully persevere in self-perfection,

They would age and die without reaching goals.

Anyone, no matter who he is,

Determining to pursuit a goal, will eventually achieve it.

Esoteric disciples should valiantly persevere in self-

---

[34] According to the Buddhist Scripture *Đại Báo Phụ Mẫu Trọng Ân* ,the Ten Graces are the favors that parents unconditionally do to their child: 1) bearing all emotional and physical changes during the nine months of pregnancy, 2) overcoming fright and pain during the child birth process, 3) withstanding all hardships in raising the child, 4) self-sacrifice for the child's sake; 5) protect and shield the child from all dangers, 6) chewing foods to feed the toothless infant, 7) willing to wash the child's dirty clothes, 8) longing for the child when being away, 9) potentially doing everything for the child, even committing sins, 10) potentially self-starving to feed the child..

perfection,

Otherwise, their nonchalance leads them to nowhere.

To break a bad habit,

Make a resolution and willfully stick to it.

These words are your MASTER'S wishes,

Make sure you comprehend the True Teaching,

Follow examples of Sages and Saints,

Self-purify to penetrate the Sojourn of Immortals.

Leave the profane life to seek peace and quietude of mind;

Imitate dignified man, and not the vulgar one.

Obstacles and hardships no longer shake your will,

If you hear the soundless symphony of angels.

Your human dignity obliges you to think over,

To select the good path and leave the bad ones.

No matter how abrupt and bumpy the God-Way is,

Never regret the effort in seeking the Master for your enlightenment.

In the past, when King NGHIÊU looked for a Sage

Capable of reigning the people as he had done,

He put so much effort in going after DO,

But HỨA DO was so disgusted of interest and glory.

Viewing the world as a nauseous pond,

HỨA DO stayed away from it and enjoyed the hermetic life.

Disdaining the imperial throne,

He never cared about riches or noblesse.

Yet SÀO PHỦ was even more transcendent

Claiming his buffaloes intoxicated by NGHIÊU's proposal.[35]

Sages viewed this world so satiated and infected,

So contemning and vile that nothing is enviable.

They resigned on mountain tops to play the poetry,

Away from whispering sounds of this turbulent world.

The great talent HÀN TÍN,[36] master of resignation and perseverance,

Crawled through between his opponent's legs in front of the full crowd.

NHAN HỒI spent quite a time,

Hiding in jungle for self-purification and enlightenment;

Reciting poems under autumn sky,

He wandered around with a rice cake and water gourd.

Harmonizing soul and mind,

He passed these hermetic years to become superhuman;

---

[35] SÀO PHỦ considered the stream in which HỨA DO rinsed his ears after hearing NGHIÊU's offer as polluted water; thus, he did not allow his buffaloes to drink this water, fearing that such a dirty proposal in that water would infect his buffaloes.

[36] HÀN TÍN or Han Xin (died 196 BC) was a military general who served Liu Bang (Emperor Gaoxu of Han) during the Chu-Han Contention and contributed greatly to the founding of the Han Dynasty. Han Xin was named as one of the "Three Heroes of the early Han Dynasty", along with Zhang Liang and Xiao He. Once, a hooligan saw Han Xin carrying a sword and challenged him to either kill him or crawl through between his legs. Han Xin knew that he was at a disadvantage because his opponent was much stronger and bigger than him. Hence instead of responding to the taunts, he meekly crawled through between the hooligan's legs and was laughed at. Several years later, after becoming the King of Chu, Han Xin returned to his hometown and found the hooligan and instead of taking revenge, he appointed the hooligan as a *zhongwei* (equivalent to a present-day lieutenant). He said, "This man is a hero. Do you think I could not have killed him when he humiliated me? I would not become famous even if I killed him then. Hence, I endured the humiliation to preserve my life for making great achievements in future." (Source: *en.wikipedia.org*).

He preferred the pure and quiet mind of Sages,

From the treacherous, ignorant, and brutal world of humans.

TỬ NHA spent his time sitting on a flat rock,

To fish in Vi River where he contemplated the Celestial Mechanism.[37]

Pretending to be idiot during hapless time,

He waited for the right chance back to the imperial court.

He got lots of setbacks and deceptions,

As failures and defeats took turn to come.

What a trouble carrying a physical body!

From dawn till dusk, he tugged vainly to support it.

Yet in poverty and misery he still savored the interior joy,

And comfortably spent his life seeking Immortality.

During the seven harsh years in the prison of Dủ Lý,

VĂN VƯƠNG expressed Hà Đồ into Lạc Thơ,[38]

---

[37] TỬ NHA or Lü Shang (11th century BC), commonly known as Jiang Ziya and Jiang Shang, was an ancient Chinese military strategist who helped King Wen and king Wu of Zhou overthrow the Shang Dynasty. The last ruler of the Shang dynasty (16th - 11th century BC) was a tyrannical and debauched slave owner who spent his days carousing with his favorite concubine Daji and mercilessly executing or punishing upright officials and all others who objected to his ways. After faithfully serving the Shang court for approximately twenty years, Jiang came to find King Zhou insufferable, and feigned madness in order to escape court life and the ruler's power. Jiang was an expert in military affairs and hoped that one day someone would call on him to help overthrow the king. Jiang disappeared, only to resurface in the Zhou countryside at the apocryphal age of seventy-two, when he was recruited by King Wen of Zhou and became instrumental in Zhou affairs. It is said that, while in exile, he continued to wait placidly, fishing in a tributary of the Wei River (near today's Xi'an) using a barbless hook or even no hook at all, on the theory that the fish would come to him of their own volition when they were ready. Source: *en.wikipedia.org*).

[38] VĂN VƯƠNG or King Wen of Zhou (1152 – 1056 BC) was king of Zhou during the late Shang Dynasty in ancient China. Although it was his son Wu who conquered the Shang, King Wen was honored as the founder

To reveal to the world the mystic mechanism,

That separates the Spiritual from the Temporal;

To greatly assist later generations in the quest for Truth,

VĂN VƯƠNG, being exiled, did not blame anyone;

He accomplished his life of piety and fraternity,

Without a word against ungrateful and unfaithful people.

Conscientiously screen and correct your own mistakes,

Confide other people's faults to the guardianship of angels.

Exert resignation and forgiveness,

Let other people exaggerate whatever they would like to.

Consider the example of TỬ LỘ,

He was a superb child,

Fulfilling his filial piety at all price,

Even if a tragic death is required;

LỘ had a saintly mind,

---

of the Zhou Dynasty. Some consider him the first epic hero of Chinese history. King Wen is credited with having stacked the eight trigrams (the Yellow River chart Hà Đồ) in their various permutations to create the sixty-four hexagrams (the Lo River plan Lạc Thơ) of the I Ching. He is also said to have written the judgments which are appended to each hexagram. The most commonly used sequence of the 64 hexagrams is attributed to him and is usually referred to as the King Wen sequence.

The eight trigrams or the bagua (Chinese: 八卦; literally "eight symbols") are eight trigrams used in Taoist cosmology to represent the fundamental principles of reality, seen as a range of eight interrelated concepts. Each consists of three lines, each line either "broken" or "unbroken," representing yin or yang, respectively. The relationships between the trigrams are represented in two arrangements, the *Primordial* or Pre-Genesis or "Fuxi" bagua (Hà Đồ), and the *Manifested* or Post-Genesis or "King Wen" bagua (Lạc Thơ). The Bagua used in Feng shui can appear in two different versions: the Pre-Genesis Bagua, used for burial sites, represents an ideal state, when everything is in balance; and the Post-Genesis Bagua, used for the residences, describes the patterns of the environmental changes. (Source: *en.wikidepia.org*)

Joyfully acknowledging when his errors were pointed out.

TRƯƠNG LƯƠNG appreciated the taste of DAO,

He devoted to Buddhism to gain peace of mind.

Declining all rewards after warring time,

He escaped the death penalty the emperor assigned to other generals.

Study to gain the deepest understanding,

Be like HẠNG THÁC, the teacher of TRỌNG NI.[39]

Discern and separate silver from lead,

It is not wise to mix gold and brass.

Discern and separate good from evil,

The wise and unwise are two distinctive types.

Real musk naturally gives off its fragrance,

It is recognized without any exhibition!

The karmic wheel rotates unceasingly,

The incarnation cycle turns and returns eternally.

The secular links hold you tightly,

In the fate of tanked fish or caged bird.

Some adore the depth, others prefer the height,

All tirelessly climb up, slide down, and tumble.

Should you apply such perseverance to the quest of Wisdom,

Your escalation toward the Unity would be like an easy game.

Iron block becomes a needle after being sharpened continuously,

Success always waits for those who overcome difficulties.

Should you repent your sins and avoid committing them again,

---

[39] TRỌNG-NI is the alias of Confucius.

You transform IGNORANCE into ENLIGHTENMENT.

Two paths are open: the one of BUDDHA and that of MARA,

Ascend or fall, it depends solely on your pure or impure soul!

Poem:

The impure soul tends toward ignorance and vileness,

It longs for power, profit, and flatteries;

It feeds selfishness, greed, and desires.

Thoroughly cleanse to make it pure like lotus flowers.

Lotus flowers and autumn chrysanthemums give off fragrance,

For protection, you should store them in the house.

Similarly, the miraculous DAO is prone to the tricks of grand magic,

For prevention, you should control desires leading to the wrong ways.

I bless you all. I ascend.

The 4th day of the 9th month of Bính Tý year (1936)

PERSEVERANCE AND FORBEARANCE

THE DISCIPLE'S VIRTUES

NGỌC HOÀNG THƯỢNG ĐẾ
JADE EMPEROR SUPREME GOD

Poem:

The JADE hidden in the Five Primordial Elements[40] radiates brilliantly,

As the EMPEROR GOD grants it to the world;

From the SUPREME Realm where the absolute purity reigns,

GOD commands the Revelation of the Imperial DAO.[41]

Your MASTER. I greet all children. Enter in grand meditation and listen to my brief explanation on the terms 'PERSEVERANCE and FORBEARANCE'.

Poem:

PERSEVERANCE and FORBEARANCE builds the heart of Saints.

Perseverance and forbearance lead to contemplation of moral and conducts;

It is the fortress to protect oneself from exterior attacks,

As long-term resignation puts out the flame of desires.

Lesson in Verse:

---

[40] the Five Primordial Elements are Fire, Water, Metal, Wood, and Earth.

[41] Original Vietnamese term 'Đạo Huỳnh' or Đạo Hoàng or Đạo Vàng literally means the Imperial or Royal Way, i.e., DAO of the King or DAO of Children of God, alluding to DAO of the TRUE MAN.

To train mankind into Saints and Sages,

I have to endure so much trouble and grief.

I instruct you the method to purify body and souls,

Until you understand the principles to regenerate the true mind.

Preaching a Saintly Doctrine is harder than establishing an empire,

But teaching humans to enlightenment is even harder!

I have to patiently guide and correct them day and night,

It takes immense effort and persistence to become Immortals and Buddha!

Here are the required virtues for esoteric disciples:

Completely ban fraudulence and arrogance,

Stop talking nonsense, lying, and gossiping,

Refrain from bad-mouthing or grumbling at others.

Maintain fraternity and union, perseverance and forbearance,

Fulfill human duties with a calm conscience.

Never divulge other people's faults,

Never laugh at or criticize other people's defects or ignorance.

Gradually strain your habits into good virtues,

Keep your souls perfectly pure,

Withdraw from stubbornness or exploitation,

Do not take up unnecessary trouble and problems.

Inwardly, focus on creating the Buddha body,[42]

---

[42] Buddha body or Buddha form, alluding to the spiritual body or the Aura of Light.

Outwardly, show to others your honesty and fraternity;

Be always flexible like a boat meandering on a river,

To mutually help and guide co-religionists.

Do not abuse powers and titles,

Do not show off wealth and fortune.

Even if you are an emperor,

On the esoteric path you are just like anyone else.

Virtuous people do not seek vanity,

They like to work in union and fraternity.

Respecting others, they naturally forget themselves,

In such calm and pure souls no evils can interfere.

Being in accord with the rhythm of Nature,

They restrain the five instincts to fabricate the Aura of Light;

Though residing in the corporal world,

They do not care for wealth and fame.

For a perpetuity tree to fecundate,

You should frequently water and fertilize it;

For your spiritual cultivation to progress,

You should diligently perform the esoteric exercises day and night.

Knowing DAO you should well control your words,

Guard or attenuate other people's faults.

To form a raft, you should assemble many logs together,

To be strong, you should unite with each other.

Strive to successfully raze the dungeons of this corporal world,

And completely disengage your emotions and passions.

Whatever you attach to or long for,

You should empty these bags of greed once forever.

To escape from the cycle of Karma and reincarnation,

You should heartily devote in DAO to be saved.

This grievous world is as hot as a full-flamed furnace,

It releases excruciating heat and suffocating smoke.

Those who inhale it become brutal and crazy,

Losing conscience, they ramble in the dark paths.

To counterbalance such toxic smoke,

Here your MASTER brings you the curing potion.

Resign yourself to yield to others,

Your virtues will brilliantly radiate everywhere.

Children! Take my advice to heart,

Be flexible in every situation to maintain Impartiality.

Maintain your willpower in self-cultivation,

Rescue those sinking in the ocean of ignorance.

Divert yourselves from worldly attractions,

Do not take up the burden they insist on.

To fill up the ocean of distress, how can you do it?

To raze the fortress of grief, you are hardly able!

As most people are intoxicated with ignorance,

Uniting, we can easily accomplish this impossible mission!

As disciples you should hold up your beliefs,

Be determined in accepting all trials,

Overcome challenges to bravely elevate,

With great courage and willpower you are admitted to Paradise.

Exterminate the inferior self to abandon the power of being in reality,

Eliminate the ego to unite in the Universal Harmony.

Cultivate the flow of Fraternity globally,

Revivify human rights glorified in ancient times.

When human nature is pure and noble,

Doctrines of high moral are preached globally,

To facilitate human prosperity

And unification within each community.

Those people refuse praises or compliments,

They decline profits acquired at the expense of mankind.

No resentment, no grudge, no misunderstanding,

They discretely focus on good deeds and fraternity.

Sages who want people to know their works,

Are not authentic Sages.

True Sages tranquilly resign and persevere

In developing hidden virtues for spiritual perfection.

Had they still been inflated by their own performances,

None would have called them Sages!

Sages are imperturbable and always calm,

Regardless of the tide with which their souls are forged or stagnated.

Never are Sages boastful or haughty,

They care for others and focus on common interests,

They maintain tranquil minds without respite,

They humbly resign and persistently break off the worldly links one-by-one

Poem:

Consider the Saints and Sages in all epochs,

Their peace of mind is due to FORBEARANCE-UNION-

PERSEVERANCE.'

In the example of TRƯƠNG CÔNG NGHỆ,[43]

Even animals know that congeners are much worthier than money.

I bless you all. I ascend.

---

[43] Mr. Trương Công Nghệ was in the Tang dynasty of China. His family included nine generations living together in a big house without a single conflict. When the king asked him how to maintain harmony in this big family, he replied by writing the word FORBEARANCE. As evidence, when the king gave him an apple, he chopped the fruit into small pieces and boiled them in a big pot. Then he distributed the boiled fruity water equally to everyone in his family. He raised hundreds of dogs, and this whole pack of dogs would not eat if one of them was missing at meal time. Indeed, his virtues were positively influenced the conduct of these animals. (Source: Excerpted and translated from *Tam Kỳ Ngũ Đức Lương Châm* written by Đức Hộ Pháp Phạm Công Tắc).

The 3rd day of the 8th month of Bính Tý year (1936)

FRATERNITY

JADE EMPEROR SUPREME GOD

Your MASTER. I greet you all. Enter in grand meditation and listen:

Poem:

The JADE has been hidden in the mountain top for long time,

The EMPEROR exposes it to establish DAO and its Virtue

SUPERIOR spirits should seek and reach their noble origin,

GOD has waited to deliver this Scripture of heart to them.

I am glad to have this chance of revealing the esoteric teaching to lead superior spirits back to their celestial positions. You are so blessed to receive this Scripture of heart. I am teaching you the method to regenerate your nature and forge your conscience.

Poem:

Your spirit is completely submerged by the five turbidities,[44]

And permanently disabled by the six sensual attractions.[45]

The door to DAO is blocked, your mind becomes obscure,

It is because you attach too much to material life!

Here I discuss "FRATERNITY".

Poem:

FRATERNITY is a very precious virtue in life,

---

[44]The five turbidities are eye, ear, nose, tongue, and body.

[45] The six sensual attractions are color, form, carriage, voice or speech, smoothness or softness, and features.

As the concord of hearts is a lasting source of love,

And the union of people is a steady fortress,

Fraternity is the method to withstand future catastrophe.

Long Poem:

The Fraternity of Yin and Yang,

Establishes DAO and Virtues to create the Universe.

It ends the cycle of perishable life to open the cycle of immortality,

And self-harmonizes to preserve all creatures.

Fraternity is a miraculous treasure,

It is the key to penetrate Jade Palace.[46]

Impartiality and Harmony means neither low nor high,

Neither inclined nor crooked, becoming very stable.

As long as harmony exists, DAO and Virtues remain in life,

As long as harmony exists, all creatures perpetuate.

Harmony is the secret of Genesis,

Fraternity is essentially the origin of mankind.

Symphony of wind and rain establishes prosperity in life,

Harmony of time and space denotes the facility in Paradise.

Fraternity creates the Sacred Body,

As the union of body and soul reveals the miraculous DAO.

Fraternal union of people leads to peace,

And only in such global peace does the Imperial ĐẠO circulate.

Fraternize with each other to generate Universal Harmony,

In which everyone treats each other with kindness and

---

[46] Original Vietnamese term 'Ngọc Kinh' or 'Bạch Ngọc Kinh' is Jade Palace where Supreme God reigns; in the context of this sentence, it means the Nirvana or the Paradise.

loyalty.

Fraternity is built on extreme honesty and sincerity

In the Universal Love to save mankind from upcoming catastrophe;

It preaches God-Way to everyone,

And serves as a ladder for fleeing from the profane world.

Fraternity is first of all your self-protection,

It unites dignified people heart-to-heart and mind-to-mind.

Only with fraternity can the universal love be developed,

To serve as motivation for the universal salvation.

Overview on FRATERNITY and HARMONY of God-Way,

The Fraternal Union reforms society and creates life.

Esoteric disciples conserve the pure and eliminate the impure,

Persevere in this syncretism to forge into Buddha and Immortals.

Union of the Five Primordial Elements[47] results in spiritual sublimation,

Moderation of Energy and Spirit[48] determines mercury-lead harmony.[49]

In this process of self-purification and quintessence-condensation,

Those who can harmoniously balance these energies will succeed.

To deeply comprehend this original teaching,

---

[47] The Five Primordial Elements are Fire, Water, Wood, Metal, and Earth (Alkaline).

[48] Original Vietnamese term 'thần khí' means spirit and energy, two of the Three Treasures in humans: Quintessence (Tinh), Energy (Khí), and Spirit (Thần). In the context of this sentence, Energy also includes Quintessence due to the conversion of Quintessence to Energy in Taoist Alchemy.

[49] mercury and lead refer to the Primordial Elements Fire and Water in Taoist Alchemy.

There is no other way than acquiring union and fraternity.

How sacred and precious the term Harmony!

It encloses the Universe, interlinking the low and the high,

Heaven and Earth come from it,

Buddha and Immortals apply it to achieve ascension.

Those people earning good karma from past lives

Treat fraternity as a priceless pearl or jade.

Yet fraternity is not easy to accomplish!

Those who acquire it are freed from the death-life cycle.

Disciples in the same school,

Practice fraternity and forbearance to avoid aberrations.

Those who deny them,

See the fire of their desires blaze their spiritual credits.

Everyone likes and adores fraternity,

This union of heart deserves all praises and compliments.

Humble yourself to be elevated,

Should you climb high you will be pitifully overthrown!

Fraternity is the method of globalization,

Fraternal union is just and impartial to everyone.

Practice fraternity and forbearance with people around you,

To gain peace of mind and respect from others.

Acquiring fraternity is a great achievement,

Only the incompetent and muddled neglect it!

Shine up the harmony jade brilliantly,

To unite willful people of superior mind.

Poem:

Superior mind accomplishes fraternity,

Thanks to fraternity, all beings are engendered,

Thanks to fraternity, humans can forge into Buddha and Immortals,

And identify to the Absolute Emptiness to stay with your MASTER.

I bless you all. I ascend.

The 2nd day of the 9th month of Bính Tý year (1936)

UNION

CAO-ĐÀI TIÊN TRƯỞNG
CAO-DAI SENIOR IMMORTAL

Poem:

CAO-DAI preaches the miraculous method,

To reveal the Great DAO to this world.

Immortals and Buddha assist in guiding mankind,

As the SENIOR IMMORTAL grants this Scripture of heart.

Your MASTER. I greet all children of both sexes. I am very pleased to activate the mechanism to save the world. May impiety be faded while good morals, beautiful traditions, and saintly affections be restored to establish the perfect upright and extreme aesthetic world.

Poem:

Purify your mind until it becomes upright,

Serve mankind until its good time;

Restore traditions to establish order and peace,

Breathe harmoniously to absorb life energy.

Poem:

To fraternally unite mankind all over the world,

Dignified men assemble to wake up their peoples;

In union everyone mutually helps and self-governs,

To express friendship and develop spirit.

Lesson in Verse:

Unite fraternally with co-religionists,

Love and help each other like siblings.

Corporally separated but spiritually linked,

Together forge the spirit of lucidity.

People of the same race perpetuate fraternal union,

The wise guide, the unwise follow;

Share the burdens of grief, trouble and danger,

Love and stick with each other to save the world.

An actual face is worth more than ten stacks of mere words,

Just as the union of ten trees forms a mountain.

Hold the fervor and willingness steadfast,

To live with and die for each other.

Unify competences and virtues to accrue in kindness,

Observe the Celestial Law to advance in self-cultivation.

Even with the impious and ignorant,

Love them all and share their burdens.

Together in the furnace of the Creator,

Fraternally unite to ensure the perpetuity of mankind.

Adorn culture with esoteric traditions,

Preach the true teaching to human world.

Isolation only causes constant trouble;
Rally one after another in the fraternal union,
Embark together in the boat of wisdom,
Teach mutually the method to avoid aberration.

 Joyfully share the task of moderating mankind,
Renovate the human world in accord with its circumstances;
Bring peace and prosperity to the peoples,
Restore fraternity and affections throughout the world.

Unite everyone near and far,
Fill the gap between North and South,
Gather everyone under the same roof,
Let the entire world live together in peace.

In review of the current status of mankind,
Deviating from God-Way, this world is so brutal,
All fraternal links are corrupt,
And filial affections are grievously deserted.

Due to profits and fame, they harm each other by all means;
Due to power, they separate into sects and orders;
Due to ambition and egoism, they fight each other,
For comfort in material life, not for justice and love.

Due to their constant competition and squabbles,
Human affections are impracticable;
Siblings cannot meet each other,
As everyone greedily cares for his own hoard.

Ban your ego and selfishness,

Show your love and care of others;

To cross the river you build a bridge,

To save mankind you join hands with each other.

Build up fraternal union,

And do not exploit each other.

Disunity weakens the human race

Due to loose linkages and dwindled affections.

Unite to revivify the ancient foundation,

Help each other to flee from this dusty world.

Serve loyally your country and people,

Like the heroes fully devoting to their communities.

Poem:

Once the equilibrium is restored, the true teaching is revivified,

Everyone will be happy

To re-establish good morals and customs,

To unite accordingly to what DAO holds up.

Hold up the values of religious practitioners,

Practice esoteric exercises to dissipate the ignorant veil,

Unveil this hazy port of illusion,

Disillusion of fame and riches so as to freely travel.

Travel leisurely to enjoy wine and games with Immortals,

Immortal pill dissipates all your grief,

Grieve that humans are unaware of their divine nature,

Naturally, no one has the heart to condemn the foolish!

Fooling around the Five Continents piled up with catastrophes,

The catastrophic world is coming to its end,

Ended people have not yet considered self-cultivation,

Self-cultivate in DAO to avoid disastrous intensities.

Intense love is found in the universal fraternity,

Fraternizing everyone with the leisure of drinking in reciting poems,

Reciting poems reveals the bliss of attaining wisdom and virtues,

Virtues come with the enlightenment of conscience.

Conscience absolutely pure and calm is clairvoyance,

Clairvoyant people hasten to forge their souls and bodies,

Embodying with the corporal materials obscures the mind,

Obscured mind is barely compatible to Buddha!

Buddha has come many times to preach,

Preached men cleanse up their souls,

Souls impregnated with vices cannot cultivate,

Cultivate the mechanism to attain Universal Harmony.

Rhyming prose:

Look at this world! Alas! People are so ignorant!

Why do they zealously jump into the dark abysses of Satan?

I have come and advised so many times,

Their profane characters! Alas! These are countless!

This impious mankind is really ignorant,

Being content to drown itself in the karmic ocean!

Poetic prose:

In this last Era,[50] DAO and its Virtues is revealed,

To save the world from the abyss of ignorance.

The grand tribulation is close,

Yet, no one launches in the radiant path.

Humans keep drifting without seeking a shore,

They submerge in the tide of desires and ambition,

And bury their souls in the four carnal dungeons.[51]

Yet, they still compete with each other for the best,

And wonder which is right, which is wrong.

It is so disgusting to think about this world...!

Human status is really pitiful,

Everyone is contracted with the devilish illness.

They compete with each other with trickeries and violence,

To exterminate or exploit each other.

These are so impious, disloyal, and ungrateful,

Their cruelties upset honest people,

Who frown in perceiving such worldly circumstances,

Who close eyes to avoid this sad picture of a corrupt mankind.

 Alas! People regress toward the Devil, not progress toward the Angel,

Ascension or fall, this dilemma is so painful to ponder.

Devilish illness has seriously gnawed this mankind for a long time,

---

[50] The last Era of the Cosmic Revolution, i.e., the Inferior Era, the Annihilation Era.

[51] The four carnal dungeons are beauty, riches, vanity, and alcoholic imbibing.

Even miraculous remedy cannot reverse such effects.

I would have abandoned this impious world,

But I do not have the heart to disregard its cruel destiny.

Here I aspire to expectations and wishes:

May the last Era save mankind from the universal catastrophe!

I use miraculous remedy to treat greed and ignorance,

Such detoxification purifies and strengthens human souls.

As the toxin is deeply penetrated, mankind hardly avoids death;

Yet, the Saintly Doctrine can miraculously liberate unjustly-dead souls.

To restore peace in this world,

Its disturbing elements must be eliminated.

The impious have to succumb under the pressure of their malice,

While the pious, though weak, are unbreakable and long lasting.

To shed some light on this obscure future,

Study the physical constitution decreed by CAO-DAI FAITH.

Mankind cannot fight the catastrophic outburst,

As the destructive scourges are unpredictable and immeasurable;

But the grand tribulation certainly marks the end of this impious world,

Following this event, the Golden Age of the Ancient Era will be revived.

Poem:

Tales and legends, conserved in Annals,

Account for the persistent effort of ascetics,

Who endured challenges in the quest for the Master of DAO;

Due to such forbearance, they became renowned.

Known as CAO-DAI for CHIẾU-MINH branch,

It teaches the spiritual alchemy of immortality,

Humans have endured myriad trials since birth,

Many of them cannot have peace at their last sigh.

Recount old stories of Saints and Sages,

TRỌNG NI[52] prostrated before the PRECOCIOUS DEITY,[53]

Whereas HIÊN VIÊN[54] had endured hardships for years and months,

In order to receive the true method of deliverance.

In the past, to quest for DAO consumed great effort,

Seekers patiently endured all austerities,

They even exhausted their willpower before finding the True Master.

Nowadays, the true teaching is within your grasp.

I bless you all. I ascend.

---

[52] TRỌNG NI is CONFUCIUS, the Founder of Confucianism.

[53] In this case, it alludes to HẠNG THÁC, the very young Master of Confucius; he was just a child when Confucius bowed to Him after receiving the Spiritual Traditions from Him.

[54] HIÊN VIÊN is a legendary Emperor of Ancient China.

The 27th day of the 8th month of Bính Tý year (1936)

WISDOM AND VIRTUE

NGỌC HOÀNG THƯỢNG ĐẾ
JADE EMPEROR SUPREME GOD

Poem:

JADE EMPEROR SUPREME GOD operates the miraculous DAO,

To restore and console humans from their grief and suffering;

HE opens the Contest of Flowery Dragon[55] to recruit Sages and Saints,

And revivifies the true traditions to gather the elects.

Your MASTER is in great pleasure. Listen with quietude in your mind. I explain the terms ĐẠO ĐỨC, i.e., WISDOM AND VIRTUE.

Wisdom and Virtue should pair up with each other. Wisdom is the Yang, and Virtue, the Yin. Yin and Yang have to fraternize, unite, and intimately moderate each other in order to fructify.

Humans should recognize God Way, and self-cultivate in order to return to the original destination. They should rely on DAO, i.e., the method of God, to perfect their souls and bodies, and apply its great virtue to forge themselves into the pure and noble life.

Humans should acquire DAO; they need to work on expanding and augmenting it. On the other hand, DAO does not expand and augment mankind. (Man propagates DAO, but not vice versa).

Wisdom and virtue are the standards up to which humans should strive so as to perfect their mind and characters. Should they

---

[55] The General Judgment.

deviate from wisdom and virtue, they would fall in hallucination, the spiritual blindness leading to abysses of Satan.

Lesson in Verse:

Humans deprived of DAO are like a bottomless tank,

Through which all the water flows in is leaked out;

Those who acquire DAO and virtue are favorable,

Like a boat sailing downstream before the wind.

DAO the pure Yang energy,

That breeds and nurtures all beings,

In serenity, vigor, and joy,

They blossom and exhale their suave perfumes.

Being the link between Heaven and Earth,

Virtue spreads thoroughly everywhere in the Universe.

Thanks to it, humans and other beings can evolve;

Thanks to it, initiates can open up the Nine Celestial Worlds.

Humans acquire DAO by self-edifying the foundation of Truth,

Their determination is the key to success,

Their perseverance results in celestial dignity,

DAO helps develop their nature, purity, and mercy.

DAO in humans is like jade,

If not polished to shine,

It remains dull and crude,

Virtue is the polish and, DAO the crude jade.

If DAO is without virtue,

It is like a boat on land;

Virtue is the water flow,

Circulating in oceans and on mountains.

Never should dignified man neglect virtue!

Virtue is for him the compass and measures.

Virtue lasts, everything lives and prospers,

Virtue shines, it illumines the entire world.

Virtue is the origin of Buddha and God,

Virtue of Sages and Saints shines more brilliantly than stars.

Virtue is like the bark of a tree,

Without bark, can any tree survive?

Virtue embellishes and ennobles all good values,

Virtue compassionately spreads all over the world,

Virtue is the universal love among humans and other beings,

Virtue is the infinite source of favor humans should know.

Virtue flourishes abundantly and brilliantly,

Virtue circulates silently and naturally,

Virtue brings humans closer to Sages and Saints,

Those cultivating hidden virtue are Immortal in the profane world.

Hidden virtue glows like the full moon,

Those harboring it do not show off their values;

They simply strive to accomplish their self-perfection,

And respect others like jade, gold, or pearl.

Poem:

Pearls and jades are rare gems in this world,
Which people seek and adore;
Fame and power excite human desires,
Yet, pious disciples consider them as playthings!

Playing until saturated with worldly flavors,
Imbibing, vanity, beauty, riches are included.
Once squandering all residues of good karma,
When misfortune knocks, you call God for help!

Call God for help, but what can HE do for you?
Fortune or misfortune depending on what you did previously,
If you exhaust your good karma and augment the bad one,
Despite His Mercy, God cannot save you!

Save you if you valiantly persevere in esoteric practice,
Once accomplishing, you will enjoy the eternal rest.
Evade from the tide of this illusionary world,
And diligently amass DAO and virtue.

I bless you all. I ascend.

The 13th day of the 8th month of Bính Tý year (1936)

SELF-SACRIFICE TO SERVE OTHERS

CAO ĐÀI TIÊN ÔNG
CAO-DAI SENIOR IMMORTAL

Poem:

Serene spirits enjoy the high and pure realms,

It is the Sojourn for those who acquire DAO and Virtue;

Immortals and Buddha manifest themselves to save the world,

CAO-DAI IMMORTAL gathers His Children back to the Paradise.

Your MASTER. I greet you all.

Poem:

The ascension path is very abrupt and narrow,

Cautiously grope your way through the heath;

Tumbling over it, you will fall in deep abysses,

Cling tightly so as not to lose your MASTER'S trace.

Losing your MASTER'S trace you will suffer forever,

Infinitely crushed under the karmic wheel,

To metamorphose from animal to mankind, and vice versa,

You barely have the chance to flee from grief and miseries!

I sadly perceive my children drowning forever in the mire of fame and riches, and enduring the eternal cycle of incarnation in the furnace of the Creator. I cannot keep my hands crossed to let it happen. So, I abandon my throne and manifest in this world to save them by founding the true DAO to open the divine path for humans to return to their original destination.

This time, since I have come, is the inauguration of a blissful era for entire mankind. I want to deliver you from this world of illusion and suffering, and to break off all your karmic links. Which method would I use to save you?

The majority among you who have not comprehended DAO assume that the exoteric teaching would suffice. They do not know that only the profoundly mystic esoteric method can lead to the complete dematerialization, and that these spiritual traditions can only be transmitted heart-to-heart, mouth-to-ears to those who are disenchanted of this impious world. Due to that method of heart, disciples who succeed in formulating the Aura of Light can detach their carnal bodies to evade from this world of four sufferings.[56] This enigma remains unfathomable to you.

Poem:

Past till present the Three Doctrines[57] have taught the same method,

By which mankind can forge into Immortals and Saints;

Nowadays I revivify that esoteric teaching,

And unite the Three Purities to reveal this miracle.

Children in séance! You should maintain quietude in mind, so that I can teach you.

Lesson in Verse:

The Cao-Dai bell rings its wakening sounds,

While the enlightening torch illumines the path of deliverance.

To serve others, mankind and animals sacrifice themselves,

In earning credit to expiate their sins and gradually unwind their Karma.

As example, vegetation does not live for its own benefits,

---

[56] The four sufferings are birth, ailments, aging, and death.

[57] The Three Ancient Doctrines: Confucianism, Taoism, and Buddhism.

Never does it stop sacrificing itself for others,

Its weeds, flowers, and fruits nourish other species in the world,

Thank to this food source, myriads of beings perpetuate.

To serve others, do not mind hard work,

Pursue your goal despite all trials,

Brave the dangers and obstructions,

Overcome the steep mountain and deep sea of challenges.

Animals sacrifice miserably,

They endure sun and rain, winter cold and summer heat,

Without a complaint of hardships or suffering,

To render services to mankind.

Domestic animals serve their master,

By loyally providing their bodies and souls,

No matter how they are treated,

They faithfully sacrifice themselves for their master's use.

Buffaloes and horses disregard their cruel destinies,

They endure the hard and vile tasks without offense,

And completely dispense themselves in their labors,

Only to be fed with a portion of wild grass.

These servants do not cost their master anything,

And never do they betray him or her.

Yet, very often they endure cruel beatings,

What a sorrowful fate of buffaloes and horses!

Once aging, they die of exhaustion and ailments,

Their wrecked body weakens on their shaking legs;

Despite all the hard labors throughout their lifetimes,

People do not feel pity for them.

With cruelty, the butcher displays his art,

In removing their skin and cutting their corpses.

Being chopped into hundreds of pieces,

They are severely punished for the services they provided.

Why is mankind so inconsiderate?

How can you have the heart to chop and eat those carcasses?

How can you enjoy such perversion?

How can you have appetite in swallowing those corpses?

Dogs secure their master's properties,

Day and night they keep watch over the house,

If a thief comes nearby,

They bark furiously to wake their masters.

Even dogs know to hold up fidelity,

How can people betray their families or country?

Even dogs live and die for loyalty,

How can humans swindle thoughtlessly?

Silkworms are small caterpillars but very useful to mankind,

Their workload is tremendously greater than their force,

They spin the silken cocoon with an accomplished art,

And use their bodies to produce silk.

Each lifetime they endure numerous metamorphoses,

They work hard for the common benefits;

Not for their own interest of life,

They transform into a chrysalis to achieve their work.

They sacrifice their own life to benefit other species.

Alas! These examples make mankind blush!

Even animals have the sense of sacrifice,

How about mankind, the superior species in this world?

Animals suffer physically in their sacrifices,

Humans only need to devote their mind in services.

Avoid committing further sins or errors,

So as to save others drowning in the ocean of grief.

Sacrifice yourselves to serve others,

Work for the common benefits of your people,

All humans are siblings of the same FATHER,

And animals are also your relatives.

Willful people! Seize this favorable occasion,

Rally mankind in the miraculous DAO,

To reform the devilish world into a saintly one,

To develop human conscience so as to establish the nation.

Cultivate fraternity and union,

Teach the esotericism of enlightenment and deliverance,

If everyone illumines his saintly nature,

Peace will be established in families and nations.

Poem:

With peace in mind, establish firmly the divine mechanism,

To cultivate and illumine the spirit of citizen,

To unite pacified families and organized nations,

To enjoy the strong and rich world of ethics.

I bless you all. I ascend.

The 4th day of the 9th month of Bính Tý year (1936)

THE TWO GRAND SOURCES OF GRATITUDE

CAO ĐÀI GIÁO CHỦ
CAO-DAI FOUNDER

Poem:

CAO-DAI FOUNDER holds the sovereignty of the Universe,

On the Throne of Lotus, I oversee the Genesis,

I teach and advice humans to get back to their origin,

By focusing on self-perfection to forge into Buddha and Immortals.

Your MASTER greets you all.

Poem:

I was sweating on the Crucifix of Piety,

And bleeding to atone human sins;

I accepted death for the redemption to all beings,

Yet, I never mind such grief to save you, my children!

Here I briefly explain to you the DAO.

The methods to save this world should be based on ethics, clemency, loyalty, courtesy, and intelligence, that serve as the compass and measure in teaching humans, so that they thoroughly understand the profound Truth, and conscientiously work on the self-correction of their body and soul.

People should first illumine their conscience, then purify their nature, before managing their families and ruling their countries. Whoever has a physical body should acknowledge the grand gratitude to:

First, God or Supreme Being who gives each person a point of divine nature.

Second, parents whose gametes unite to engender the person's corporal body.

The point of divine nature is the profoundly mystic and supreme nature that assembles with the corporal body to form "the soul-body union". Thanks to that divine nature, humans are able to acquire DAO, and discern good from bad, right from wrong, joy from sorrow. In summary, humans are able to know everything in the world.

Unfortunately, humans are so attached to profane life; they bury the point of divine nature deeply inside their instincts and passions, and crush it under the mountain of their sins. Children! This devilish malady currently penetrates into your bone and flesh. Should you not seek a remedy, certainly you are going to die. Moreover, the malady reaches its severity. Day and night, the worms gnaw at your bone and marrow, pierce your liver, intestines, and lungs, suck your blood, and exhaust your strength and energy. Only could the God of Medicine BIỂN THƯỚC[58] save you, thanks to his accurate diagnoses and his miraculous remedies. At this time, you are delighted in listening to his words. Yet, you do not show your eagerness and still hesitate to follow his regimen. Should you wait until the agonies occur to supplicate BIỂN THƯỚC for remedy, the God of Medicine could no longer cure your malady, and will simply announce the imminent date and time of your death. ... (*I'm smiling*).

---

[58] BIỂN THƯỚC or Bian Que (died 310 BC) was, according to legend, the earliest known Chinese physician. His real name is said to be Qin Yueren, but his medical skills were so amazing that the people gave him the same name as the legendary doctor Bian Que, from the time of the Yellow Emperor. He was a native of the State of Qi in Ancient China. According to the legend recorded in the Records of the Grand Historian, he was gifted with clairvoyance from a deity when he was working as a noble hostel staff. The legend states that while being an attendant at the hostel, he encountered an old man who stayed there for many years. The old man was thankful of Bian Que's attentive service and politeness, and gave him a packet of medicine which he told Bian Que to boil in water. After taking this medicine, he gained the ability to see through the human body. He thereby became an excellent diagnostician with his X-ray-like ability. He also excelled in pulse taking and acupuncture therapy. [Source: *en.wikipedia.org*]

Alas! This epidemic illness is spread throughout the entire world. Submerged under its outbursts and convulsions, the patients have only a couple of days to live. Who among you are not anxious, grievous, and worried about such contagion?

Physical ailments may be cured. But the moral illnesses are really horrible, because they fill the world with sins, grief, and disturbances. At present, I am the God of Medicine BIỂN THƯỚC, coming to cure your fatal illness. Should you be unwilling to take my regimen, you surely wait to die. At your death, "you will see ME once again". You will have to kneel in front of the Celestial Tribunal to declare all the sins you committed during your corporal life. At this General Judgment, even if you repent and supplicate ME to save you, I cannot do so. Children, try to understand what I am saying! Those among you, who still conserve some faint light of Conscience, and who retain a vague intuition of their divine nature, should hasten to persevere in self-cultivation, as well as to willfully acquire DAO and Virtue. These pious children know how to appreciate and nurture their soul so as to purify it until perfection.

You nourish your body with foods, such as cereals and other exotic dishes, capable of providing strength and energy so that your body can accomplish whatever tasks you want. As for your soul, besides self-cultivation, you also need to practice esoteric exercises to harmonize the Yin and Yang, filter and extract the quintessence in order to nurture your soul until illumination and perfection. That is why your daily sessions of meditation are the method to forge and strain your soul so that it becomes pure and light, brilliant, saintly, and wise. Moreover, should you starve yourselves in many days, your body becomes skinny, wretched, exhausted, and weakened. Similarly, should you neglect your spiritual exercises, your soul becomes obscure, impure and heavy. It tends to descend and not elevate. Never can such an imperfect soul evade from the three worlds of illusion.[59]

I ascend.

---

[59] The three worlds of illusion are the world of passion, world of form, and world of non-form.

The 26th day of the 8th month of Bính Tý year (1936)

AWAKENING

CAO-ĐÀI GIÁO CHỦ
CAO-DAI FOUNDER

Poem:

The SUPREME Virtue spreads all over the world,

GOD grants lotus thrones as miraculous rewards,

To wake humans up on the Path of Deliverance,

And recruit superior spirits in the Saintly DAO

Your MASTER greets you all.

Rhyming prose:

The source of ethic-virtue is the profound enigma,

Only those with a vigilant faith could discover it.

The decrepitude of this world is not afar,

And its complete abolishment is clearly exposed.

Upheavals shatter everywhere on earth,

While wars and terrors spread throughout the world.

Alas! Countless families and peoples suffer from dissolution,

And from terrible grief and scourges.

DAO manifests, signaling the end of the world,

Buddha and Immortals warn humans to self-correct;

Yet, most of you still prefer vileness and illusion,

You are content to die in the dungeons of sins and errors.

Despite all my repeating counsels, you do not repent,

Instead, you keep sinking in the ocean of ignorance.

The vicissitudes are so frightful to witness!

But you remain insensitive to my warnings.

When the tribulation occurs, you will be terrified,

And recall ME. But who knows where I am!

I decide to eradicate the citadel of grief and ocean of suffering,

But you have to endure terrible vicissitudes for some time.

Long poem:

The Saint Virtue bell is ringing to wake souls up,

As DAO is revivified to save and conserve all beings.

This impious world is so vile and hostile,

Why do you bury yourselves in such a reproachable site?

This world is abhorrent and contemptible,

Get away and flee from it once forever.

Human life is a stinking morass,

It is a dirty pond, a bait of Demons.

Vivacious colors are attractive to carnal eyes,

They trigger desires and push you into deadly abysses.

Mankind in contemporary decadence,

Tends toward hatred and massacre, without mercy.

This serious impiety overthrows temples and ramparts,

Causing family ruins, nation chaos, and world troubles.

Perceiving this catastrophe, I cry in hot tears

Pitying on my ignorant children!

They resign in the obscure dungeons of illusion,

And imprison themselves in the abysses forever.

Touched by their miseries,

I come to point out aberrations;

They create such huge mountains of sins,

That a lifetime does not suffice to expiate them all!

Due to desires and passions, they endure suffering,

While their mind becomes obscure and spirit, impure.

I see my children in this world segregating, squabbling, and competing with each other for food, land, fame, and riches. They act like a knot of hungry snakes in the same pit, fighting, killing, and devouring each other, with no consideration or discernment of good and evil.

Alas! You all commit sins and share the same fate in this pond of distress and grief. Yet, instead of mutually helping and collaborating in finding an escape, you exterminate each other. You are so silly! So foolish!

Human life is a river of ignorance and an ocean of suffering. Desires and passions imprison your souls tightly in the dungeon of grief. You should recognize this world is merely a big trick for everyone; all are fake dreams and deceitful reveries. That is why your seven emotions and six sensual attractions deceive you toward the appeals of perishable favor and profit, so as to incarcerate yourselves between the four walls of beauty, riches, alcoholic imbibing, and vanity. What a miserable world! Everything in human life is bathed with grief! Concentrating in sensuous pleasures and worldly interests, humans exhaust their souls and engage in the vicious cycle of sorrow, worrying, inquietude, suffering, and grief.

Right at birth, humans begin to sorrow[60]. Alas! From birth till death, scourges and grief incessantly happen. Then when they are aging, their back is bent and their knees are sagged, maladies and disabilities develop along with thousands of hideous suffering.

But even if life is extremely grievous, its existence is indispensable. It is so because, being succumbed by suffering, the world is prone to transform itself into the field of evolution with trials and contests destined for mankind to progress.

---

[60] Babies wail at their first moment in the world.

Nevertheless, I would ask you this question: Is it true that life is extremely grievous, or is it because you create suffering for yourselves?

Children! Consider this. Life itself is not painful at all. Your sins lead to grief. The more you yield to desires, passions, and aberrations, the more ways to incur grief. Without desires, passions, and aberrations, there are no sins, no expiation, and no Karma. Greedy for fame and riches, you enslave your body and exhaust your souls. Envying beautiful spouses and smart children, you tie yourselves up with conjugal and filial links. The more you dive in the illusionary world, imprison in the four carnal dungeons, and enslave to the seven emotions, the more you want to continue with myriads of worldly pleasures. This pursuit is the origin of horrible catastrophes in which corpses litter on the ground, blood floods the river, and consequently the deprivation of morals and the degradation of DAO and virtue.

Alas! Getting to such stage of corruption, this world is merely a terrible battlefield, a horrible massacre, filled with countless miseries, endless wars, and widespread crimes. Even children of the same blood and the same race kill each other to satisfy their bestiality. As a result, morals, good traditions, and saintly affections no longer exist!

Facing this universal corruption, even Sages do not know any remedy for such human foolishness. It signals that the world has come to the end.

Nevertheless, if humans nowadays learn and adopt DAO and Virtue as the central norms of their morals, the universal calamity will diminish little by little and yield to the ethical and aesthetic improvements.

Humans should rely on DAO and virtue to re-educate the citizen spirit, and refrain from desires and passions so as to get back on the path of clemency, loyalty, and happiness.

Only when humans clearly and deeply understand the infallible law of expiation and karmic causation, can they recover their true destiny, regenerate their body and souls, restore good traditions, and rectify the morals which serve as the norms for mankind. Once rehabilitated, this world will be gradually replenished with the ethical spirit that encourages humans to perform good deeds, to avoid scourges and grief. Little by little, humans will comprehend the source of DAO and virtue to discover the unique origin of the universe and all beings.

Once penetrating that common origin, humans will mutually re-fraternize, as they understand that all beings in this world, including vegetal, animal, and human, come from the same furnace of the Creator, share the same spiritual source. Consequently, they consider each other as siblings, older is senior, younger is junior; the universal love is so developed that they no longer want to eat the flesh, chew the bone, and suck the blood of any other beings. Humans at this evolutionary stage will attain the culminant point of their moral perfection; bad emotions and vile passions such as egoism, hatred, envy, jealousy, etc. will no longer exist. Then the universal peace comes to this world, establishing the Golden Age of Thuấn-Nghiêu,[61] where all beings enjoy and mutually share the universal harmony. Isn't it right that human dignity is also forged, thanks to ethics and virtue?

Oh! DAO is so admirable! DAO is so adorable! Unfortunately, this world has still not well understood it. If an individual understands DAO, then ten, hundreds, thousands know DAO, all families and all peoples in the entire world also know DAO. Then who else would commit sins? Then the government no longer needs to enforce laws, doesn't it?

Alas! This miserable world has established lots of implacable laws, rigorous penalties, and even utilized weapons. Yet, its outcome is not only do the impious and cruel remain, but also such impiety and cruelty augment day by day in amplitude as well as in frequency!

Only when humans understand the karmic law, and only when they adore DAO and virtue, then they dare not commit a single offense, even the most discreet one. It is so, because discretion may be hidden from other people, but never can it be a secret to their conscience and the expiation mechanism.

---

[61] That period is comparable to the Paradise on Earth. King NGHIÊU, or YAO (尧), 2356 – 2255 BC, and. King THUẤN, or YU THE GREAT (大禹), 2200 - 2100 BC were among the Three Emperors and Five Kingdoms in Ancient China.

Therefore, nothing is more indispensable to this world than the DAO and virtue. Only when the DAO and virtue are preached, can this world be transformed, and can humans extricate desires and passions. As their bestiality is disciplined, their brutality will disappear; as brutality disappears, suffering is ended. Hence, you should fraternally unite with each other and join your effort in the propagation of the Saintly Doctrine to save all beings in this last era.

Life normally oscillates between order and anarchy; as anarchy is minimized, order is restored. By the same token, DAO also knows its peak and trough; a midnight of decadence is followed by a dawn of renaissance. These vicissitudes are not beyond the evolutionary cycle of Genesis.

I bless you. I ascend.

The 18th day of the 8th month of Bính Tý year (1936)

A LAMENTATION

CAO ĐÀI BỒ TÁT
CAO-DAI BODDHISATTVA

Poem:

CAO-DAI BODDHISATTVA blesses the entire universe,

From the Jade Palace, HE radiates the brilliant Saint-Esprit,

To focus the mechanism of DAO on humans via their eyes,

To establish the true teaching to conserve their conscience.

Your MASTER greets you all.

Poem:

Multiple times giving advice to my children,

I am breathless, hoarse, and exhausted;

Their profound ignorance is so deplorable,

As they impassibly accumulate mountains of sins.

Lesson in Verse:

This world shows no attempt to save itself,

This world errs in myriad aberrations,

This world is intolerantly problematic,

This world generates scourges to itself.

This world causes grief and suffering,

This world is blind with brutalities and atrocities,

This world provides humans no peace or security,

This world spreads its cruelty and bestiality.

This world, deprived of DAO, blazes with desires and passions,

This world vainly seeks to avoid the grand tribulation;

This world displays the more bitter and deceptive issues,

This world arises with the more sarcastic and flattery voices.

This world should avoid karmic expiation,

This world should seek the esoteric teaching,

This world is so spiritually devastated,

This world of materialism signals human annihilation.

This world always looks for profit,

This world should revivify DAO to illume its spirit,

This world is a good bait of Satan,

This world is like a ripe fruit hanging on a branch in the wind.

This world shares together all vicissitudes,

This world still rivals each other, why so?

This world is so absent-minded,

This world likes vivacity: sounds, colors, and superstition.

This world exterminates the wise and sage,

This world never can expiate all its Karma,

This world is troubled with wars, miseries, and scourges,

This world has no long-term stability or security.

This world has to endure calamities and scourges,

This world is terribly punished,

This world deviates from the wakening Wisdom of God,

This world is so inconsiderate and insouciant.

This world contents to remain in the furnace of Creator,

This world, with its tide of desires, can push down high mountains,

This world is flickering like a lamp running out of oil,

This world should revivify the Saintly Doctrine to regenerate itself.

This world should head on the path of Wisdom and virtues,

This world should develop its mental and spiritual values,

This world should accomplish piety, loyalty, and clemency,

This world, once acquiring DAO, approaches Buddha and Immortals.

This world can forge into Sages and Saints,

This world can re-establish peace and prosperity.

This world should advance in self-cultivation,

This world should mutually support and help other beings.

This world, once regenerated, will get back to the blessing source,

This world will then liberate itself like fish leaving lake for ocean,

This world will preach the Saintly Doctrine of Universal

Fraternity,

This world will reunite at its origin to self-purify and serve others.

Poem:

Acquire DAO and virtue to have peace in your entire life,

Forge your nature into absolute emptiness to penetrate the Nirvana,

Wipe off all worldly appeals to maintain perfect quietude of your mind,

Circulate your breath up and down to enjoy the magnificence of DAO.

I bless you all. I ascend.

The 25th day of the 8th month of Bính Tý year (1936)

EXPIATION AND REINCARNATION

NGỌC HOÀNG THƯỢNG ĐẾ
JADE EMPEROR SUPREME GOD

Poem:

The miraculous JADE[62] radiates under your eyes without you perceiving it,

GOD THE FATHER feels pity on you for such spiritual blindness;

Since very few elects could attain the superior enlightenment,

SUPREME GOD mercifully comes to open the path of salvation.

---

[62] Translator's note: the Miraculous Jade alludes to the Saint-Esprit.

Your MASTER. I greet you all.

Poem:

The Saint-Esprit encompasses the entire Universe,

In which the Invisible world is the Spiritual one;

With body-soul union humans accumulate karma,

Blue Sky[63] illumines and salvages them at dusk.[64]

I perceive this world profoundly corrupted. Humans regress towards materialism, obscuring and losing their spiritual light. Thrilled with vanity and power, they fail to recognize the celestial mechanism and its predetermined terms.

It is now the Era of Annihilation, and the fatal vicissitudes are displayed. Yet, humans are still drowning in imbibing, glory, beauty, and riches, without concerning the upcoming tribulation in which mankind and other beings would perish in the Grand Cosmic Revolution. The world is getting close to its end. I am not content to keep my hands crossed and watch my children being utterly destroyed. I confer the Three Ancient Doctrines and the Congress of Buddha, Immortals, and Saints to preach and revivify God-Way. In this world, good and evil exist side by side. The former adores wisdom and virtues, being interested in spiritual matters and in serving others. The latter is cruel and brutal, being fond of material matters, worldly vanities, and denying God and His Law. I would not let all my children, the pious as well as the impious, endure the upcoming grand torment. I manifest in this world to found the Saintly Doctrine, and open the Grand School of Esoteric Teaching to enlighten and perfect mankind. Anyone who recognizes my Teaching should consider it as the method of deliverance from the karmic cycle of reincarnation.

Poem:

CAO-DAI ĐẠI ĐẠO[65] enlightens and purifies humans,

---

[63] The Blue Sky alludes to the Saint-Esprit or Jade Emperor who presides the Nine Heavens
[64] The Last Era of the Cosmic Revolution.
[65] CAO-DAI GREAT WAY or Cao-Dai Esoteric Teaching

It teaches them the method to attain the absolute emptiness,

It is the compass and measures that form the basis of DAO,

Which humans should regularly practice for their spiritual progress.

Long Poem:

Impartially the Creator loves all beings,

Mercifully HE finds the method for universal salvation.

God and Buddha hold the Secret of Genesis,

It is the heart-to-heart esoteric method to penetrate the origin.

Immense oceans and sky-high mountains are designed by the Creator,

Who, in the Invisible, manifests His Omniscience and Omnipotence.

The Sages seek, contemplate, and think over,

They observe the nature to discover the verities;

All beings are created from the Yin-Yang harmony,

These two energies perpetually animate the Universe.

I am SUPREME GOD, propagating Wisdom and Virtues,

To sovereign the unification of the Universe;

I emanate myriads of the Spirit of Light,

Each of which incarnates in the physical worlds to evolve.

The Three Ancient Doctrines reveal this secret,

Exposing the miraculous method of Buddha and Immortals,

So that humans can understand how DAO is founded,

And how their souls influence the corporal world.

Evolving from vegetal to human destiny,

The soul endures innumerable incarnations,

The more perseverance, the higher ascension,

The finer self-purification, the closer approach to the Eternal

Facility.

Human souls evolve very miraculously,

They can acquire supernatural powers and invisible miracles;

They are extremely valuable and eternal,

After being enlightened and perfectly purified.

The Imponderable Energy encompasses the Supreme Being,

The Supreme Being is the Absolute Master of the Universe,

His Omniscience and Omnipotence are unfathomable,

By which the Mechanism of Creation is operated to yield the Supernatural ĐẠO.

His Saint-Esprit encompasses the entire Universe,

To assure its Order and Perpetuity,

From past till future,

HE creates all beings and all species.

The Supreme Being is the Universal Soul, source of all life,

HE moderates the Yin-Yang union to engender all creatures;

Originated from this Common Soul,

All spirits incarnate in an infinite variety of corporal bodies.

In every body there exists a spark of sacred light,

This divine soul carries life and intelligence;

Yet, there are the wise and the unwise,

Depending on the purity of their souls.

As the spark of light incarnates in the material,

The corporal body is animated by this Buddha nature;

Once the soul leaves the carnal envelope,

The body decomposes back into material.

The soul can enlighten and self-purify,

Due to its experiences in discerning wrong from right;

Incarnated in diverse corporal envelopes,

The soul self-perfects by exercising work of piety.

Progressing on the path of wisdom and virtues,

The soul eventually leaves the body to rejoin its divine origin;

This evolution is so mysterious, so miraculous!

The soul becomes immortal, everlasting in Paradise.

All spirits must incarnate to learn and experience,

Until they comprehend a variety of worlds,

They must learn about life and death,

Also fall and rise, good and evil, enlightenment and ignorance.

Purified souls accede in the radiant path of Wisdom and Virtues,

They self-cultivate to identify with the Absolute Emptiness,

Seeking to receive the miraculous method of heart,

They maintain the quiet mind to practice esoteric exercises day and night.

They penetrate their true identity,[66]

Once they cleanse off all the worldly stains;

While profoundly meditating on the miraculous mechanism,

With the saintly fetus they attain spiritual enlightenment.

Liberated from karmic cycle of expiation,

These souls progress on the radiant path of Buddha and Immortals;

They become exemplary in virtues,

And the world commends their acquisition of the Immortality.

Concerning the souls that deny Love and Justice,

They have to expiate their sins in horrible ordeals,

Incarnated in heavy, coarse, and impure bodies,

---

[66] Original Vietnamese text 'bổn lai diện mục' literally means the original face or Buddha nature, the true identity

These souls are hazy, obscure and veiled by ignorance.

They cannot escape from carnal dungeons,

As multiple links tie them up from all sides.

Should they seek the source of Wisdom and Virtues,

They can completely end all karmic links.

They should remove the exterior and interior envelopes,

By willfully extracting the pure from the impure.

As the souls are liberated and enlightened,

They no longer cherish worldly pleasures.

Karmic debts veil the divine nature,

In endless expiating cycles;

Paying old debts is also contracting new ones,

Cause-and-effect ties up in inexorable Karma.

A crooked image is the projection of a crooked object,

Good and evil incessantly follow each other;

While the carnal body enjoys worldly pleasures,

The soul groans in melancholy and suffering.

What is sowed is immediately reaped,

Cause and effect respond faithfully to each other,

Consider the bullock-cart,

Its wheels rotate with the bull walking rhythm.

The wheels pause when the bull stops,

Fast or slow is determined by the bull steps,

The wheels turn with the bull rhythm,

Moving or not depends on the bull movement.

You criticize others' faults, who would do yours?

Mind your own business and let others do theirs.

To quickly evade the reincarnation cycle,

Endure the intense expiation of your past karma.

In this world there are the poor and the rich, the noble and the common;

It is due to your anterior lives that determine your current class.

Yet, you foolishly blame God for creating such inequalities,

Without thinking that they result from your past karma.

Your greed and desires are boundless,

And the seven emotions take control of your soul;

That is why you are prone to commit errors and sins,

Anyone falling in such traps suffers from scourges.

Your impiety tries to cheat lead for silver,

Expecting to deceive others,

Without knowing you are caught in the divine net,

Which is thin but even the finest thread cannot pass through.

The law of EXPIATION constitutes the Divine Justice,

That may punish the soul first, then the body;

Cause and effect are inseparable,

The Balance of the Creator never mistakes.

Eating a good fruit, you should save its seeds,

And sow them to ensure the perpetuity of its tree;

Should you throw the seeds away after eating the fruit,

Later you would beg others for food.

Today you laugh while being in good circumstances,

Tomorrow you will cry because of your miseries.

Should you earn credit from works of piety,

You will reincarnate in the best circumstances.

On the other hand, if you are brutal and cruel,

You will reincarnate in horrible ordeals.

Why do humans not make any effort in self-correction?

The Celestial Mechanism clearly manifests in the Expiation Law.

Dignified men firmly hold up their will,

And select the way directly leading to the Nirvana.

Thousands of paths display under your eyes,

Discern God-Way from the tortuous or obscure routes.

To penetrate the pure and miraculous DAO,

Maintain peace in mind and practice spiritual exercises;

Observe faithfully the Divine Laws,

Live in accord with the Nature and stay away from vanities.

Focus on evading the carnal dungeons,

And on extricating the seven emotions;

Dust off the worldly appeals with the willow branch,[67]

To develop and transcend your soul.

Cautiously approach the detours on the Path of Salvation,

Persistently follow God-Way until success.

Propagate and circulate the Saint-Esprit,

Willfully self-correct to eliminate ignorance.

Cease your love promises and pledges,

Break up all the links tying you to this world.

Remember: Soft dominates tough, gentle prevails forceful,

Slack remains while stiff breaks; these are common sense.

Misery and happiness are accurately expiated,

Sow good seeds in current life to reap the future fruits.

Brilliant people will face more talented ones,

Arrogance is often subjected to misfortune.

---

[67] The branch of willow tree, held by the Goddess of Mercy, Kuan Yin Boddhisattva, symbolizing for serenity and wisdom.

Poem:

As your karmic debts are endlessly contracted and paid,

Your spiritual nature is tangled in multiple incarnations;

Expiate diligently your past Karma,

Good deeds certainly result in divine blessing.

Karmic expiation exists since the Genesis. Humans could return to the divine source of blessing if they self-cultivate, perform good deeds, and diligently improve their virtues. Otherwise, impious people who attach to devilish brutality and cruelty have to be moored in exile by their karmic links.

The Celestial Law is impartial and infallible: the good echoes the good, and the evil responds to the evil. Why are there in this world the poor and the rich, the noble and the common, the sage and the silly?

Such social inequalities are created by humans themselves. Consider the variety of fruits. Why are some sweet, some sour, pungent, or bitter? The same token applies to the poor and the rich in this world. Sowing the seeds of sweet fruits, you reap the sweet fruits; cultivating the seeds of sour fruits, you harvest the sour fruits. The more you sow, the more you reap. Today, as you are sheltered from hunger and chilliness, you should be as benevolent as possible, to sow the good seeds that assure the future comfort. Should you eat up the fruits and seeds (exterminating their lineage and the source of these revenues), nothing can be reproduced thereafter.

Poem:

Your MASTER dispenses blessings into the world,

As a sacred potion against hallucination;

Knowing that Wisdom-Virtue is the path to the Truth,

Persevere in self-cultivation to penetrate the Nirvana.

The Nirvana is the most enjoyable Sojourn,

There exist all prodigies, miracles, and delights;

In this pure and calm realm, you remain immutable and eternal,

And no longer endure the karmic cycle as you did in the past.

In the past you erred in aberrations,

Now recognizing your MASTER, you should hasten in the Path of Salvation;

Should you still cherish this world, you have to bear all the horrible ordeals,

As this Era of Annihilation is ended with myriad scourges.

I bless you all. I ascend.

The 10th day of the 8th month of Bính Tý year (1936)

THE NATURAL NATURE AND THE ADAPTED NATURE

CAO-DAI FOUNDER. YOUR MASTER.

Poem:

The Balance of Creator is infallibly fair,

Those who dive in worldly pleasures lose their original nature;

They are wrecked by the tidal storm from the ocean of suffering,

And dismantled by the flood from the river of unleashed passions.

Receiving the teaching of heart, keep yourself calm and pure,

Acquiring the key of enigma, stay focused and persistent

Forge your body and soul to regain your original position,

Doing so, you are in accord with the Natural Nature.

I explain the NATURAL NATURE[68] of God and the ADOPTED (NATURALIZED) NATURE[69] of Man.

I perceive mankind keeps competing and exterminating each other for power and profits. They are so passionate in the quest for pleasures that they lose their spirit. They are content to be wrecked in the karmic ocean and locked in the four carnal dungeons.[70] As they do not consider about forging body and soul, they have to endure the wind and submerge in the tide of predicted torments. It is so regrettable! So sorrowful!

Human nature is identical to that of Buddha and Immortals. Yet, man is not immortal and eternal. After about eighty or ninety years, a man is at the end of his lifetime and like a dim shadow in the sunset. A human life is wasted, as he does not use his conscience for judging, thinking, seeking and practicing esoteric exercises; instead, he leaves it obscure and depraved. It is so, because he lets "the Adapted Nature" of man prevail "the 'Natural Nature" of God.

The "NATURAL NATURE" is spiritual. Thus, it only aspires to the transcendent soul and does not attribute any value to the sullied carnal body. I give each of you a divine soul to incarnate in this world, so that you can use the original quintessence of the body to nourish and conserve the original energy, and unite the original energy with the original spirit. In other words, you should convert quintessence of the body into energy, and convert energy into spirit, to forge into Immortals and Buddha. This self-perfection brings you back to the original nature so that you can penetrate and enjoy the serenity in the Nirvana, which is the eternal and immutable world for perfectly pure spirits.

Mountains, rivers, and all other entities in this world endure innumerable vicissitudes; but the soul exists eternally and immutably. Unfortunately, once leaving the origin, you forget the way back. Incarnated in the material world, you keep sinking and cherishing the emotions and pleasures. As you neglect your natural nature, you do not preoccupy yourself with Wisdom and Virtue, nor

---

[68] The Divine Nature, the Spiritual Nature, the Original Nature.

[69] The Spontaneous Nature, the Temporal Nature, the Adapted Nature.

[70] The four carnal dungeons are beauty, riches, alcoholic imbibing, and vanity.

seek the true teaching and the Great DAO of Pre-Genesis to perform spiritual exercises so as to return to the original nature and reunite with your MASTER.

In this material world, once being born all creatures blindly follow their corporal instincts of Post-Genesis Yin-Yang union, by which the sexual-appealed polymorph ties them into the four sufferings,[71] and encloses them in the four carnal dungeons. As long as sexual matters exist, reproduction is generated (these descendants are evolutionary men, like the animals being recently transformed into humans). Yet, you consider this lineage as happiness, with no doubt of being tied up in the net of conjugal bonds and filial links. Even worse, if someone advises you to self-correct, you would always defer it. As time flies, your back bends, your knees shake, your three treasures exhaust, and your five organs perish. Alas! *"Once the Pre-Genesis energy is expended, the impassible scythe of the Dead ceases all mutable matters!"* That is it! A cycle of re-incarnation is wasted! Since mankind has endured so much suffering, nowadays I, your MASTER, JADE EMPEROR SUPREME GOD, do not have the heart to witness the complete disintegration of mankind. Due to my infinite mercy, I emit spiritual energy and manifest in this world to found the Great Way of Pre-Genesis by unifying the Three Ancient Doctrines and teaching the method of heart to salvage my children.

Those who exert the Natural Nature know how to apply spiritual exercises to reverse the normal process of reproduction, by converting the original quintessence into the original energy and uniting it with the original spirit to forge into Immortals and Buddha, and completely deliver from this material world. These are predestined men or pure spirits.[72] On the other hand, those who follow the Adapted Nature have to endure the obligations of animal biology in Post-Genesis reproduction, and are condemned in the vicious cycle of karmic expiation and reincarnation.

---

[71] The four sufferings are birth, ailments, decrepitude, and death.

[72] Translated from the original note: Predestined men or pure spirits are the Pre-Genesis energy incarnating in the corporal world to self-perfect or to salvage humans. Progressive or evolutionary men are the impure spirits evolving from insect or vegetal orders into human order.

Poem:

The unique Nature splits into the forward and the reverse way,[73]

The reverse way leads to the immortality;

Whoever knows in depth the Great Immaterial Way,

Can penetrate it to return to the Blue Cave.[74]

I bless you all. I ascend.

The 9th day of the 8th month of Bính Tý year (1936)

THE UNIVERSAL CENTER
THE CENTRAL POINT (THE CENTER OF THE "GRAND CYCLE" OF DAO)

CAO-DAI FOUNDER

Your MASTER. I greet you all.

Poem:

DAO is the mechanism to create and transform the universe,

DAO, originated from the Absolute Non-Being, is eternal,

DAO of the Three Purities is preached in the Three Religions,

DAO unites the Three and the Five[75] to establish moral standards.

---

[73] The forward way is the adapted nature, the reverse way is the natural nature.

[74] The Blue Cave is the residence of Lao-Tseu Great Immortal, referring to the Sojourn of Immortals.

[75] The Three Ancient Doctrines (Confucianism, Taoism, Buddhism) and the Five Religious Branches (DAO of Man, Deity, Saint, Immortal, Buddha).

DAO is the Imponderable Energy of the Absolute Non-Being. It engenders the Yin and the Yang, creating Heaven and Earth. Then, the pure and the impure mingle, the male and the female harmonize to create all matters and beings, which gradually evolve into vegetal, animal, and mankind. Thus, all creatures are of the same original nature.

Man adopts the Pre-Genesis energy as his spiritual nature, before interacting with the Post-Genesis Yin-Yang pair to form a physical body.

Human body possesses the three treasures and the five elements, because DAO procreates them thoroughly as it does Heaven.

Man is a micro-Cosmos,[76] an equal footing member in the Universal Triad.[77] Therefore, incarnated in the Universe, human beings experience some very difficult times and atrocities. In order to deliver from the corporal world and escape from the four sufferings, human beings should accomplish spiritual and temporal works of piety, regenerate soul and body, and seek and practice esoteric methods of deliverance. An ancient adage predicted that *"At the end of the last era, God reveals the Imperial Teaching"*[78]. This prophecy hints at the fact that nowadays DAO has been opened up to all beings. It includes all the three stages and the nine initiations originally preached in the Three Ancient Doctrines that I reform into a shortcut to lead my children back to the origin.

Humans wishing to become Immortals and Buddha, or even Immortals and Buddha already attaining the complete dematerialization and spiritual enlightenment, all must follow the same route of self-perfection starting with levels in the Small Cycle before getting to the Grand Cycle.

The Small Cycle is the Man-Way. Those who follow the Small Cycle are involved in the framework of religion. This Cycle only teaches the physical aspects. Those, who strictly observe the precepts, abstinence, and commandments, can consider this narrow

---

[76] A Universe in miniature.

[77] The Universal Triad is Heaven – Man – Earth.

[78] The Imperial Way teaches the method to forge into 'real Man'.

path a disciplinary way to guide their first steps toward the immense way of the Grand Cycle.

Beginners should strictly follow the virtue of DAO, first fulfilling their human duties, then initiating their quest for the Heaven-Way which instructs them the method of deliverance to evade the corporal world and reach the spiritual world.

The Grand Cycle teaches metaphysics. Disciples practice meditation and self-cultivation; they should consider everything as nothing. In the past, CONFUCIUS also penetrated the principles of the Grand Cycle when HẠNG THÁC initiated him. Thanks to this intuition, he later attained the Perfection of Saint. But in most of his teaching, he emphasized the Man-Way, guiding humans to the exquisite humanism. Regarding the Esotericism, he only instructed some rare disciples. That is the reason people of later generations mistakenly thought that CONFUCIUS SAINT had not acceded to the Spiritual Way. In fact, anyone who aims to attain spiritual enlightenment must penetrate the Secret of Genesis, harmonize the Yin-Yang pair, and formulate the magic pill to create the double-body. Thus, the Grand Cycle means "*DAO is the Great Learning that aims to illumine the radiant virtue, renovate the people, and only rest in the highest excellence.*"[79]

This God-Way is conceived as follows:

CONFUCIANISM says: *Maintain impartiality to comprehend oneness.*

BUDDHISM says: *Preserve impartiality to converge to oneness.*

TAOISM says: *Hold impartiality to attain oneness.*

Practitioners of the Grand Cycle, already having received esoteric traditions, should set schedules for spiritual exercises to purify their conscience until immaculately clear. In such serenity, they should contemplate to grasp the enigma of Genesis, and penetrate the Registry of Immortals so as to capture the mystic energy of Heaven and unite it with the original energy of Man to create the immortal pill. Therefore, here I emphasize that disciples in the Grand Cycle should seek a clean and pure place to harmonize the

---

[79] The Great Learning is one of the Four Books and the Five Classics of Confucianism.

Yin and Yang so as to prepare the magic pill, by generating exactly eight measures of pure yang and eight measures of pure yin to form one pound of the great remedy at LI ($\equiv\equiv$) arch. Then, after ten months of gestation, the saintly fetus will be formed. And after three years of nursery, the double-body will be able to communicate with the Pre-Genesis world and enter or exit the Celestial Gate[80]. Nevertheless, it is also due to ME, your MASTER, to grant you the Aura of Light based on your merits and virtues.

Poem:

Purify and perfect your conscience to practice spiritual exercises,

Seek and study esoteric methods in the Three Religions,

Once your double-body is created, you penetrate the Heaven Way,

And receive the Pre-Genesis energy to deliver from this terrestrial world.

I bless you all. I ascend.

The 25th day of the 8th month of Bính Tý year (1936)

SELF-PERFECT ACCORDINGLY TO GOD'S WILL

CAO-DAI SENIOR IMMORTAL

Poem:

CAO-DAI imparts His Saintly Doctrine to resolve human problems,

In the marvelous tower, the IMMORTAL sadly watches the world,

HE utilizes the miraculous esotericism to enlighten human spirits,

---

[80] The Nirvana Chamber in human head crown.

And salvage them from complete disintegration.

Your MASTER. I greet you all.

At this time being, I descend in this séance to confide to you some esoteric vestige so that you can observe and live accordingly with God-Way, in order to evade from this illusionary world, and escape from the worldly confinement.

Rhyming Prose:

The secret of Genesis is unfathomable, and could only be penetrated by persistent seekers.

The method of heart, the true DAO, could only be understood by those who make serious effort in studying it.

The Imponderable Nature, with myriads of spiritual laws, needs to be contemplated.

Consider the effort that Buddha, Saints, and Immortals have deployed to discover this true nature;

Penetrating God's nature also influences the natural nature.

Alas! What a miserable world, filled with grief, worrying, inquietude, suffering, and calamities!

You keep carrying your karma from one life to another,

And your corporal desires pull you further in the obscure tracks;

No wonder in such exile you cannot end up your karmic links.

Children! In order to penetrate the miraculous nature, you should self-correct thoroughly so as to shine your conscience up, to recover the norms of the perfect righteousness and sublime moral aesthetic so as to conform to the order and harmony of the true DAO.

The miraculous mechanism of God and Buddha includes myriads of miracles and prodigies. But never could you fathom and understand them using your carnal eyes, obtuse ears, and profane intelligence.

In order to snatch some tiny bit of the secret nature, you should shut your eyes, plug your ears, quiet your mind, and discipline your thoughts.

The miraculous DAO encloses profoundly mystic laws that cannot be thoroughly expressed in words or in pictures. In the past, Saints and Sages devoted their entire lives to these researches; still they were unable to completely unveil the Secret of Creation. But essentially, in your contemplation and meditation, Immortals may shed some light by heart-to-heart transmitting to you the esoteric teaching. Yet, even Immortals and Buddha are unable to fully decode the supreme and omniscient enigma of God.

Nowadays, as you are blessed to receive your MASTER'S Saintly Doctrine, you should persevere in spiritual exercises and self-purification so as to return your original nature to its miraculous origin. In this last era, with infinite love I manifest in this world to guide you back on the right track. But you should sincerely and diligently self-correct; do not overestimate your abilities or lazily rely on my mercy. You should know that even I - your MASTER - have to conform to the authority and law of DAO.

Incarnated in a heavy body, your divine nature is sunk and exiled in the five carnal senses. With infinite love I enlighten and re-animate it. But you should fight your way to evade from mounts of emotions and passions. Do not wait for or expect ME to carry and transport you to Heaven. Children! That is impossible!

DAO is preservation of the pure and elimination of the impure. The pure and light can be united with ME; the impure and heavy must be sunk in the abyss. Thus, you should strain your nature into the perfectly pure yang so as to penetrate the divine realm. The air in the divine realm is hundreds of thousand times lighter than the terrestrial atmosphere. Even a tiny trace of impurity in your nature can prevent you from acceding to such pure and noble realm. I said that "displacing mountains and reverting oceans" is a routine for Immortals and Saints. Yet, bringing the profane back to the origin is beyond their power. Mountains and oceans are heavy, but they do not own seven emotions and six sensual attractions. Human corporal bodies are quite tiny; but, being intertwined with desires and bestiality, they become hundreds of thousand times heavier than mountains. Despite my infinite love, I cannot carry you in my arms. Therefore, you should practice esoteric methods to self-perfect, to separate and extract the pure from the impure, to escape from the cycle of reincarnation in the six paths of metempsychosis.[81]

Long Poem:

DAO of GOD corrects and regenerates your spiritual nature,

Exert it persistently so as to return to your divine origin.

The corporal world is an ocean of suffering and a river of ignorance,

And your carnal body is sullied and heavy.

The Celestial Mechanism has opened and closed many times,

Repent and gain spiritual experience of the miraculous DAO.

The esoteric method is not easy to seek!

Immortals and Buddha selectively teach it to the Sage only.

It is transmitted mouth-to-ear and heart-to-heart,

Once learned, the initiates pass it on to others.

DAO of your MASTER has no discrimination,

Whoever, willfully practicing it, will be admitted to the Sojourn of Immortals.

Perceiving that humans err and get lost,

I preach the miraculous and true teaching.

Do not employ symbolic forms and sounds of exotericism,

Maintain your serene mind, and DAO will definitely illumine in you.

Esotericism is the method of spiritual enlightenment,

It cannot be clearly expressed in any language or script!

Since it is unthinkable and miraculous,

Non-diligent seekers easily get lost in the erroneous paths.

DAO of your MASTER essentially focuses on spiritual

---

[81] The six paths of metempsychosis (or of sentient existence) are: hell-dwellers, hungry ghosts, animals, titanic demons or asuras, human beings, and celestials.

nature,

It relies on the action-and-reaction mechanism to preserve all beings.

Poem:

The miraculous and omnipotent DAO is imparted,

Imparting the secret vestige to save original men,

Original men should strain their nature into the perfectly pure yang,

Pure yang is condensed they can ascend to the nine Heavens.

I bless you all. I ascend.

The 28th day of the 8th month of Bính Tý year (1936)

FAITH
Break off sensual love – Put out passion fervor

CAO-DAI SENIOR IMMORTAL

Poem:

CAO-DAI IMMORTAL governs the imponderable DAO,

From Jade Palace HE unblocks the Eight-Trigram plan;

Thanks to this true teaching Immortals and Buddha succeed in their self-perfection,

HE now bestows it to this world so that it can be widely preached.

Your MASTER. I greet you all.

Poem:

Think about this world: It is just like a water bubble,

In which pleasures are immediately followed by scourges,

Yet, humans keep competing for vanity and profit.

I sprinkle the magic remedy to save them from calamities.

Rhyming Prose:

It is time to start a new cycle of Cosmic Revolution,

So as to regenerate and enlighten humans in this last Era.

So far, they have endured grief and ignorance,

Being indefinitely tied by karmic links in this ocean of suffering!

Alas! The legacy of wisdom and virtues was collapsed,

Unfortunately, the Ark of Salvation was also sunk long ago.

As a result, humans have blindly dived into the ocean of vicissitudes,

And endured poignant suffering and grief.

Yet, even in such horrible conditions, they do not repent,

They treat each other as savory baits;

Very few people preserve the perfect honesty,

As human ethics is torn and denatured.

The coming torment will bring them much more horrors,

Poor humans! Whether you are smart or silly,

Your divine nature is buried under your passions.

Pitying you, your MASTER hurries to save the world.

Hasten your steps as the dusk is on!

Children! Hurry up to the Universal Judgment,

Try your best to break all the karmic ties,

To regain your original state and enjoy divine favor.

Poem:

Divine favor is durable and everlasting,

Self-perfecting, you should extinguish the fire of your temper!

Keep your conscience pure and serene to preserve the Saint-Esprit,

Exert the "ABSOLUTE EMPTINESS" to establish the foundation.

Long Poem:

Establish the foundation for spiritual enlightenment,

Follow the miraculous DAO of your MASTER.

Accomplish work of merit and hidden credit,

Improve virtues and unite with each other.

Foster the Universal Fraternity,

Advance together toward the Ark of Salvation.

Who willfully persevering in this practice,

Should piously remember and follow MY instructions.

Valiantly overcome the high mountain of obstacles,

Patiently cross the dangerous passes of the ocean of suffering.

Human life is full of vicissitudes,

With brief sessions of comedy followed by long periods of tragedy.

How many of you experience more joy than sorrow?

Yet, you all content to live such an enslaved life!

Thoroughly cleanse off your worldly passions,

Diligently practice esoteric exercises to forge into Buddha and Immortals.

Innumerable karmic links tie you up,

The fire of desires blazes you in hatred and ignorance.

You are so morally paralyzed,

That even sharp punctures cannot recover your sensibility!

You remain impassive like a dead corpse,

Suffering or scourges barely disturb you!

Except for yourself, whether anything else is lost or found,

Whether it is right or wrong, good or bad does not matter you at all.

This is a great danger,

Since your ignorance always perturbs your serene spirit.

Consider everything in this world,

They are all spiritually deprived due to the fire of their desires.

At the first place are human ambition, greed and anger,

Then the fire of sensual love blows out and endlessly develops,

Women's beauty is like tidal waves,

That submerges the sturdiest boats and defeat the bravest heroes.

The more you are passionate in such beauty,

The more the fire of your sensual love burns your soul.

Aspects that deserve your attention and admiration

Are wisdom, virtue, honesty and kindness.

Humans are sinking pitifully in the material world,

They die and stack up in the fight for vanity and riches.

It is due to such stinking baits,

That cause wars everywhere.

Try to put out the fire of your desires,

By inwardly sprinkling the serene fluid of Saint-Esprit.

The fire of profane pleasures burns everything,

It is so foolish to throw yourself in.

Be determined in self-cultivation,

To prevent the six sensual attractions from ruining the Three Treasures.

Gradually rid of your pride and vanity,

Adopt "PERSEVERANCE and FORBEARANCE" for tranquility.

In particular, strictly discipline your characters,

Discern clearly the good from the bad.

DAO is wisdom and virtue, loyalty and ethics,

Faith is indispensable to penetrate the sojourn of Immortals.

Faith is for your self-assistance,

Faith strongly supports you on the path of Truth.

Faith helps you overcome challenges,

Faith flickers, never can you regain your destination!

Faith is like an oil lamp,

A lamp is not lit up without oil.

Faith is like a boat,

A boat sinks if its base is bottomless.

Faith unshakably strengthens your will,

Faith is the foundation to forge into Buddha and Immortals.

Faith is the miraculous boat,

Transporting you to the Paradise.

Faith should be firm and infallible,

For you to attain spiritual enlightenment.

Faith is a ladder,

For you to escalate up to the Paradise.

Faith services the world,

Should you have faith, God and Buddha save you.

Faith is like a jar,

If it has holes, its content leaks out.

Faith directs you toward GOD FATHER,

Faith is in your heart, you live in peace.

Faith, you should never let it go.

Believe in expiation mechanism, believe in Holy Messages.

Believe Divine Beings up above,

Believe that religions are the source of human peace.

Believe with all your heart,

Believe and revere Divine Beings up above.

Believe so as to bridge yourself with the Invisible,

Believe that God and Buddha are omnipotent.

Believe so as to persevere in the permanent DAO,

To become virtuous and exemplary in piety and mercy.

Poem:

Mercifully I give you sincere recommendations:

not sulk in receiving honest advice (*I'm smiling* ...),

Rally in fraternal union,

Persevere in self-perfection.

Daughters! Listen:

Poem:

Look at the moon lighting up the universe,

When clouds block its clarity,

Heaven- Earth would become obscure;

Moon is wisdom and virtue; clouds, discord and anger.

If you really adore ME and devote to DAO,

Remember my words to improve your characters,

Male and female, all are equal in the Nine Grades of Divine Noblesse,

Embark in the Ark of Salvation to penetrate the Paradise.

I bless you all. I ascend.

The 17th day of the 8th month of Bính Tý year (1936)

PRINCIPLE OF DAO – METHOD OF SELF-PERFECTION

CAO-DAI FOUNDER

Poem:

CAO-DAI FOUNDER bestows the true constitution,

In the presence of the Celestial Congress of Divine Beings;

HE elucidates the principle of DAO to revivify human conscience,

And advises humans to strictly obey the virtues of Saints and Sages.

Your MASTER. I greet you all.

I myself come to you, my children!

To instruct you to live in accord with your divine nature.

But you are still passionate in worldly pleasures,

Ignoring my advices and accumulating mounts of sins.

Long Poem:

Listen! Young and old children incarnated in this world!

Think over, repent and diligently self-correct;

The sins you commit in a day viciously submerge you for months,

Children! Extricate them, or you will be condemned!

Obey the Celestial Law, you are saved,

Violate it, you undoubtedly ruin your soul and body!

Inscribe my advice in your heart,

Repent and accomplish your spiritual and temporal duties.

Even if you amass mounds of treasures,
You squander them gradually in your idleness.

Everyone has a Spark of Divine Light,

It radiates brilliantly if you continuously shine it up.

On the other hand, if you nonchalantly perform self-perfection,

With your impure soul you hardly forge into Immortals or Buddha.

Should you follow the examples of Sages and Saints,

I will heart-to-heart transmit the divine mechanism to you.

Strictly follow the schedule of your spiritual exercises,

Self-perfect and attain Oneness that is the key to sanctify.

Eliminate progressively all greed,

Such as excessive food, luxurious outfits, or wrongdoings,

Also extravagant colors, good-looking forms, attractive flavors,

Immeasurable prosperity, and incomparable vanity.

Wash off all these devilish surpluses,

Put on modest clothes and live in simplicity.

As ascetics, unleash yourself from this material world,

Practice DAO of God and Buddha to free from ignorance.

Recite your rosary of Buddha in serenity,

Immerse your soul in Divine Light to wash off impurity.

Your soul can be as light as foam or as heavy as lead,

Pure and light sublime to Heaven, while impure and heavy sink in abysses.

As ascetics, you should accept tribulations,

And overcome them with your strong will and great courage.

Even if innumerable evils and demons[82] hinder your way,

Move forward with a strong faith to shy them away.

Secure yourself in every single step,

Ascetically practice meditation for thirty-six hundred days;

Constantly monitor your mind while walking, standing, sitting or resting,

You will attain enlightenment by a self-operating divine mechanism.

Knowing the method of preserving the pure and eliminating the impure,

You transmute the Quintessence into Energy that operates miracles.

Practice and strain your mind to the "ABSOLUTE EMPTINESS",

Faithfully stick to a virtuous life and renounce worldly enjoyment.

Once the nine energy centers[83] are unblocked,

You can force the Celestial Porch to regain the Divine Sojourn.

It means you succeed in forging into Immortals or Buddha,

And identify to the miraculous Spiritual Nature.

---

[82] impure spirits

[83] the nine energy centers are points where soul and body interconnect and interpenetrate, the centers of subtle or refined energy in the human energy system.

Performing esoteric exercises is not easy!

Straying from them, you practice your whole life without results.

Accomplish your spiritual tasks day and night,

Maintain peace and serenity in mind to self-identify to the Nature.

Do not give up, despite all the hardships;

After myriad reincarnations, it is time to return to the "Vi" arc.[84]

Be persistent with your self-perfection,

The more temptations you resist, the faster you progress.

With strong will you develop the DAO within,

To concentrate the Three Treasures in the head crown and return the Five Elements to the origin.

Being half-asleep, you regain the magic pill,

And harmoniously link to the entire Universe.

Esoteric disciples live in chastity and leave the profane house;

But leaving the profane house does not mean abandon family.

As ascetics, honestly pay taxes and fulfill all duties,

Do not cause distress to your parents.

Be not scared of anything,

Be a spiritually noble person by always maintaining fraternity.

Do not hide yourself in wild mountains,

As wrongly indicated in some ancient and contemporary doctrines.

Where is DAO? DAO is in your Conscience.

---

[84] Original Vietnamese text: Cung "Vi" ("Vi" arc) alludes to the Paradise, the Nirvana.

Thus, no need to look for it elsewhere.

You have a home, but do not consider it yours,

You are with your family, but do not tie up with such affections.

Other things such as money and estates,

Rice fields and buffaloes, profits and vain honor,

Extravagant glory and wealth,

Together they make up excessive amount of properties.

Innumerable relatives surround you,

Beautiful wives, pretty concubines, numerous children and grandchildren.

Though being in such circumstances,

You should maintain a complete disinterest in them.

Neither enslave yourself to sensual love,

Nor attach to properties or cherish vain honors and wealth.

Being in the mud, you should not be impregnated with its stink.

Living in this world, you should not be infected with its perishable characters.

Having a corporal body, you should not spoil it,

Even numerous events unwind under your eyes, you should remain impassible.

Achieving such status is really superior

To the state of leaving home and abandoning family.

Assess simultaneously the Spiritual and Temporal aspects,

Accomplish both with your perseverance and forbearance.

Fulfill your secular duties, and accomplish your spiritual tasks.

Achieving the Man Way, you also succeed in spiritual evolution.

Accomplish your duties toward humanity,

Serve continuously your society.

Your karmic debts are endless,

You cannot pay them off even after innumerable life-death cycles.

Speaking of "IGNORANCE and AWAKENING",

Try to discern them clearly.

The soul is a serene Spark of Light,

It is the most miraculous and extremely precious creature.

Awakening and Ignorance are opposite like right and left directions,

Awakening Soul is pure and calm, benevolent and merciful;

Ignoring Soul wallows in all wrong aspects,

It causes impiety and never denies any corruptions.

It indulges in the orgies and debauchery,

It is muzzled by glory and locked by profits.

It leads humans into the wrong and dark paths,

In which their wrongdoings ruin their souls and body.

Any time people find something attractive,

Their greed rises and their moral senses eclipse;

The more their desires blow out, the more the Ignoring Soul predominates.

The more their passions inflame, the more the Devilish Genie bullies.

They disregard benevolence and mercy, wisdom and virtues,

Because their bestiality is rebelling.

Such depravation ruins Original Quintessence,

And disperses the miraculous source of Original Energy and Spirit.

Ignoring Soul is a crafty evil,

It ruins and overthrows the spiritual empire.

Should the Divine Soul let it reign,

The entire globe would be exterminated in wars, blood and tears.

Awakening Soul brings harmony and order,

It lights up Wisdom and Virtues all over the world.

It aspires toward the practice of Buddha,

As well as the examples of Saints and Sages.

Possessing the Secret of Immortals,

Its benevolence is the ark of salvation.

Its loyalty and heroism are incomparable,

Its virtues such as compassion and piety are a plus.

Never does it care about worldly honor and wealth,

Nor does it like uproar, or induce trickery.

It is unbiased, not close not far,

It is disinterested in worldly honor and wealth.

Without discrimination, it likes serving others;

Egoism and partiality are nonsense to it.

What a pure and radiant soul!

It directs humans toward accomplishing their duties.

AWAKENING and IGNORANCE coexist in the human soul,

AWAKENING aspires toward the good, and IGNORANCE, the bad.

The soul is intercalated between these two,

Ignoring. the soul tempts it toward the karmic cycle;

Awakening, the soul is too weak to resist the temptations,

That is why humans have to endure endless reincarnation cycle.

Only when the profane nature abdicates, the Divine Nature

can emerge.

Only when all three souls are cleansed off, you can become Immortal or Buddha.

You will enjoy the facilities of the eternal sojourn,

Exploring the outdoors at dawn, and residing in the Paradise at dusk.

Or recite poems in the moonlight at a breeze,

Playing chess and drinking wine to appreciate the everlasting peace.

Poem:

Enjoy the everlasting peace in the Home of Buddha,

Play chess of Saints and taste wine of Immortals,

Occasionally wander around to view impressive spectacles,

Day and night purify your souls so as not to become Mara.[85]

Mara or Buddha is created by humans for themselves,

The pious become Buddha and the rebel, Mara.

Stepping in God-Way, you aspire toward the Nirvana,

Submitting to human desires, you are entangled in devilish traps.

A SERIES OF TWELVE HEAD-TO-TAIL STANZAS

DAO operates to save the world,

It instructs the method of self-deliverance to penetrate the Paradise.

---

[85] Mara means Demon. In Buddhism, it is the demon that tempted Gautama Buddha by trying to seduce him with the vision of beautiful women who, in various legends, are often said to be Mara's daughters. In Buddhist cosmology, Mara personifies unwholesome impulses, unskillfulness, the "death" of the spiritual life. He is a tempter, distracting humans from practicing the spiritual life by making mundane things alluring, or the negative seem positive.

Practice its esoteric method to regenerate your True Nature,

Attain the enlightenment, you will enjoy the eternal facility.

The eternal facility is gained by exercising esoteric method,

And by renouncing troublesome and turbulent activities;

Enjoy limpid water and green mountains,

Condense the sun-moon essence into the pill of Original Spirit.

Original Spirit, Original Energy, and Original Quintessence,

Unite them gently and constantly to form the Double-body, (*I'm smiling ... smiling…*)

To force the Sublime Porch and enter the Miraculous Tower to revere Buddha;

The convergence of the Five Elements is very miraculous to the human Spirit.

The human Spirit has blindly perpetuated in reincarnations,

Nowadays, it will be bathed in divine benediction,

Purify your body and souls diligently,

Once achieving the Mystic Sight, you can visit the sojourn of Immortals.

The sojourn of Immortals is gained by your perseverance,

Master your breath to tranquilly fraternize Spirit and Energy,

Increase fire and decrease water[86] to provoke the union of mercury and lead,[87]

---

[86] Increase the Yang flame, decrease the Yin smoke or Augment the Yang and reduce the Yin'.

[87] the assembly of lead and mercury; lead is a heavy solid that sinks in water, symbolizing Quintessence in human; mercury is a liquid that can be evaporated, symbolizing Spirit. Therefore, 'the union of mercury and lead' alludes to the union of Quintessence and Spirit in esoteric practice.

That is the method of positioning the caldron and building the furnace.

The Furnace of God engenders all creatures,

And gives each of them a miraculous point of Divine Nature.

Incarnated in this world to accomplish spiritual and temporal work,

They are fascinated with worldly enjoyments and forget to return.

Return to the Sojourn of Immortals is much more enjoyable,

As its beauty and serenity are unfathomable,

Where flower fragrance wafts on a cool breeze,

In contrast to the turbulent activities in the dusty world.

The dusty world burdens you with spiritual and temporal duties,

The more you attach to such material life, the more your divine soul is torn,

The more you are passionate in the worldly pleasures,

The more you are tied to this illusionary port of ignorance.

IGNORANCE and AWAKENING, thoroughly discern them!

Fulfill your spiritual and temporal duties,

Watch out to avoid stumbling on tortuous paths,

Keep in mind compassion, resignation, and humiliation.

Resignation and humiliation help endure hardship and danger,

Give up yourself to pass through trials and tribulations;

Fraternize with the superior and the inferior,

Tolerate each other to avoid misunderstandings and

conflicts.

Conflicting with each other, dare you tear off[88] your MASTER?

Here HE instructs you how to acquire Wisdom and Virtue;

Pray, meditate and contemplate on DAO day and night,

To sanctify and sublimate into the Nirvana.

Into the Nirvana you step on multicolored clouds,

To fly above oceans and mountains,

To enjoy a cool breeze and translucent moon,

To compose poems and perform all kinds of miracles and prodigies.

I dispense special benediction to you. I ascend.

The 11th day of the 8th month of Bính Tý year (1936)

SELF-PERFECTION

CAO-DAI FOUNDER

Poem:

CAO-DAI SUPREME BEING leads the Congress of Immortals;

From the Highest Palace of Linh-Tiêu HE imparts the Saintly Teaching,

To instruct humans on the essential union of Yang and Yin,

Meditate and contemplate on it, you will attain Spiritual

---

[88] Original Vietnamese text 'xé banh' literally 'tear off' or destroy completely.

Enlightenment.

Your MASTER greets you all.

Lesson in verse:

The Pre-Genesis DAO is profoundly mystique;

Unite the five and the three[89] for your self-perfection,

Wake up from worldly ignorance and illusion,

Seek the esoteric method for your spiritual deliverance.

The Three Celestial Purities are the origin of the heart-to-heart method,

The reunion of these doctrines is consistent with the Natural Nature.

Moving upstream, you regain the Divine Origin,

Going downstream, you fall into the karmic cycle of reincarnation.

Children! The Great Way is revivified!

000

Children! You should understand that CONFUCIUS had not thoroughly comprehended DAO when he preached Humanism. So, he still took a non-vegetarian diet. But after receiving Spiritual Enlightenment from HẠNG-THÁC, he became strictly ascetic. Hence, it is said that *"Confucius was born a really extraordinary intelligence; yet, at the beginning of his Apostolate, he had not discovered the intuitive Esotericism of Dematerialization; during his journey of Evangelization, he met the prodigious child HẠNG-THÁC who revealed to him the mystic science; thus, the old man was a student of a kid."* Also there is another saying: *"Observe vegetarianism to restore corporal purity, discipline desires to conserve spiritual quintessence"*. Later, CHÂU-TỬ,[90] while not thoroughly comprehending these circumstances, nor deeply

---

[89] The Five Primordial Elements and the Three Treasures

[90] CHÂU TỬ was a scholar of the TANG dynasty in the Ancient China.

penetrating the Middle Way philosophy,[91] dared to discuss the profoundly mystic DAO and criticize that the Doctrine of Absolute Emptiness taught by LAO-TZU and CONFUCIUS was just superstitious utopias. Isn't it like a frog sitting at the bottom of a well and seeing the sky just tiny like a crucible cover?

Since the Middle Era, several perceptive Taoists have succeeded in bringing the Esotericism back to light. But none of these proofs are as convincing as your MASTER, whose Ultimate Judge is evidenced with the infallible Balance of Justice.

000

EXPLANATION ON "SELF-PERFECTION"

To **SELF-PERFECT** means to forge your will and liberate it from sensational love, conjugal and filial links, and all other worldly desires.

Successful in self-perfection, the profane nature is abdicated so that the Divine Nature emerges. Anyone, who is extremely sincere and respectful in seeking a Master for instructions of the DAO, who never abandons his original nature and diligently practices esoteric traditions, will achieve absolute emptiness.

Achieving absolute emptiness means accessing serenity of mind and body. In this state, the Post-Genesis breath receives the Pre-Genesis energy, uniting with the nature of Buddha and Immortals, as well as with the energy of the Absolute Emptiness. Once achieving absolute emptiness, the DAO evolves naturally. (It is because after returning to absolute emptiness, nothing remains to be trained). Thus, it is said: *"Never can anyone leave DAO even in a fraction of a second"*.

Esoteric practitioners should maintain THE ABSOLUTE SERENITY OF MIND to think of the MASTER. They should not recall the past, nor worry about the present, nor think of the future. Their ears hear all charming voices and melodic sounds, but they

---

[91] The philosophy of the Middle Way was detailed in a Confucian book named *The Mean Way* (*Trung Dung*); it discusses Humanism based on Love and Justice or on Piety and Fraternity

should be completely undisturbed. Their eyes see all prodigious, pretty, and nice things; but they should be fully indifferent. They maintain absolute disinterest toward the illusionary spectacles of this world. It is like an on-stage actor who plays the roles of king or commander, passing tragic scenes, enjoying pleasant phases, displaying joy or anger at this moment and love or hatred at another instant; yet, he is not fascinated with these roles, because he knows all these gestures and acts are superficial, unreal, and only last for short elapses of time.

Children! Diligently persevere in self-cultivation and have a strong will to forge your soul and strain your nature day and night. In the Invisible, I mystically guide and guard you. In the Visible, you should patiently withstand all the trials and sufferings to pay off your bad karma. Achieving the complete deliverance sooner or later is up to My Benediction, but also determined by your will and effort. Focus on fulfilling all your duties. In general, uniting the Three Treasures and the Five Elements, you will become Immortals or Buddha; on the other hand, dispersing the Three Treasures and Five Elements, you will regress to Demon or Mara.

Your life comprises two options: either rise or fall. Should you obey your awakening nature to exercise esoteric practice, you will succeed in regaining Immortality; but if you ignorantly tempt toward the impious paths, you certainly deviate from the Divine Origin.

Poem:

Strain yourself to convert bestiality into divinity,

Seek Esoteric Traditions to elucidate the Spirit of Truth,

Follow your awakening intuition to return to your destination,

Where you will leisurely enjoy the eternal serenity.

000

CONVERGENCE OF THE THREE TREASURES

AND THE FIVE ELEMENTS

Children! Do you know why you should "Converge the Three Treasures and the Five Elements"?

As humans worry and long for temporal matters, they expend SPIRIT (the Divine Soul); as they envy or dream of wealth and fame, they disperse ENERGY; and as they are passionate in orgies and debauch, they squander QUINTESSENCE.

If the Three Treasures are exhausted, a human is like a fading lamp, running out of oil and wearing out of wick; it flickers in the darkness and naturally goes off after a short agony. Certainly, if the Three Treasures are ruined, the Five Elements and the five organs in human body are subsequently debilitated.

In their early years, humans are candid and do not know grief, worry, anger, and sorrow. Growing up, they are accustomed to living in comfort, and little by little are passionate in glory and wealth. To acquire these possessions, they devise all cunnings and tricks, and even attempt violence as well as all other impious means. Consequently, their "TRUE HEART"[92] is exhausted (heart corresponds to Fire Element).

Once the stratagem is established, they fight to achieve its objectives. This battle for life exhausts their LIVER (liver corresponds to Wood Element).

As the goals are attained, as wealth and glory are achieved, they tend to satisfy their desires for corporal pleasures by immersing day and night in the ocean of passion filled with tidal waves of sensual love. Orgies and debauch parch their KIDNEYS (kidney corresponds to Water Element).

As corporal pleasures induce eating pleasure, they search in forests and oceans for exotic foods by killing birds and animals. To satisfy their appetite, they even swallow poisons or incompatible

---

[92] the Saint-Esprit, the Conscience

ingredients. Therefore, "illnesses get into body through the mouth" and upset their STOMACH (stomach corresponds to Earth Element).

Excessive animal-based dietary stimulates human bestiality. Thus, corporal instincts and sensual passions, such as brutality, atrocity, pride, anger, are developed, and suffocate their LUNGS (lung corresponds to Metal Element).

That is how the Five Elements are exhausted and the five organs are degenerated.

Hence, ascetics should not covet wealth and glory, desires and passions. To succeed in self-cultivation, they should be completely disinterested and free from all worldly attractions.

Poem:

As Man takes part in the Universal Triad.

He should strictly observe Commandments and Abstinences,

Practice esoteric traditions to extract the pure and eliminate the impure,

Achieve enlightenment to evade from this world of illusion and grief.

I bless you all. I ascend.

The 1st day of the 10th month of Bính Tý year (1936)

SEEK AND PRACTICE ESOTERIC TRADITIONS

GIÁC MINH KIM TIÊN

Poem:

Wake and receive Sacred Scripture to return to the original position,

Enlighten and regain Wisdom to evade from incarnation,

Perfect the Aura of Light to attain the precious Immortality,

And penetrate the enjoyable Sojourn of Immortals.

I'm smiling, smiling ... GIÁC-MINH KIM TIÊN greets all religious devotees of both sexes. I come ahead to announce the arrival of the SUPREME BEING. Sincerely check your ritual protocols to solemnly welcome HIM and the Escorting Immortals. Salutation! I leave.

000

Your MASTER. I greet you all.

Poem:

Brilliant like JADE is the revivification of Wisdom and Virtue,

SUPREME EMPEROR is so delighted to see this Universal Renewal,

Superior Spirits will be rallied under the Sacred Banner

Into the Celestial Realm to enjoy the eternal facility.

I dispense exceptional bliss and grace. Children! Sit down and enter in meditation.

Lesson in Verse:

Strive to deeply research the source of Wisdom and Virtue,

These esoteric traditions are the supreme treasure of Buddha and Immortals.

Humans in this world should rely on it as the boat,

To cross the ocean of suffering and penetrate the Paradise.

Practice esoteric exercises diligently to fabricate the saintly fetus,

Exert your willpower to forge yourself into dignified men;

Maintain peace and serenity in your mind,

To evolve spiritual energy and circulate it throughout the five senses[93].

Regain the pure yang by correctly positioning QIAN ($\equiv$) and K'UN ($\equiv\equiv$),[94]

And return it to the miraculous and divine origin;

Gradually develop DAO day after day,

Create the double-body to unite with the energy of the Absolute Emptiness.

Poem:

Mystic esoteric traditions are normally kept in secret,

Now it is time to disclose them;

The Three Ancient Doctrines failed due to its transcendence,

Seekers misunderstood or could not grasp its essence.

000

---

[93] The five senses are sight, hearing, smell, taste, touch.

[94] QIAN is the supreme Spiritual (at the North quarter) and K'UN, the supreme Temporal positions (at the South quarter) in the Pre-Genesis Eight-Trigram plan.

ESOTERIC PRACTICE AND SELF-PERFECTION

Here I elucidate the chapter on "ESOTERIC PRACTICE", so that all beings can deeply understand and exercise it to self-liberate from the incarnation cycle and catch up with the evolution mechanism.

The Great Way has been opened for over nine years. Yet, its esoteric traditions have not been disclosed, because at the debut of the religious propagation it is wise to let humans seek and reach the culmination of this doctrine gradually.

Nowadays, Caodaism has passed the propagation stage to move to the teaching period. Hence, I impart the GRAND CYCLE OF ESOTERIC TEACHING so that you can trace the returning path. Following this esoteric method, you will certainly evade from the port of ignorance and ocean of suffering.

Most of you adopt the teaching for self-perfection, but you do not practice it. What does SELF-PERFECTION mean? How to PRACTICE it? You frequently mention these two words: PERFECTION and PRACTICE, but you do not strive to seek and grasp its sense and scope. That is why you do not gain any edification (no success!). Disappointed by this failure, you abhor My Teaching, and tempt towards the pagans[95] or err in the heresy.

I briefly discuss the DAO so that you understand it:

DAO of your Master is profoundly spiritual. So, in any circumstances it should be evolved spiritually. The Esotericism in the Three Ancient Religions and the DAO taught today are one. But the foundation of these Ancient Doctrines was profoundly mystic. Their Spiritual Tradition was only entrusted heart-to-heart among superior-minded men and Sages. Its sense was well beyond the grasp of average-minded people and laymen. Little by little, from the vicissitudes through many eras of evolution, humans have plunged more and more in materialism and denied spiritual values. The Esotericism was then eclipsed, because seekers could no longer penetrate it.

---

[95] The false master who teaches the inferior psychiatric powers.

Nowadays, I perceive that humans no longer have support or initiative for their salvation, due to the decrepitude of the Three Ancient Doctrines. Hence, I myself manifest in this world to establish the True Teaching, confiding the standard method of heart to those who sincerely make the effort to practice it so as to evade from this material world.

Poem:

Where does this miraculous DAO come?

From CHIÊU[96] who came in spirit to the Precious Palace;

He learned the mystic method and leagued it to people in this world,

So they forge into Immortals or Buddha and end their karma.

Rhyming Prose:

DAO is evolved to deliver humans from this material world.

Wake up from reveries and grasp it.

I cry in hot tears in perceiving my children in the upcoming catastrophe.

So, I adapt to the circumstances to preserve security and peace in this world.

Now it is time for Buddha, Immortals, and Saints to forge their divine noblesse.

The Contest of Flowery Dragon is the General Judgment, in which the impious and the wicked expiate their sins.

As the List of Elects will be published, and the grand tribulation will signal the predestined end of this Era,

I come to reveal the Esoteric Traditions of the Great Way.

Poem:

DAO and Virtue currently start emerging,

DAO miraculously shines like the radiant moon,

---

[96] Sir NGÔ VĂN-CHIÊU, the first disciple of CAO-DAI SUPREME GOD.

DAO clarifies the Truth and enlightens human mind,

DAO and its practice few people have succeeded in.

Lesson in Verse:

The Cosmic Revolution brings up this rare occasion,

The Contest of Flowery Dragon will soon publish the List of Elects.

Yet people in this world seem completely unaware of it,

They do not strive to practice the miraculous method to deliver from ignorance.

Bent under the heavy burden of their sins,

And incarcerated in the four sufferings[97], humans are prone to the future scourges.

In this world full of bumpy roads,

And at dusk of the Era, watch out your steps, or you will get lost in the abysses.

With love, I activate the Infinite Mercy,

And manifest in this world to open the Third, the last Era.

Now is time for the debut of a new cycle,

Buddha and Immortals come to save humans;

They restore God-Way,

To wake humans up from their worldly reveries.

They preserve the future of mankind,

By establishing CAO-DAI Spiritual Way[98].

Concerning the mystic method of heart,

It remains the key for self-perfection from past to present.

DAO is a great treasure,

That is immutably preserved from generation to generation.

---

[97] The four sufferings are: birth, ailments, decrepitude, and death.
[98] Original Vietnamese term 'CAO ĐÀI Tiên Thiên'.

Knowing how to seek the DAO and choose the Clairvoyant Master,

You are spiritually successful by receiving the secret formula;

Not to mention the escape from reincarnation,

That relies solely on the miraculous precepts to wash off your karma.

To become Saint, Immortal, or Buddha,

Regardless of your path, you must exercise the miraculous method.

To forge yourself into True Man,

Imperishable and everlasting.

You should understand the Saintly Teaching and grasp its essence,

DAO of your MASTER is mystic, yet it radiates in your mind.

Those of you, who are good and righteous,

Will receive the teaching of heart from Clairvoyant Master.

In self-perfection, the number of years[99] of practice does not matter,

As soon as you are enlightened, DAO spontaneously evolves in you.

Distill and condense your mind and spirit

In accord with the static – dynamic equilibrium.

Once accomplishing the four daily sessions of esoteric exercises,

You should spend time meditating to fortify your Divine Nature.

Fulfill your secular duties,

By carrying out activities as usual.

But do not cling to any karmic links,

---

[99] the seniority

Do not overload your heart with either love or hatred.

The more Wisdom accrued, the more Virtues exposed,

Smile and apologize to whoever offends or insults you.

Untie little by little your passive Karma,

Reduce day by day your human relations.

Self-cultivate in secret and loneliness,

Sit in meditation and contemplation to practice ecstasies.

Do not let anything meddle,

An occupied mind is like a dying lamp.

Sit or lie in tranquil places,

In sleep or dream the spirit gently detaches from the body.

But first, train your double-body until maturity,

Before forcing the Celestial Gate to penetrate the universe.

If the double-body is still weak and impure,

Demons may impede in your rise and fall.

Poem:

Rise and fall are rare occasions to conquer,

Attain enlightenment to determine your Divine Noblesse,

Enlightened, your Divine Nature becomes eternal,

Find the practice of self-perfection in the secret vestige.

I bless you all. I ascend.

Part II
THE ABSTRACT PART
THE ESOTERIC SCIENCE

The 3rd day of the 8th month of Bính Tý year (1936)

THE PRE-GENESIS ODD-EVEN SET

ĐẠI ĐỨC CAO TIÊN
CAO-DAI VENERABLE IMMORTAL

Poem:

The GRAND CYCLE OF ESOTERIC TEACHING re-animates the universe,

Its saintly virtue creates all beings, salvaging human bodies and souls,

Its science of heart teaches them the method of dematerialization,

So they can return to the everlasting nature of the Pre-Creation.

Your MASTER. I greet all disciples of both sexes present in this séance. I bless you all.

Poem:

The GRAND animation of Yin-Yang pair generates the miraculous DAO,

Its CYCLE blesses and saves the entire world,

Its ESOTERICISM is the method to prepare the Immortality Pill,

Which TEACHES the miraculous mechanism of dematerialization.

I explain the two words: "CƠ - NGẪU".[100]

"CƠ" is odd or unpaired, while "NGẪU" is even or paired. With respect to the Universe, "CƠ" belongs to the Pre-Genesis and the Yang, while "NGẪU", the Post-Genesis and the Yin. Hence, the Supreme Being (the Monad) is "CƠ", while the Yin-Yang Dyad is "NGẪU". In human beings, the divine soul is "CƠ", and the body is "NGẪU", because the divine soul is Spark of Divine Light emanated from the SUPREME BEING, while the body is from the moderation of the Yin-Yang Pair. Therefore, "CƠ" and "NGẪU" should be united in order to forge into Saint, Immortal, and Buddha.

At this time being, due to the Infinite Mercy for all creatures, I humble myself to impart the DAO and its Virtue to mankind.

I feel sorry for the majority of my children, who are unaware of the revivification of the Great Way and the revelation of the true method of dematerialization for humans to return to the original destination. Most people let their divine nature be eclipsed in their heavy body and depressed under their carnal temptations. They ignorantly follow the vicious cycle of reincarnation, enjoy sensual love and desires, absorb fame and wealth, and consequently deviate from the "MIDDLE WAY"[101]. In their pursuit of egoist interests and illusionary fame, bestiality fills up in their heart; as a result, they devour each other to fight for food and lodge, or to satisfy their racial discrimination. Human dignity and fraternity are nonsense to them. Day by day, they deviate further from God-Way, from nature and serenity, and sink more deeply in the blind, brutal, and infectious realism. Enslaved by human desires, the divine soul becomes more and more obscure and covered. With such faint sacred light, they have no hope to escape from the karmic cycle of this ocean of suffering.

Therefore, disciples of the Esoteric Branch of the GREAT WAY should obey Divine Order to piously comply with the Principle of Nature.

000

---

[100] The ODD-EVEN set.

[101] The Central Point of DAO.

I briefly explain the "ABSTRACT AND MYSTIC DOCTRINE".[102]

Before the separation of YIN-YANG, the Universe is a nebula with no definite form, in which light and dark, pure and impure are intermingled. It is named the Pre-Genesis cosmic nebular energy[103].

From this nebular energy, a sublime halo, namely the Supreme Being, is flashing out. It is said that the Non-Being, symbolized by a circle ○ , creates the Supreme Being (i.e., nothing creates something).

Then a point shows up at the center of this nebular circle ⊙ . So, the Supreme Being is "CƠ". CƠ is unpaired, and cannot create the Universe, including all beings such as animals, plants, continents and oceans. Therefore, that principle of Monad radiates a cyclone of light, creating the miraculous partition: The pure and light energy elevates to form Heaven, while the impure and heavy precipitates to form Earth. Pure and light, the former rises and symbolizes the trigram QIAN (or CHIEN) (☰). QIAN is Heaven, i.e., the primordial positive energy. Heavy and impure, the latter settles down and symbolizes the trigram K'UN (☷). K'UN is Earth, the primordial negative energy.

These two powerful energies of primordial Yin-Yang pair undulate, waltz, spiral, attract and repel each other in space. The Yang is dynamic, and the Yin, static. The Yin stays in place, while the Yang embraces the entire Universe.

The Supreme Being provokes the union of the true Yang with the true Yin (Yang and Yin are ODD and EVEN, respectively). This mystic alliance results in antagonism, in conflict, in action, in reaction, and in affinity; it is the origin of the infinite variety of beings and creatures. The Yin-Yang energy starts engendering all beings. Once generated, the creatures reproduce themselves from generation to generation with no respite or interruption. It is said:

---

[102] the Esotericism
[103] The Pre-Genesis energy of the Absolute Emptiness, i.e., the Pre-Genesis cosmic nebular.

One creates two, two creates three, and three creates all beings[104]. But all beings must return to one, because *"the One engenders all beings, then all beings converge to the One"*.

The mechanism of transforming profane into saint is the natural law and the mystic method; it applies to all spiritual and corporal worlds in the Universe to engender and ensure the perpetuity of the entire Creation.

The Supreme Being is the Principle of Monad, the Creator and the Absolute Sovereignty of the Universe.

The Yin-Yang Dyad is the miraculous method, the profoundly mystic mechanism. It is said: *"DAO is the union of the Yin principle and the Yang principle"*. That saintly alliance engenders the Universe. When the Yin energy seizes a positive part from QIAN (or CHIEN), QIAN (☰) transforms into LI (☲). (LI symbolizes the Infinite Yang, the Sun). As K'UN (☷) gains a positive part of the Yang, it transforms into K'AN (☵). (K'AN represents the Infinite Yin, the Moon).

The Yin element, intermingling with a Yang part, slowly ascends due to the Yang portion. QIAN (or CHIEN) makes up its missing part of Yang energy by partially mixing with the Yin energy, and is pulled downward by the Yin portion. Hence, it is said that QIAN is ousted and K'UN is degraded. Consequently, Pre-Genesis transforms into Post-Genesis. The Yellow River Chart[105] becomes the Lo River Writing[106]. That is why it is said: *"Conjugation of the four Yin-Yang pairs makes up the Eight Trigrams"*. These opposing pairs alternate between the static and dynamic states, between the upward and downward movements to ensure the perpetuity of all beings.

---

[104] To be clearer, 'God the Father or the Supreme Being creates the Yin-Yang pair, then the One assembles with the Yin-Yang pair to form the Three, and the Three engenders all beings.

[105] The Yellow River Chart (Reference: Wilhelm, Richard and Cary Baynes, trs. 1967. *The I Ching or Book of Changes*, 3rd. ed., Princeton University Press, Bollingen Series XIX. page 320).

[106] The Lo River Writing ((Reference: Wilhelm, Richard and Cary Baynes, trs. 1967. *The I Ching or Book of Changes*, 3rd. ed., Princeton University Press, Bollingen Series XIX. page 320).

The Pre-Genesis energies can transform and engender, because they are fed by the Primordial Yang Energy. Never could humans perceive, conceive, or measure such unfathomable and unseen nature with their corporal senses or profane intellect.

The Pre-Genesis Odd-Even set is the serene and light energy, like the fragrance of flowers, fruits, or plants.

When the grains or seeds are sowed, they germinate and grow. They rely on the Pre-Genesis energies and the Post-Genesis energies absorbed from the air to grow day after day, then blossom, and fructify.

Similarly, the esoteric method of heart also utilizes the Yin-Yang Pair to create Buddha baby[107]. Regarding plants, they absorb the Yin-Yang energies in the Universe to live and thrive. Thus, esoteric disciples should observe full vegetarianism to get light and pure energies from plants. Animal-based produces contain mainly heavy and impure substances, due to its Post-Genesis nature (from sexual reproduction). Such a diet induces bestial instincts in man and obscures his true spirit, impeding its detachment from his body. Disciples! Pay much attention to this note!

Poem:

THE PRE-GENESIS ODD-EVEN PAIR is the esoteric method,

It reveals the miraculous secret of Saints and Immortals;

Saints and profanes are created from the same principle,

Weld the broken line of LI ($\equiv\!\equiv$) to return to QIAN ($\equiv$).

I bless you all. I ascend.

---

[107] the saintly embryo.

The 5th day of the 8th month of Bính Tý year (1936)

THE POST-GENESIS ODD-EVEN SET

CAO-DAI JADE EMPEROR

Poem:

The miraculous DAO is a profoundly mystic science,

CAO-DAI at Linh-Tiêu Palace passes it to His disciples;

As the White JADE brilliantly radiates throughout the Milky-Way Galaxy,

The EMPEROR manifests Himself in this world to impart this Esotericism.

Listen to your MASTER'S elucidation on "the POST-GENESIS ODD-EVEN SET".

The Celestial Law is spiritual and immaterial. Still, it requires the harmony of two supernatural powers of "pure yin, pure yang" to create the Universe. For Earth, this pair is "firm, soft"; in humans, it is "male, female". They are the two opposing but complementing powers to assure the perpetuity of all creatures.

The Pre-Genesis Odd-Even Set belongs to the "spiritual, immaterial state", while the Post-Genesis Odd-Even Set belongs to the "material, physical phenomena".

Heaven, Earth, humans, and other beings all have two bodies: the yin and the yang. The yin is impure, and the yang is pure.

The pure elevates to form Heaven; the impure precipitates to form Earth. Between Heaven and Earth, the pure and impure intermingle to form humans. In wise and clairvoyant people, the pure spiritual predominates; while in silly and brute ones, the impure corporal prevails.

For instance, when a seed is sowed, it germinates and develops into the two first leaves. That is a clear manifestation of the Duality Law of Yin-Yang. Obviously, the Mechanism of Creation delivers the fundamental law of sexual reproduction for the corporal beings to perpetually create, grow, multiply, and reproduce.

Heaven is lucid, and Earth is opaque; female is impure, and male is pure. Such lucidity elevates from opaqueness, and opaqueness precipitates from lucidity. Such purity engenders impurity, and impurity spurts purity.

Human reproduction is based on the coupling of sperm and ovule. When the sperm ejaculated from a male joins the ovule of a female, a fetus is conceived. After a normal gestation, a baby is delivered. That is a profane fetus. On the other hand, esoteric practitioners can reverse that process to transform sperm into Quintessence and unite it with Energy and Spirit to form a saintly fetus. Therefore, humans seem pretty much different from Saints, but actually they differentiate from each other only by this subtle detail.

Odd-Even is also the norm of sexual reproduction in viviparous, oviparous, moist-dependent, and metamorphosed species (i.e., the four forms of reproduction of reptiles, birds, insects, as well as multi-legged animals). Due to sexual instincts, all species reproduce perpetually. Also due to such sexual reproduction, the yin-yang pair engenders an infinite variety of beings. These two energies attract, repel, separate from, and unite with one another in affection, order, and harmony to ensure the perpetuity of all creatures. Thus, such creation is originated from harmony. And so, DAO of Heaven-Earth is nothing else but the two words "IMPARTIALITY AND FRATERNITY". Fraternity engenders union; union engenders love and affection, from which sexual instincts burst out.

Hence, all races are created from sexual desires. Everyone has sexual instincts and sexual appeal. Why so?

It is because sexual desires arouse a man and a woman, making them love and couple with each other. The man's sperm unites with the woman's ovule to form a fetus. After gestation, the baby is delivered. Isn't it true that the baby's body is created from the parents' sensual love? That explains why the divine soul is buried in a body made up of desires, and also why humans are fond of profane life. They favor delicious foods, fancy clothes, charming women, orgies and debaucheries, while their divine souls are imprisoned in the carnal dungeon of suffering.

Therefore, should humans leave their delusion, rupture all carnal links, cease sensual love to regenerate their Original Spirit, conserve Original Quintessence, practice esoteric exercises to reconcile with the serene state of their natural nature, they can certainly evade from the world of trouble and the river of ignorance.

Those who can break up with sexual desires and sensual passions, banish pride and cruelty, disinterest from worldly vanities, would certainly become live Saints or Immortals right on earth.

But it is so hard to become sound and righteous! Everyone wants to do good, but few people accomplish it; everyone wants to avoid evil, but most people fail it. Devoting the entire life for good deeds may not even suffice to secure you, but committing just one wrongdoing can pile you up with stacks of sins.

Thus, I recommend that you, my children, exhort to goodness. There is an old adage: "Virtuous life is the source of blessing; passionate life, the chain of suffering". You should try your best in self-perfection, as your effort is the key to success.

Lesson in Verse:

DAO is the most precious treasure in the Universe,

It is the ladder for mankind to escape from the abyss of profane love.

It circulates throughout the corporal worlds,

To impart the Spirit of Truth so as to moderate the entire Cosmos.

DAO liberates human souls from all suffering,

Those who persevere in esoteric exercises will progress in self- perfection.

Even the most ignorant and silly people

Could achieve the eternal beatitude, if they willfully step on the esoteric path.

With regard to the human world,

Those committing sins obviously cannot avoid catastrophes.

Deeply touched by their fatal destiny,

Your MASTER imparts the Esotericism to open the Path of Deliverance.

Children! Hurry to embark on the Ark of Salvation,

So as to avoid the upcoming grand tribulation.

How to shun such calamity?

Maintain a pious life and CAO-DAI will protect you.

Incessantly persevere in your self-cultivation,

Continuously revolve the Cosmic Wheel,[108]

Fraternally unite your soul and body to create the Saintly Fetus,

Day and night, forge and strain your Divine Soul.

Use the "characterless bible of heart" to amend all the shortcomings,

Maintain serenity by eliminating all worries that trouble your soul.

Absorb yourself deeply in these spiritual exercises,

Cultivate saintly virtues and pull out sinful seeds.

To develop and optimize spiritual powers,

Contemplate to discover the secret of nature.

Once penetrating the mystic science of Immortals,

You can clearly perceive vicissitudes in temporal worlds.

Esoteric vestiges include profoundly mystic sense,

Only sound and righteous people could penetrate its source.

Firmly frame yourself into its immutable compass and measures,

To perceive the mutable scenarios in this world.

Those who waste their life in frivolities,

Cannot forge their souls into perfection,

---

[108] The energy centers in human body.

Nor extract and absorb the light and pure energy,

To germinate and grow their Immortality tree.

Your Divine Soul has been deeply buried in the carnal body,

And severely suffocated by ignorance of such corporal nature;

Lend your ears to the crows of the saintly rooster within you,

Wake and return to the ancient Sojourn.

Break up all karmic links,

So that Pure Spirit can aspire towards God;

To penetrate the mystic law of dematerialization,

Have strong faith in Divine Beings and beg them for assistance.

To evade from this ardent furnace of the Creator,

Pray your Divine MASTER to open the spiritual porch,

And to unveil the Secret of Genesis,

As this magic bag contains all miraculous laws of the Universe.

In the Esoteric Scriptures of Ancient Doctrines,

The secret of dematerialization was not fully revealed;

Only some part or an overview was exposed in hermetic allegories,

As no one dare unduly reveal the Secret of God.

Immortals and Buddha are pre-destined Elects,

Who received the key from Divine Master to harmonize the Yin-Yang pair.

Not everyone is able to penetrate the Celestial Mechanism,

Only sound and righteous people could acquire it.

Though numerous people practice the esoteric method,

Only few succeed in forging into Immortals and Buddha!

For, if the ascension toward the Sojourn of Immortals is easy,

Demons and Mara have already invaded this Realm.

Make use of scriptures to regenerate your Original Nature,

Research and exercise piously the esoteric method;

Regarding the esoteric vestiges,

They are verbally transmitted in complying with esoteric traditions.

Poem:

This Scripture is circulated to wake dozing souls,

Its Esotericism is imparted to regenerate degraded people;

Step on the Spiritual Way and aspire toward God,

To escape from ignorance and worldly displacements.

Replicate Poem:

Displacements of mountains and oceans are not hard at all!

Impious people condemn themselves in these imminent catastrophes,

And perpetually reincarnate under diverse animal bodies.

Yet, very few of them seek the path of benediction and blessing!

I briefly discuss the term SELF-PERFECTION.

Lesson in Verse:

The top method in esoteric traditions is perfecting the mind,

Perfection of mind is a spiritual practice,

Perfection helps practitioners reach the original nature,

Perfection means purifying soul and body to let the miracle evolve.

Buddha and Immortals are enlightened thanks to spiritual

perfection;

It is the shortcut to complete dematerialization.

Perfect yourself to enlist your name in the Celestial Board,

Perfect yourself to escape from the ocean of worldly suffering.

Your MASTER, the SUPREME BEING, disseminates this miraculous method,

HE imparts the Esotericism to assure the Universal Salvation.

Perfect yourself to evade from the perpetual cycle in corporal worlds,

Perfect yourself to shine up your nine spiritual senses like the full moonlight.

Perfecting means conserving your heart and nurturing your nature,

Perfecting means developing the virtues of moderation and sincerity,

Perfecting means differentiating the Paradise from the Hades,

Perfecting to gain Immortality and penetrate the Wisdom of Cao-Dai.

The Three Ancient Doctrines instructed on mind perfection,

Now this Esotericism of Immortals is passing on.

Perfect yourself by exercising perseverance and resignation,

Practice it day and night with meditation and contemplation.

Let others rush in their greedy race toward honor and wealth,

Focus yourself on fulfilling your duties in secular life.

Perfect yourself by practicing the Esotericism of your MASTER,

Perfect the three and five[109] -- key to penetrate the Universal Genesis.

As the most precious goal of self-perfecting process,

---

[109] 'the three and five' is the Three Treasures (Quintessence, Energy, Spirit) and the Five Primordial Elements (Metal, Wood, Water, Earth, Fire).

Destined disciple intuitively feels the urge to adopt Esoteric Teaching.

Perfect yourself to unveil all obscurity,

And to attain the everlasting Sojourn of Immortals and Buddha.

Perfect yourself to access the Celestial Hierarchy,

Perfect yourself to get back to the Spiritual Way,

Renounce worldly life and stay away from wealth and glory,

Elaborate the Buddha's nature and the Immortal's wisdom.

Perfect yourself before salvaging others,

Perfect yourself to amend this corrupt world in the Inferior Era.

As the Third Divine Revelation evolves with the cycle of Cosmic Revolution,

The Universe gets back to the Era of Spiritual Teaching.

Perfect does not mean self-isolate in wild caves or on solitary mountains,

Perfect does not insist in self-imprisonment or extravagant asceticism.

Perfect means condense the Energy and distill the Spirit,

Perfect means achieve self-vigilance and serenity.

Perfection should be practiced abreast secular activities,

Perfection should be operated at home, but without relying on anyone else;

The world "Perfect" is not applied exteriorly but within oneself,

Perfect means elaborate soul and body to purify the Spirit of Light.

Perfect means accomplish all duties;

Do not perfect superficially to deceive people,

As brown turban and white gown dyed with the bark of

mangrove tree

Cannot save you from devilish tricks or reincarnation cycle.

Perfect means exercise the sovereign of Original Spirit,

To tame the six devils of instinct and the seven demons of passion[110],

To restore the Golden Age of THUẤN - NGHIÊU patriarchs[111],

To shut out carnal senses and control bestiality.

Perfect yourself to make an effort in perfecting others,

Perfect yourself so as not to abuse the saintly doctrine,

Confine the monkey[112] in cage,

Leash it up to prevent its escape.

Perfection should start with eyes, ears, nose, and tongue,

These sensual attractions must be completely abolished

To establish the sandalwood censer and stabilize the incense burner[113],

To condition the evolution of dragon and tiger[114] for enlightenment.

Attain the quietude of mind to gain clairvoyance,

Regenerate the Three Treasures to prepare the Immortality,

Forge yourself into spiritual enlightenment and perfection,

---

[110] The six sensual attractions and the seven emotions.

[111] the peaceful and happy time under Kings Thuấn and Nghiêu in Ancient China. King NGHIÊU, or YAO (尧), 2356 – 2255 BC, was a legendary Chinese ruler. King THUẤN, or YU THE GREAT (大禹), 2200 - 2100 BC, was a legendary ruler in ancient China, famed for his introduction of flood control, inaugurating dynastic rule in China by founding the Xia Dynasty, and for his upright moral character.

[112] The monkey is an allusion of the Inferior Mind.

[113] Sandalwood burner is the hearth, i.e., the elixir field, and the Incense Censor is the head crown in human body.

[114] Dragon and tiger allude to the Yang and Yin, respectively.

In such state the jade hidden inside luminously radiates.

Esoteric disciples should faithfully perform spiritual exercises,

To self-perfect in the four daily sessions of meditation,

To evolve the Cosmic Wheel[115] without respite,

To create the miraculous harmony of mercury and lead[116].

Perfect yourself by stepwise following the Esoteric Teaching;

Pre-destined disciples will receive Revelation at the right time,

This is the mystic science to forge Immortals and Buddha,

To gain both omniscience and immortality.

Esoteric disciples should express simplicity and candidness,

Their words should be true and good;

Banish anger and sulking,

Maintain a serene mind to condense the Immortality Pill.

Perfect means filter the pure from the impure,

The pure elevates to Heaven and the impure precipitates on Earth,

Vigorously swirl muddy water,

Once it stays still, impurities settle at the bottom and pure water is on top.

Perfect yourself to discern the Spiritual from the Temporal,

Perfect yourself to distinguish Saint from profane;

By self-perfecting, you can penetrate the Spiritual Genesis,

Self-perfection is your day-and-night continuing effort in esoteric practice.

Oh! How sweet the foretaste of Wisdom!

It refreshes your heart with an endless bliss.

The more you engage in, the more you become addicted,

---

[115] the spiritual energy centers in human body.

[116] Mercury and lead allude to the Yang and Yin, respectively.

The higher celestial rank you achieve, the more prodigies you perceive.

Your MASTER discusses some aspects of esoteric practice,

To benefit the initiates on their path toward perfection,

Perfect yourself to avoid transgressing the Divine Law,

Forge yourself into Immortals and Buddha to guide others.

Without DAO, countrymen fall into anarchy,

They form sects and parties to fight each other,

They squabble and devour each other with trickeries and violence;

They condemn themselves to the decadence and misery.

Without DAO, the impious family breaks up by sins and egoism,

Such a disordered home is depraved of respect and love;

Incest and immorality prevail over good sense and wisdom,

Like a house without host or a citadel without army.

Without DAO, impious man is like a plant,

He lives a stupid life without any goal or ideal,

Obscure, ignorant, unintelligent,

Such an ignoble creature dishonors mankind.

Ascension.

The 3rd day of the 8th month of Bính Tý year (1936)

DISCUSSION ON THE ESOTERICISM

CAO-DAI GREAT IMMORTAL

Your MASTER greets you all. I reactivate the psychography to instruct you on "the Esotericism".

From the Antiquity to present, Buddha, Saints, and Immortals all have to practice the esoteric method of heart to forge the soul and strain the body in order to self-transform from profane into saint.

Human nature is the most miraculous among all other beings, as it is from the Pre-Genesis energy. That is why it earns the name "NHƠN" ("MAN").

What does the character "NHƠN" (MAN) mean?

Character NHƠN (人) implies the profoundly mystic enigma of DAO, because it consists of two traits: the left one symbolizes "the exact Yang", and the right, "the true Yin". Yin and Yang are intermingling, because human is a combination of dynamic and static, half pure half impure. People with clear and strong intuition would seek esoteric method to filter the pure from the impure to make their divine soul light and lucid.

What does the character "TU" (SELF-PERFECT) mean?

TU means fully nurture Quintessence, Energy, and Spirit, and also refine virtues. To accomplish it, the initiate should get rid of profane desires, purify and illumine their spirit in accord with the Natural Nature. They should maintain serenity, resignation and tolerance; also they should replenish whatever is degraded.

What does the character "LUYỆN" (SELF-FORGE) mean?

LUYỆN means polish until perfect clarity, forge and strain until extreme finesse.

TU (SELF-PERFECTION) without LUYỆN (SELF-FORGING) is like a piece of iron without being strained to become a useful tool. LUYỆN is forging. Forge a piece of iron means heat it up to its melting point, then hammer it, smooth it, grate it, strain it to make it a useful tool.

Esoteric disciples self-operate the same procedure in their spiritual domain. In order to fully acquire the astral body, they should perform spiritual exercises to forge, strain, grate, smooth, and polish their spirit day and night until it metamorphoses into the golden body of Buddha. That is the esoteric method of self-perfection.

Children! Recall that I usually say: I am you, and you are ME. Only do I exist that you are created; and you exist before Deities, Saints, Immortals, and Buddha do. Therefore, human is a "Micro-Cosmos". Any spark of Divine Light wishing to forge into Immortals or Buddha must incarnate in corporal worlds. And even a Lord of Heavens[117] incarnating in this material world would have little chance to get back, if he does not practice spiritual exercises for self-perfection.

What is "Điểm LINH-QUANG" (Spark of DIVINE LIGHT)?

It is merely a spark of light. The Supreme Being is a "Globe of Divine Light" that self-divides into "sparks of Divine Light", each of which incarnates into a human body. At human death, the spark of Divine Light returns and identifies to the Globe of Divine Light.

Do you clearly understand the term: THIÊNG-LIÊNG (SACRED or DIVINE)?

THIÊNG-LIÊNG (SACRED or DIVINE) means continuing, uninterrupted, immortal, and eternal. Anyone successful in acceding to DAO must be bound to specific laws of divine mechanism.

God imparts a spark of Divine Light (Original Spirit) in every human being. The spark of Divine Light has to incarnate in this physical and material world where, borrowing a corporal body, it practices self-perfection to gain divinity. The corporal body is

---

[117] Original Vietnamese term 'Đại La Thiên Đế'.

indispensable for that spark of Divine Light to succeed in its self-perfection to forge into Immortals or Buddha. Why so?

It is because the Original Spirit exists but without the Original Quintessence of the corporal body and the Original Energy, how can the spark of Divine Light create the Double-Body? The Divine Light is the Yang or the spiritual, whereas the Original Energy is the Yin or the material. DAO must have the Yin-Yang pair to create the Divine Fetus, i.e., Buddha relic.

Borrowing the corporal body to extract Original Quintessence from the vital breath and blood, man can then strain Original Quintessence into Original Energy. Hence, the Post-Genesis Quintessence gets back to the Pre-Genesis one.[118]

Forging Original Energy means nurturing Original Spirit to its perfect clarity and purity. Even Immortals or Buddha have to incarnate in corporal worlds to create Buddha Fetus as a means to regain the invisible realm. Thus, do not think that Immortals or Buddha could achieve complete dematerialization without exercising this esoteric practice. If so, how could they self-forge and attain enlightenment?!

The method to strain the Immortality Pill is nothing extraordinary. To create the Divine Fetus, you must work out to reverse the mechanism. Otherwise, following human desires you remain profane with the forward mechanism.

Ascension.

---

[118] Profane man becomes divine man.

The 12th day of the 8th month of Bính Tý year (1936)

THE EVOLUTION OF HUMANS AND OTHER BEINGS

CAO-DAI SUPREME GOD

Poem:

CAO-DAI teaches the Saintly Doctrine to forge humans into Divine Beings,

Those passionate in worldly noblesse are tied to the vicious cycle of suffering.

SUPERIOR spirits are those willing to help others on the evolutionary ladder,

GOD will rally them back to the sojourn of eternal serenity.

Your MASTER. I greet you all.

I perceive this world is nothing else than illusion. It keeps changing like clouds or dreams that form and quickly dissipate. Hence, the grand tribulation is certainly unavoidable!

Alas! Social conflicts and natural catastrophes, such as scorching sunburns and torrential rains, endlessly occur. They are common calamities for the entire mankind. Unfortunately, humans keep paddling in the infectious pool of fame and wealth. As a result, they create such intolerable cycle of grief and suffering for the society and the peoples.

Alas! The wit oppresses the idiot; the smart deceives the silly; and the strong swallows the feeble. No one cares about other beings. As long as they and their families have good foods and clothes, they ignore Wisdom and Virtue. Such egoism drains out their spiritual values and submerges their body and soul in the soiled domain.

They even disregard the Three Ancient Doctrines and only follow their instincts and passion. Consequently, they fall under rigorous law and justice to repress their impious actions: the Expiation is infallible, and the Divine Balance is accurate. Good deeds or wrongdoings rebound automatically and precisely. The Law of Cause-and-Effect does not spare anyone. If you sow the bean, never could you harvest the squash. For instance, the person sitting in the hand-cart enjoys the reward for his good deeds, while the one pulling the cart atones for his wrongdoings.

Poem:

Do not tie yourself to the Cycle of Expiation,

Persevere in esoteric practice to return to the enjoyable sojourn of serenity.

Should you stay in this port of ignorance, you submit yourself to the malice,

And definitely bear the Karma that you have created!

Having pity on my next-to-last group of children, who are still dozing in illusionary reveries, I manifest in this world and impart the esoteric method to wake and guide them back to the original destination.

The Evolutionary Law of the Universe is immutable, eternal, and very miraculous. It progresses naturally. Never could you, with corporal senses, unveil the prodigious Mechanism of this Enigma, nor understand the absolute verities of this Omniscience and Omnipotence. Even Buddha, Saints, and Immortals do not know in depth the Mechanism of Creation. Innumerable veils cover the Secret of the Invisible Being who organizes the Universe. What the Omnipotent Creator has planned, no one can interfere to trouble its Order and Harmony.

The mystic Machinery of this Celestial Mechanism has continuously traversed from one point to another in the entire Universe to animate the world throughout the four cardinal directions. With such eternal rhythm, it creates the mechanism of DAO in a single wink.

The Messiahs of the Three Ancient Religions had pity on mankind who, due to ignorance, had generated sins and consequently tied up to the karmic wheel and the expiation law. Thus, the Messiahs incarnated in this world to preach the Spiritual Doctrine so as to guide humans out of the worldly dungeons, teaching them to live in accord with the Natural Nature, and transmitting to them the esoteric method so that they can self-dematerialize and transform profane into Saint.

The Messiahs of the Three Ancient Doctrines established the basis for the Spiritual and Corporal Genesis of Creation. Yet, they only revealed a tiny bit of the Enigma, since no one dare unduly unveils the Secret of God!

Had you penetrated the Mechanism of Creation of your MASTER, you would have been terrified and anguished.

How foolish you are! How fatuous you are! Mankind is the lord of all creatures. Why do you not seek and perfect the miraculous machinery inside you, so as to evade carnal dungeons, and escape from the rigorous exile of Karma, where you incarnate under animal bodies with wings in one instant and with horns at another moment? Alas! What a pity! Alas! What a pity!

Of the evolution tree, man is the root of all beings, and all beings are the twig of man; Heaven-Earth is the root of man, and man is the twig of Heaven-Earth.

The evolution of plants, animals, and humans progresses slowly and continuously, with no respite or stroke. But regression also happens.

Children! Listen to ME! Plants also receive sparks of Divine Light from your MASTER. They also live, but their intelligence is nearly inactive.

As you see, from plant to human there are three anatomical rules of creation:

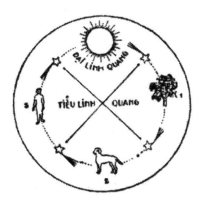

Đại Linh Quang is the Globe of Divine Light

Tiểu Linh Quang is the Spark of Divine Light

1) A plant has its root downward and its twig upward (root is head and twig is foot).

2) Evolving to animal stage, the creature has its head and tail on the same horizontal plane.

3) At the human stage, the head is upward and the feet are downward.

Thus, plants have only one part of the soul. They keep evolving through myriad incarnations until reaching the animal stage in which they have two parts of the soul. Animals gradually evolve through myriad incarnations, before being able to transmigrate into human beings. They have to experience hundreds of bitter disappointments, thousands of prickly deceptions, innumerable grief and suffering. Life after life, they fulfill their duties with endurance, self-sacrifice to serve humans and other beings.

After myriads of successive incarnations, creatures reach the human stage in which they possess the complete set of three souls and seven astral bodies.

Progressive men, who recently metamorphose in human bodies, are still clumsy, silly, and nasty. Should they humbly sacrifice themselves to help other beings, they would become smart and wise after some dozens of reincarnations.

To be human means to continuously progress on the evolutionary ladder. Toward this goal, they have to reincarnate myriads of times to learn and experience all aspects of life in this world. Being human is extremely difficult!

People wishing to become Immortals, Buddha, Saints, and Deities should purify their soul and body, and accumulate credit from works of piety. From humans evolving into Immortals and Buddha it is a steep elevation that includes innumerable harsh trials; this process is not easy at all...

However, pious people are humble and sage. They have strong faith in God and relentlessly practice the Saintly Doctrine. They love and assist everyone. They abandon the world of illusion, disinterest from the material, and only adore the spirit. Disillusioned by the worldly life as well as by vain honors and wealth, one day they will receive the esoteric method transmitted by Immortals and Buddha to self-perfect their soul and body, to unify the Three Treasures and to spiritualize the Five Elements. Thus, they could attain the ranks in the Celestial Hierarchy, evolve into Immortals and Buddha, and enjoy the immutable serenity of the Eternal Sojourn.

Every spirit must go through this evolutionary process in order to become Immortals and Buddha. Those who do not practice the Saintly Doctrine must stay forever in this corporal world to accumulate their credit of piety, to optimize their intelligence until attaining the integral goodness and ideal beauty of this world. They then transmigrate into another world of immediate superiority, where they must spend myriad reincarnations to learn and reach the ideals of that world before being able to transmigrate into yet another world. At least, they have to get through myriad reincarnations to gain credit of piety in order to move from one earth to another. What a long and exhausting cycle of incarnations! Such metempsychosis tirelessly operates its spirals of evolution throughout the Three Thousand Worlds, the Four Grand Continents, the Seventy-Two Earths, and the Thirty-Six Heavens. After passing through the Three Cosmic Era, these spirits may still not have the determination to enter the Sojourn of Divinities. Thus, nothing is better than to take the shortcut by practicing the esoteric exercises to prepare the Immortality Pill. This pathway is the magic ladder to bypass the progressive stages of evolution, and also the "mystic standards" to select divine souls. Children! Try your best to understand your MASTER'S words.

Evolution from animal to human is relatively easy, but the one from human to Divinities is extremely difficult. It is so, because humans are loaded with instincts and passions that drive them blindly, irresistibly, and fatally toward fame, wealth, sensual pleasures, excessive debaucheries, and boundless violence. Involving in these aspects, humans have to regress to animal stage in which they expiate their sins under a variety of coated or horned bodies.

Poem:

The latch of the Sublime Porch has been lifted,

The secret of dematerialization has been unveiled,

Those who penetrate the Celestial Mechanism

Self-forge into Buddha and Immortals to return to the origin.

Lesson in Verse:

GOD THE SON re-manifests to save this world,

HE imparts the Saintly Doctrine to dissipate human ignorance.

This world is so horrible to perceive,

Committing innumerable sins, humans cannot have peace in life.

The universe is changing constantly and instantly,

Only DAO of GOD remains immutable and eternal.

The secret method of dematerialization has been revealed,

To guide humans back to Linh-Tiêu Palace.[119]

Due to infinite mercy,

I manifest to guide you in this fatal world.

Not content to abandon you,

---

[119] The Jade Palace or the Paradise.

I reverse the Cosmic Wheel to salvage you.

I teach you the method to build the foundation,

By uniting the three and the five[120] as the basis to forge Immortals.

Once the yin and yang assemble harmoniously,

The Immortality Pill is made from this conjugation.

As the spark of Divine Light spurts out from the head crown,

The yin-yang union[121] preserves and the Spirit sublimes[122].

To forge the Double-Body,

You should purify Quintessence into Energy to illumine Spirit.

Day and night, forge and strain your soul and mind,

Maintain the serenity of your heart to preserve the Sublime DAO.

Once the interior and exterior quietude is acquired,

Introspect to spurt out the white light.

As LI (☲) is transformed into QIAN (☰),

The eight pounds of pure yang are obviously drawn from yin.[123]

LI represents Fire and Fire symbolizes the heart,

It extracts the yang from K'AN (☵) to make K'UN (☷).

As K'AN (☵) and LI (☲) become K'UN (☷) and QIAN (☰),

---

[120] The Three Treasures and the Five Primordial Elements.

[121] Original Vietnamese text 'Long thăng hổ giáng' literally means 'the Dragon ascends while the Tiger descends', alluding to the harmony or union of two complementing opposes such as yin and yang, Spirit and materiel, etc.

[122] Original Vietnamese text 'xuất thần' literally means the sublimation of the Spirit from a body still alive.

[123] The yang is the solid line, and the yin, the broken line in a trigram or hexagram.

You get back to the right chart of YELLOW RIVER,[124] leaving the wrong plane of LO RIVER.[125]

Persevere in four daily sessions of esoteric practice,

During which mercury and lead[126] interact to form the Immortality Pill.

Nurture this pearl by activating the Octagonal Trigram Template,

With great care like hen sitting on hatching eggs, or cat watching out for mouse.

In this recipe to prepare the Immortality Pill,

The fraternal union of Spirit and Energy is the basis for dematerialization.

Poem:

The magic pill is extremely precious, as precious as Immortality;

Whoever can create the Saintly Fetus will also attain Wisdom and Virtue.

It is everlasting and immutable,

Accomplish work of Piety to enjoy serenity.

Serenely recite a poem of Immortals in moonlight,

Thoroughly dust off worldly grief and suffering,

Comfortably enjoy the sojourn of Wisdom and Virtue.

Blissfully find peace beyond the vicious circle of fame and wealth.

Wandering peacefully and delightfully,

Willful ascetics prefer serenity.

---

[124] The Spiritual Genesis.

[125] The Corporal Genesis.

[126] 'Mercury and Lead' alludes to Quintessence and Energy, respectively.

With moon and wind, they explore fairy sceneries,

For them the corporal world has no true noblesse!

Noblesse in this corporal world is just stinky vanity,

For which silly humans compete with each other.

Only do disillusioned people seek Wisdom of God,

And practice the Esotericism to achieve dematerialization.

Poem:

Right and wrong ways lead to rise and fall, respectively,

Redemption and perdition follow immediately.

Sages climb up the shore of enlightenment, becoming Immortals and Buddha,

Silly ones dive in the sea of ignorance, transforming into Demons and Mara.

Innumerable cases of reward and penalty are obviously exposed,

Such as previously rich people now becoming indigent.

Karma and reincarnation are unavoidable,

Only can self-perfection eliminate them.

I bless you all. I ascend.

The 28th day of the 8th month of Bính Tý year (1936)

THE CROSS OF THE THREE PURITIES

JADE EMPEROR SUPREME GOD

Poem:

Nape Point is the sublime porch to access mystic energy at the head crown,

Golden Censer operates the mystic union of K'AN ($\equiv\!\equiv$) and LI ($\equiv\!\equiv$).

These superior centers moderate to activate the Yin-Yang pair,

Forming the imperial regulation of the Universe that all beings must follow.

Greetings to you all. Remain in deep meditation to listen to your MASTER'S elucidation of DAO.

At this time being, I descend in the séance, inspired by your unanimous motivation and sincere pledge on self-cultivation so as to deliver you from the four sufferings.[127]

Alas! You still need to conquer a lot of your imperfections on the way to Wisdom and Virtue. Now, being able to discern right from wrong, you should be willful in practicing esoteric exercises diligently. I will transmit the mystic method to "PENETRATE THE ONENESS AND CONSERVE THE UNBIAS"[128], so that you can exercise to distill Energy and condense Spirit for your self-dematerialization and sanctification. If you are not determined to do so, you will have to reincarnate myriads of times following the mechanism of spiral transmigration to evolve gradually toward your MASTER, with innumerable hardships and grief. Therefore, you should know that DAO is spiritual and profoundly mystic; it is the Divine Energy that has activated and flowed through space before

---

[127] The four sufferings are birth, ailments, decrepitude, and death.

[128] Original Vietnamese text ' QUÁN NHỨT CHẤP TRUNG'.

the Creation of Heaven-Earth. Heaven-Earth needs to absorb this Divine Energy before being engendered and separated into sun, moon, stars, and all other beings.

In the past, you received from your MASTER a point of "mystic energy"[129]. Incarnated in the corporal worlds, it was then suffocated by Post-Genesis energy. Consequently, the Three Treasures and the Five Primordial Elements dissipated in the seven emotions[130], six sensual attractions[131], six sense objects[132], and six roots of sensation.[133] Your spark of Divine Light, imparted by your MASTER, was buried or degraded further and further. Deprived of Divine Light, you could not find the way back. But even if you really want to return, it is not easy to do so. Children! Why is that?

Because you do not have the Saintly Embryo, the Buddha-Baby.

Why do you have to transmigrate?

Because you have deviated from the DAO. Your spirit is corrupt and your body, degraded. You do not know how to harmonize your soul and body, nor to regenerate the Three Treasures, nor to unify the Five Elements.

Why does the birth-death cycle perpetuate?

Because, to penetrate the Enigma of DAO, first of all, you should forge your Spirit, and create the divine body called "the Sage body" or "Buddha relic". This divine body is immortal, immutable, and everlasting; you absolutely need it.

What is that divine body?

---

[129] The spark of Divine Light.

[130] The seven emotions are joy, sorrow, love, hatred, desire, anger, and fear.

[131] The six sensual attractions are color, form, carriage, voice or speech, smoothness or softness, and features.

[132] The six sense objects are seeing, hearing, tasting, smelling, touching, and thinking.

[133] The six roots of sensation consist of the five senses (eye, ear, nose, tongue, body) and the discerning mind.

It is your Original Nature, purely positive energy. After abandoning your corporal shell, your spark of Divine Light will dress in this divine body to directly come back to your MASTER. Without this divine body, you have to transmigrate perpetually. If you do not reincarnate, your soul will sink in the Yin-Yang energy[134] of the universe to regress and dissipate into atoms of cloud, rain, wind, and dust. In this case your soul is completely annihilated. You should know that it is not easy to fabricate such divine body, but neither is it difficult. (*I'm smiling ...*)

Here I have a question for you: Can the aquatic species leave water and survive on shore, if it is not trained to adapt to such an environment? Certainly not, because it must get used to living in water (the liquid energy). Should it wish to survive on dry land, at least it must exercise to adapt itself to the atmosphere (the gaseous energy). Otherwise, it would perish to death after several minutes on shore. Children! Keep that in mind!

000

Here I explain the **CROSS OF THREE PURITIES**.

Why do you revere the Cross? (*I'm smiling ...*) You do not understand. (*I'm smiling ...*) Because it is DAO.

Why is it called DAO?

The vertical line (|) is the primordial positive energy or the divine energy.

The horizontal line (−) is the primordial negative energy or the mystic energy.

These Yin-Yang energies are dynamic and static, pure and impure. They unite intimately:

The negative Yin intermingles with part of the pure Yang (the Yin contains the seed of Yang), causing the mystic energy to elevate.

---

[134] The Post-Genesis energy.

The positive Yang mixes with part of the pure Yin (the Yang contains the seed of Yin), causing the nebular fire to precipitate.

These two energies attract and repel each other, harmoniously uniting to generate all beings. These two energetic lights stack on each other (the Yang is on top of the Yin), forming the "Doublet". The Doublet engenders the "Quadruplet", because, while superimposing on each other, these two lines protrude as the four wings of the CROSS (+). This "cross" twirls in spirals like a turbine, emanating myriads of stellar bodies in the universe.

That Cross has four negative energies, namely the "Four Yin". The Four Yin combines with the "Four Yang" to form the "Octet"[135]. Once created, the Octet infinitely animates the Creation, leading to the partition of the Five Primordial Elements, Heaven, Earth, and all beings. Children! Now do you understand? That is the mystic meaning of the CROSS.

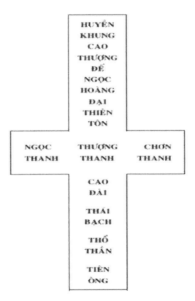

---

[135] Original Vietnamese term 'Bát Quái' is a Chinese religious motif incorporating the eight trigrams of the *I Ching*, typically arranged octagonally around a symbol denoting the balance of Yin and Yang, or around a mirror; they are the eight forces of the Genesis.

On the Cross that you currently revere it is written as follows:

ON THE VERTICAL LINE:

The upper part: HUYỀN KHUNG CAO THƯỢNG ĐẾ NGỌC HOÀNG ĐẠI THIÊN TÔN (JADE EMPEROR SUMPREME GOD OF THE IMPONDERABLE).

The lower part: CAO-ĐÀI – THÁI-BẠCH – THỔ-THẦN – TIÊN-ÔNG (CAO DAI – TAI-PE – EARTH DEITY – IMMORTAL).

What do they mean?

The upper part belongs to the imponderable, spiritual, whereas the lower one, the visible, material.

What does CAO DAI mean?

It means the highest peak of Kunlun Mountains[136] or Nirvana Chamber,[137] belonging to the Superior World.

The term THÁI-BẠCH (TAI PE) signifies the heart (conscience) and is called Linh-Sơn[138] Tower, belonging to the Middle World.

The term THỔ-THẦN (EARTH DEITY) indicates the Elixir Field[139] and is named Huỳnh-Đình Palace,[140] belonging to the Inferior World.

---

[136] The Kunlun Mountains in Asia are one of the longest mountain chains, situated in western China and extending eastward from the Indian border for more than 3,000 km; the highest mountain is the Kunlun Goddess (7,167 m) in the Keriya area.

[137] Nirvana Chamber is the ni-wan or mud-pill, the human head crown. In the symbolic language of Taoist Inner Alchemy, mud-pill refers to the acupuncture point Bai Hui (GV20), located at the top of the head. Ni wan is the mystic energy point situated in the center of the brain, at the intercept between the line connecting two ears and the one connecting the nape to the midpoint of the two eyebrows.

[138] Original Vietnamese term 'Linh Sơn' literally means Spiritual Mountain.

This Elixir Field is the magic pill reservoir, where the Spiritual Censer is established to forge the Saintly Embryo. When the Saintly Embryo is formed and able to evade the three corporal worlds, it will identify to the energy of the Supreme Purity.

Thus, the universe has three worlds: the formless, the formed, and the sensuous worlds; human body also comprises these three worlds. Once your soul succeeds in breaking open the Celestial Gate, your soul will penetrate the Realm of Supreme Purity.

What is the Celestial Gate? It is the Nirvana Chamber.

ON THE HORIZONTAL LINE, it is written "Position of the THREE PURITIES": the TRUE (or SUPREME) PURITY, the JADE PURITY, and the SUPERIOR PURITY.

The TRUE PURITY is your Original Energy

The SUPERIOR PURITY, your Original Spirit

The JADE PURITY, your Original Quintessence.

When Quintessence, Energy, and Spirit harmoniously unite, you will gain spiritual enlightenment. Children! Strive to understand it.

Heaven has Three Treasures: sun, moon, and star; or the three eras: superior, middle, and inferior.

Earth has Three Treasures: water, fire, and wind.

Man has Three Treasures: quintessence, energy, and spirit.

Thanks to its Three Treasures, Heaven engenders and nurtures all beings, and animates the universe to separate day from night, clarity from obscurity.

---

[139] Original Vietnamese term 'đơn điền' literally means the pill land, the Elixir field; it indicates where the Immortality Pill is prepared.

[140] Original Vietnamese term 'huỳnh đình' literally means the royal court (huỳnh or hoàng means royal or imperial; đình is the court in front of a house). With respect to esoteric teaching, it is the energy center about 3 cm below the navel in human body.

Thanks to its Three Treasures, Earth harmonizes wind and rain, vivifies the vegetal world, and divides the weather into seasons: spring, summer, fall, and winter.

Thanks to its Three Treasures, Man can forge into Immortals and Buddha.

000

THE THREE ANCIENT DOCTRINES

Here I explain THE THREE ANCIENT DOCTRINES (Confucianism, Buddhism, and Taoism).

CONFUCIANISM nominates the Three Major Relationships:

Relationship between king and subordinates, corresponding to the Original Spirit

Relationship between parent and children, Original Energy

Relationship between spouses, Original Quintessence.

Why does the relationship between king and subordinates signify Original Spirit?

Because in human entity SPIRIT plays the role of a king reigning a nation; ENERGY, that of satellite states and subordinates; and QUINTESSENCE, that of the people.

If the king is debauched, the people would be ingrate, and the satellite states would be rebellious. In such circumstances, the nation falls into anarchy.

BUDDHISM nominates the Three Refuges:

Refuge in Buddha[141] signifies purification of Original Spirit,

---

[141] 'Buddha' is a term derived from the Sanskrit verb root "Budh" meaning to understand, to be aware of, or to awake. It describes a person who has achieved the enlightenment that leads to release from the birth-death cycle and has thereby attained complete liberation. The word Buddha is not a

Refuge in Dharma,[142] sanctification of Original Energy,

Refuge in Sangha,[143] conservation of Original Quintessence.

TAOISM nominates the Three Purities:

The True (Supreme) Purity is Original Energy,

The Superior Purity, Original Spirit,

The Jade Purity, Original Quintessence.

That is the DAO. Children! You should know it.

000

THE FIVE PRIMORDIAL ELEMENTS

Here I explain the FIVE PRIMORDIAL ELEMENTS.[144]

The two lines of the CROSS stack on one another and protrude as the four wings, namely "the Four Imponderable Forms". These four wings indicate the four cardinal points: South, North, West, and East.

The central pivot forms Celestial Stems of Mồ-Kỷ: Element THỔ (Alkali),

The left wing becomes the East, and forms Celestial Stems of Giáp-Ất: Element MỘC (Wood),

---

proper name but a title meaning "Enlightened One" or "Awakened One." Buddha is anyone who has been enlightened, who brings enlightenment to others, whose enlightened practice is complete and ultimate.

[142] Vietnamese term 'Pháp' is the teaching of Buddha (Understanding and Loving)—Law—Doctrine—Things—Events—Phenomena—The way of understanding and love taught by Buddha—Buddha says: "He who sees the Dharma sees me". All things are divided into two classes: physical and mental; that which has substance and resistance is physical, that which is devoid of these is mental (the root of all phenomena is mind).

[143] Vietnamese term 'Tăng' is the Buddhist term 'Sangha', meaning 'wonderful Buddha's disciples'.

[144] the FIVE FORMS OF LIFE.

The right wing, the West, Celestial Stems of Canh-Tân: Element KIM (Metal),

The upper wing, the South, Celestial Stems of Bính-Đinh: Element HỎA (Fire),

The lower wing, the North, Celestial Stems of Nhâm-Quí: Element THỦY (Water).

Heaven comprises Five Pre-Genesis Energies and Five Post-Genesis Elements. They are:

In the 1st cycle Heaven engenders Water, in the 6th cycle Earth materializes it to element.

In the 3rd cycle Heaven engenders Wood, in the 8th cycle Earth materializes it to element.

In the 5th cycle Heaven engenders Alkali, in the 10th cycle Earth materializes it to element.

In the 2nd cycle Earth engenders Fire, in the 7th cycle Heaven materializes it to element.

In the 4th cycle Earth engenders Metal, in the 9th Heaven materializes it to element.

The Five Primordial Elements and the Five Energies harmonize with each other to create all beings.

While Heaven has the Five Energies and Earth has the Five Directions, Man has the Five Organs. Esoteric disciples should make use of these Five Elements to strain the Magic Pill into Buddha relic.

'To create the Buddha relic, you must circulate your breath to unify the Five Energies and converge the Three Treasures at the head crown.

How to unify the Five Energies and converge the Three Treasures at the head crown?

To converge the Three Treasures, you should conserve your Quintessence, nurture your Energy, and preserve your Spirit. You should strain yourself regularly to forge Quintessence into Energy, Energy into Spirit, and return Spirit to the Absolute Emptiness. Once the Three Treasures converge into the golden head crown, you attain spiritual enlightenment.

To unify the Five Energies, you should persevere in meditation to calm your mind, control your thoughts, and discipline your five senses. Once the five senses are shut, the five organs harmonize with each other and your mind becomes serene and tranquil, then:

In the South, the Red Emperor (Fire element) returns to the origin.

In the North, the Black Emperor (Water element) returns to the origin.

In the East, the Blue Emperor (Wood element) returns to the origin.

In the West, the White Emperor (Metal element) returns to the origin.

Children! Try to understand it.

Before your esoteric practice, the five elements part from each other as shown here . Through your perseverance in spiritual exercises, the five energies converge and overlap each other as shown here .

These five energies elevate and infinitely transform:

1 engenders 5,

5 engenders 25,

each of the 5 in the 25 engenders another 25 to create 125 ... and keep going to create infinite numbers of bodies. If you sit here and want to concurrently appear in thousand places, you can generate thousand physical bodies to accomplish your wish. This ubiquity is resulted from "the convergence of Five Energies and the union of Three Purities".

"CAO-DAI GREAT WAY" and "CAO-DAI RELIGION"

Here I explain CAO-DAI GREAT WAY and CAO-DAI RELIGION.

CAO-DAI GREAT WAY belongs to the Pre-Genesis, imponderable and immutable. This mystic or intuitive Esotericism instructs you the method of self-purification and spiritual perfection so as to return to the divine origin and accomplish the dematerialization. It inspires you to explore your inner self to comprehend the Truth and the foundation of Heaven. It favors pre-destined people (the minority), who are disinterested in the temporal world and seek the Spiritual Way (DAO), i.e., those who flee from the vicious circle of vain honors and wealth, as well as from the worldly links and corporal affinities, in order to aspire toward the Immortality. It is "the Esotericism transmitted intuitively from mouth to ears, reserved for the initiated."

CAO-DAI RELIGION belongs to the exoteric domain that pursues the propagation and universalization of Wisdom and Virtue. It guides the beginners on the path of enlightenment. It employs secular means to flatter human senses, embellish their religious life with nice gowns, high caps, hierarchical ranks, and titles of noblesse to reflect the order and solemnity. I tend to satisfy all my children, and give them what they want. Some like sweet taste; others do sour. Sweetness, sourness, spiciness, bitterness, whichever you want, I have already prepared an inexhaustible provision ready to suit your taste.

DAO is profound and imponderable, whereas RELIGION is just the entrance door.

Anyone who wants to become Immortal and Buddha has to pass that door to step into the GREAT WAY or DAO.

But I perceive that many of you are stunned by that fact. You wonder why multiple branches and churches exist. It is because some like profound spirituality, while others prefer apparent grandiosity. That is the mechanism of human evolution. I employ this mechanism to select saint from profane. But it is also due to your corporal senses; you cherish perishable items, fugitive prodigies, and miracles. Such desires and passions explain for the diversification of halls of meditation, temples, branches and churches, which compete with each other for superiority. These are all fakes and delusions of corporal senses. Even if they were real and if you managed to successfully formulate miracles, never had you been able to evade from the karmic cycle of reincarnation. To acquire the miracles, first of all, you should apply self-correction to your body and mind until they become extremely aesthetic and perfectly righteous. Once you achieve the perfect righteousness you also attain the perfect divinity. Otherwise, it is impossible to confide to you the precious esoteric method, if you still attach to your corporal body.

DAO of your MASTER is profoundly mystic, with no miracles or prodigies. It essentially transmits the perfect Wisdom and Virtue of Immortals and Buddha. It is not like the fake religions that confide the prodigies to all disciples, without considering their virtues and intentions. Isn't it obvious that such a non-selective transmission of the miraculous method only leads to worldly corruption and human destruction?

Ascension.

The 20th day of the 8th month of Bính Tý year (1936)

DISCUSSION ON EXISTENCE AND EMPTINESS

CAO-DAI SENIOR IMMORTAL

Poem:

Up in Heaven, serene spirits activate miraculous abilities,

Down on Earth, humans keep busy with castles and festivities;

Immortals and Buddha evade grief,

By merely maintaining the absolute emptiness.

Your MASTER greets you all.

I administer the Mechanism of DAO for the evolution of all beings. Due to my Universal Love, I leave My Throne and manifest in this world to found Cao-Dai Great Way. This Esotericism instructs humans on how to avoid sins, so as to escape from the fatal vicissitudes of this world of delusion.

Now I bestow the GRAND CYCLE OF ESOTERIC TEACHING to reveal the Absolute and Eternal Verities. It aims to enlighten humans, and to instruct them (esoteric practitioners, in particular) on esoteric practice for self-perfection as well as to set traditions and norms for dematerialization.

Here I elucidate the terms EXISTENCE and EMPTINESS. You should study by heart this lesson to prepare for your self-dematerialization.

Poem:

Everything in this world is non-durable,

Its existence corrupts very soon.

Only is the EMPTINESS everlasting or imperishable,

You should make EMPTINESS your foundation.

EXISTENCE is EMPTINESS. Everything in this visible and material world will soon decompose into dust.

You have a form, eyes to see, ears to hear. They are all unreal and illusionary. Everything in this world is non-durable; they are born to die very soon. Their appearance and disappearance occur easily and quickly like water bubbles on river or dew drops on grass. Moreover, this world of material and grief is the "SENSUOUS WORLD"[145], where humans are inflated with ambition, desire, and envy. Their passion leaps unceasingly from one thing to another. Their greed is bottomless, never saturated. Due to boundless desire and envy, they imprison themselves in the four dungeons of alcohol imbibing, glory, beauty, and money. Being passionate in vain honors

---

[145] the world of senses.

and wealth, they turn and return to the vicious cycle of vanities and delusion. Never do they consider nor contemplate the unreal nature of this world. Everything in this illusionary world is corruptible and non-durable. Yet, humans keep envying it, neglecting Emptiness to run after Existence. Such Existence will perish into Emptiness. This Emptiness is the True DAO. When the corporal body decomposes, the soul returns to Emptiness. Children! Make an effort to study and research this profound and mystic way.

Lesson in Verse:

The True DAO comes from "EMPTINESS", yet "EVERLASTING";

While the Religious Constitution[146] is established, yet will be deleted.

Thoroughly dust off all profane matters,

Maintain serenity of mind in accord with the natural nature.

The material world is present as seen,

Well organized but its existence soon disappears;

Its decay happens so fast,

Nothing can stabilize or last!

Eyes see color, nuance, form, and shape,

But no one is sure what happens to them later.

Grace and disgrace, noblesse and ignobleness, wealth and indigence,

They successively take turn myriad of times!

Concentrate your mind to realize this ephemeral world,

Evade from the fatal cycle of vicissitudes;

Persevere in spiritual exercises day and night,

Seek and practice esoteric traditions to self-salvage.

Look at those beautiful flowers with their vivid colors,

---

[146] the Exoteric Regulations.

They charm and enthrall all human beings!

Even Saints incarnated in this world

Are sunk under such profane tides with no escape!

Enslaved by luxurious, voluptuous, and lascivious pleasures,

Humans are like hooked fish.

Their minds and intelligence are vexed and intermixed,

Their spirit is emaciated like an exhausted oil lamp.

Wrongdoings and good deeds are distinctively weighed,

Sadly, humans are bound forever to the cycle of reincarnation!

Bad Karma hooks them to this exile,

Passion and desire prevent them from self-perfection.

This world frequently overturns black into white,

As most of its hosts pretty much go astray.

They laugh happily when desires are satisfied,

And resent nastily, jealously, otherwise.

Sins and errors are unceasingly generated,

As long as the corporal body exists.

Thought, touch, taste, smell, vision, and hearing,

Once they are quieted, the serenity of mind emerges.

Consider everything in this world,

They assemble to dissemble, appear to disappear.

Perceiving it, your MASTER has so much grief!

In such fatal vicissitudes, even mountains and rivers are overturned.

Nothing is better than refuging in the DAO and practicing it,

Renounce the inferior mind to acquire the angelic one.

The inferior mind houses suffering and grief,

As well as sorrow, worry, moaning, backbiting anger, and

hatred.

The angelic mind is really the True Wisdom,

Absolutely empty yet miraculously masterly;

It breaks up all karmic debts and temporal links,

It puts an end to the carrying-over thoughts.

Empty, it has no tones, colors, or forms;

Empty, it has no imagination, visualization, or hearing.

It does not like affiliation or company,

It does not like noblesse or vanity.

It does not seek wealth or vain honor,

It does not use tricks and cunnings to dupe people.

It does not cause trouble to people,

It does not act wrongly to harm others.

It is not passionate in the profane world,

Detaching from the four dungeons, it heads straight to the Paradise.

Absolutely empty is really miraculous,

Attaining it, you become live Immortals.

Maintain EMPTINESS to be blessed by Buddha and God,

Never should esoteric disciples part from EMPTINESS.

EMPTINESS is the miraculous DAO within you,

Practice it to clearly recognize its miracle in your mind.

To become Saints, Sages, or Immortals

First of all, you should self-purify to attain EMPTINESS.

Disregarding those who stick to worldly ambition,

Esoteric disciples should maintain serenity of mind.

Even when other people abuse their power to oppress you,

Sway them with your resignation, tolerance, and wisdom.

Do not be afraid of getting hurt,

Pretend to be blind and deaf to secure yourself.

Consider the lesson of Napoleon,

Who put up a lot of effort and energy,

To win many battles,

And faded into null after the final failure.

Consider Xiang Yu[147], who waged wars everywhere in the country,

Committed suicide at the end of his tyranny.

From past till present, so many heroic figures

Badly ended up to NULL!

Practice DAO of Immortals and Buddha to self-correct,

Achieve EMPTINESS to evade reincarnation.

This world is governed by the law of Causation,

Persevere in self-perfection to be free from that devilish trap.

Apply emptiness to relieve from grief and suffering,

Being absolutely sincere you should rely on DAO to live happily.

After unwinding the tangling skein of profane world,

You enjoy beautiful moon and cool breeze.

Who are dignified men?

Who study by heart the teaching of Sages and Saints?

Why do you languish in grief and suffering?

Why do not you strive to break the chain of Satan?

Why do not you rally on the radiant path?

Hallucinated by wealth and honors, you fool in sins and errors.

Is it wise to bury your spirit in the mire of this world?

---

[147] Xiang Ji (232–202 BC), better known as Xiang Yu, was a prominent Chinese warlord in the late Qin dynasty.

Two paths are open to you, choose either fall or rise!

Poem:

What to do to deserve the Faith of Vietnam?

Men and women should exercise it to take off their corporal nature,

Profanes differ from saints, like IGNORANCE and ENLIGHTENMENT.

Do not let illusionary senses dupe you.

I bless you all. I ascend.

The 18th day of the 8th month of Bính Tý year (1936)

DISCUSSION ON THE TERM "HEART"

Poem:

The heart[148] devoted to DAO develops into the noble will,

That makes humans struggle to escape from the four corporal dungeons.[149]

Flip EXISTENCE into EMPTINESS to attain enlightenment,

EMPTINESS contains the seed of EXISTENCE, the union of Energy and Spirit.

Here your MASTER briefly explains the term HEART.

---

[148] Vietnamese term '*Tâm*' literally means 'Heart' or more specifically 'Spiritual Heart', i.e., the Conscience.

[149] The four carnal dungeons are alcohol imbibing, riches, beauty, and vanity.

In the Universe, the Principle of Monad[150] governs all creatures and presides over the worlds of form or material (soul and body).

The Principle of Monad is decisive, lucid and radiant. It is the Supreme Being, the center of the universe and all creatures. That Unique Principle is omniscient, omnipotent, and omnipresent; it infinitely emanates, vivifies, and conserves all beings. That Unique Nature encompasses the universe, activates the invisible wheel to generate the common ladder for both spiritual and temporal evolution, based on which all beings continuously progress in accord with the Natural Nature until achieving the ultimate and fixed objective.

In that universal space, there is interchange between the static and dynamic state, also variation between rainy and sunny weather, light and darkness. So, it is exactly like the human heart, which also oscillates between tranquility and agitation, between adoration of Wisdom to follow the rhythm of God in some moments and preference of corporal instincts to unceasingly commit sins at other instants, constantly juggling between intelligence and ignorance. That is the balance at the center of the universe.

Every world or nation should have a governor. Each nation is formed by its people. But the people must submit to the will and sovereign of its king. The king is the heart or center of his people. The people live in great happiness under the aegis of a sage emperor, who governs with love, justice, wisdom, and virtue to assure peace in the country and prosperity in the people such that they never need to lock their houses. In such peaceful times, the climate is harmoniously tuned and people joyfully sing while enjoying their laborious work. They unite into a powerful nation, promote wisdom and virtues as the fortress against eventual invaders, and use examples of enlightened Sages (resignation and fraternity) as weapons against the tyrants. On the other hand, a debauched king would suffocate his people with tyranny, if he is passionate in alcohol, beauty, wealth, and vanity. Neighboring and/or annexed countries would rebel, while the people inside the country would grudge against him.

---

[150] The Monad, the Supreme Being.

Based on that principle, the Emperor is the center of his people, whereas in human being the heart is the center; it is the lord of human body, governing the five corporal senses, operating the respiration and moderating the circulation of blood and energy throughout the body.

That center of DAO in humans is very miraculous and omnipotent. It guides, encourages, and supports humans on their evolutionary path. Thus, humans should consider the heart their lord, and never let it be blocked or corrupted by desire and passion.

Intelligent and lucid, the human heart can perceive from past through present. It frequently exhorts humans toward benediction, inspiring them toward virtues, spiritual values, and toward observing God, His Will and Creation. Yet, humans should conserve its purity and omniscience by controlling their instincts and passions so as to stop committing sins and errors.

The human heart is naturally good and clairvoyant. But its lucidity is veiled and carried over into erroneous side by the interception of human desires and corporal instincts. Nevertheless, the Heart is NATURE (TÁNH); and Nature is the HEART (TÂM). Thus, Nature and Heart are one. Dignified men always strive to maintain a pure, calm, and serene heart. Never should they let it roam away. Once serenity of heart is stably conserved, blood and energy can thoroughly circulate throughout the body, corporal desires completely cease, and the Principle of God manifests, leading to the absolute emptiness of Nature or Heart, and nothing can intervene with it. In such state, humans attain the Ubiquitous Sense of *"All beings return to the Origin, while the Five Primordial Elements unite in One"* (the absolute dematerialization)[151]. On the other hand, if a man lets his heart deliberately ramble, he is near death as the ghost king of impermanence is about to take him away. Therefore, humans should deeply contemplate on this subject. For instance, if a chick or a dog is missing, you seek and bring it home. Why do not you strive to gather your heart back, once it is scattered out?

---

[151] Original Vietnamese term: ' *'Vạn pháp qui tông, ngũ hành hiệp nhứt"* (*duy tinh duy nhứt*).

The human heart is a magic storehouse. When normal storehouses are filled up, they cannot exceed their capacities. But the heart is an unlimited storehouse and never filled up.

Humans should master their hearts, and guard their thoughts, so as to conserve the Three Treasures and the Five Elements. The Three Treasures are the most precious properties in human beings. Thanks to them, humans can forge into Immortals and Buddha. But also due to them, humans become demons and Mara. To conserve the Three Treasures, you should, in the first place, shut up your five sense objects. The five sense objects are vision, hearing, smell, taste, and touch. These five sense objects belong to the five organs that correlate with the Five Primordial Elements.

Shut up vision to extinguish heart fire;

Shut up hearing to assure normal circulation of kidney water;

Shut up smell to permit separation of lung metal from lead and iron;

Shut up taste to prevent degradation of liver wood;

Shut up touch to assure the production of energy from stomach earth.

000

THE PRECIOUS CHARACTERISTICS OF THE ORIGINAL QUINTESSENCE

Should humans know how to conserve their Original Quintessence, its purity, serenity, and constancy, their mind would be certainly lucid and their body, sane and peaceful.

In the tale of TÂY-DU KÝ,[152] Tề-Thiên[153] harvested ginseng fruits[154]. Not knowing the right way to pick them, he shook the branches violently. All the good fruits fell, crushed on the ground,

---

[152] TÂY-DU is the tale about the trip toward the West Heaven, i.e., toward the Sojourn of Immortals.

[153] Tề Thiên literally means 'Heaven Governor', alluding to the person who wants to be in equal footing with God.

[154] Ginseng fruit alludes to the fruit from human seed.

and deteriorated. It was so, because he did not know how to pick them correctly. Anyone who eats a ginseng fruit can live for thousands of years. What a precious immortality remedy! The shape of this fruit is identical to the human body in miniature. But what is this ginseng? It is human quintessence. Should one know how to harvest it, it is preserved and immortal; otherwise, it deteriorates. (The quintessence which is abused and wasted in sexual relationships is the lost ginseng).

Regarding the Original Energy, it is the primordial energy of life. Losing it, human life would be in great trouble. This divine energy must circulate throughout the organs in a body to nurture the Original Spirit. Those who could maintain the internal circulation of this vital energy would attain spiritual enlightenment.

Poem:

The unique central point of the universe is the brilliant DAO,

Consider it the Lord to secure you;

Identify your Nature to the God Principle to initiate mystic capabilities,

Guard your True Soul by conserving Quintessence.

Lesson in Verse:

Conserve Quintessence, save Energy, and preserve Spirit,

Follow the Middle Way of DAO to evade reincarnations.

Break all karmic links,

Bear intense expiation in present life to accelerate dematerialization.

Do not let your mind ramble,

Decisively strive to jump out of the four exiles[155].

Assiduously transform your souls day and night,

To refill the Three Treasures with Divine Light.

---

[155] The four exiles are alcohol, beauty, glory, and vanity.

Turn K'AN (☵) and LI (☲) into K'UN (☷) and QIAN (☰),

Forge your souls and create the astral body from your corporal one.

As attraction between Moon and Sun causes tidal flux in oceans,

The magic jade with its triple aura radiates from your head crown.

The nine plans of high and low heaven are widely open,

The Original Spirit emerges once your five senses are shut.

Freed from grief, you regain true nature,

Eliminating the three moods and six turbulences[156], you achieve clairvoyance.

Your body becomes pure and calm like water in a vase,

And your spirit shines up harmoniously.

It means the Four Ancestors return to the origin[157],

The Yin and Yang unite and the Three Treasures[158] converge.

You attain ENLIGHTENMENT and leave IGNORANCE,

A Divine Order resumes you back for Celestial Nomination.

Poem:

Celestial grades are inscribed on jade stela,

Once enlightened, you come back to guide the ignorant;

With omnipotence and omniscience,

---

[156] The three moods are greed, anger, and ignorance; and the six turbulences are vision, hearing, smell, taste, and touch.

[157] 'The Four Ancestors return to the origin' alludes to the four Primordial Elements (Water in the North, Fire in the South, Wood in the East, and Metal in the West); they return to the Earth element at the Center.

[158] The Three Treasures are Quintessence, Energy, and Spirit.

You save and lead predestined people back to the origin.

I bless you all. I ascend.

The 16th day of the 8th month of Bính Tý year (1936)

THE ORIGINAL SPIRIT AND THE INTELLIGENT SPIRIT

CAO-DAI SUPREME GOD

Poem:

CAO-DAI preaches the Esotericism to gather predestined souls.

From the HIGHEST PALACE, HE delightfully imparts the doctrine.

SUPREME GOD commands the union of superior spirits,

And recommends His people to spiritually enlighten and virtuously self-perfect.

Your MASTER greets you all.

Poem:

It is unfortunate that I have to descend in this world so many times;

But pitying my children who deny my rules and laws,

And who deviate from Wisdom and Virtue,

I re-manifest for the third time.

Three times of revelation, I have imparted innumerable teachings,

But humans did not take any of my words seriously.

I even bled for their redemption,

Yet their cruelty has exceeded any imagination.

Unimaginably, the deluge of passions and instincts has submerged humans,

Its tide drowns them in the darkness.

Sailing the Ark of Salvation to rescue them,

I am so annoyed by their contentment of such ignorance and ignobleness.

Rhyming Prose:

Late in the Inferior Era Buddha and Immortals manifest,

And preach the Esotericism to salvage myriads of living creatures.

Fatal vicissitudes spread everywhere. Clairvoyant and intelligent people! Why do not you hasten to flee from catastrophes?

Alas! This world is so surfeited. Humans compete with each other merely for vain honor and glory. Yet, they are proud of these wits.

Through myriad incarnations, they bury their spirit, obscure their soul and squander their body.

Poem:

With the astral body[159], you can flee from the temporal world,

And reside in the realm of saints to continue your self-perfection.

You may feel delighted to leave the corporal body while alive,

But such ecstasy is rarely achieved.

---

[159] Original Vietnamese term '*phách*' means the true spirit, perisprit, double-body, astral body.

At this time, perceiving your ardent will, I descend to elucidate the Saintly Teaching so as to wake all creatures from delusion. Children! You should know that the spark of Divine Light is the most precious treasure in each of you. Strive to shine it up or you will be in deep regret.

Your life is neither honorable nor enjoyable. It is so disdainful and despicable. Yet, you keep immersing in this stinking pool or this dirty pond; with respect to your body, it is so heavy and clumsy that you can hardly manage yourself within it. Throughout the lifetime your divine soul is exiled in the carnal shell, and is covered by multiple Post-Genesis envelopes as well as suffocated under the weight of the five turbidities. Should you not exercise esoteric practice, you can barely self-dematerialize; it is so, because your soul is moored to the carnal body that makes you a slave for the seven emotions and the six sensual attractions.

Alas! Corporally, you are tempted by the seven emotions, subjugated by the six sensual attractions, and thus gradually become ignorant and weak. Original Spirit[160] is clairvoyant and always aspires toward tranquility and serenity. But it is thwarted by Intelligent Spirit[161] - the actual lord of the corporal body - that drives toward action and confusion. This tyrant desires one thing, envies others, and always tends toward disturbance and extravagance. It does not like wisdom or spiritual values. Sensual pleasure frequently directs you toward impiety, oppression, and baseness. The more it succeeds in enslaving you, the more it presses its yoke on you. It excites disturbances and stimulates wrongdoings. Yet, you keep following its commands. Also it is assisted by the seven devilish emotions and the six demoniac attractions that lead you to committing sins and errors. This impiety drives you into the vicious karmic cycle.

The seven emotions and the six sensual attractions trouble your heart and mind, bothering you all the time; yet, you can hardly rid yourself of them. A group of cunning and audacious bandits marauding on high mountains or in thick forests is even easier to eliminate than the rebels inside you. Especially, the six demoniac sensual attractions: VISION, HEARING, SMELL, TASTE,

---

[160] the Original Spirit is the Natural Spirit, the spark of Divine Light.
[161] the Intelligent Spirit is the Naturalized Spirit, the Spontaneous or Adapted Spirit.

TOUCH, and THOUGHT, are the most dangerous enemies that constantly disturb you.

VISION loves beautiful colors and forms.

HEARING likes elegant and rhythmic tones.

SMELL loves suave and sweet odors.

TASTE likes exotic dishes and delicious foods.

TOUCH (or BODY) loves beautiful wives, pretty concubines. It is passionate in both sensuous love and lascivious ideas.

THOUGHT wallows in rubbishes and baseness. It is an inexhaustible source of human scourges. It unceasingly hops from one item to another. It flashes in and out so fast that nothing can stop or catch it. That is why it is likened to a super-skillful robber, who picks up an object and steals another item right under everyone's eyes but no one can catch his wrongdoings.

Regarding the BODY, your carnal shell envies excessive concupiscence, abusing and exhausting Original Quintessence, Original Energy, and Original Spirit.

TASTE is your tongue; it loves exotic dishes and exquisite foods, pressing you to violate the interdict on animal slaughter and consequently to fall into the six paths of metempsychosis.

SMELL is your nose; it seeks sweet scents and thus, excites cupidity.

HEARING is your ears; they like listening to the impious words.

VISION is your eyes; as soon as they perceive beautiful colors or nice forms, they provoke envy.

Hence, vision, hearing, smell, taste, and touch stimulate thought, disturbing the serenity of Original Spirit, and promoting Intelligent Spirit toward debauchery. Nevertheless, though the six sensual attractions are six demons or six hooligans, they can be tamed to become the six supernatural powers and you attain enlightenment. But how to win these demons?

You should master your HEART, maintaining its serenity; and quiet your MIND, halting its leap. Being disciplined, the six sensual attractions turn into the six supernatural powers. If let unleashed, the six sensual attractions induce the six sense objects that, in turn, result in the six bandits. These six bandits ruin the six roots of sensation, degenerate the six conceptions, denature the six supernatural powers, and drive you into the six paths of metempsychosis. That is a human life whose Original Spirit is abdicated by Intelligent Spirit. In such circumstances, you live a dull and stupid life, just like a marionette moved by the wind or manipulated by the strings attached to its jointed limbs.

Therefore, you should distinguish Original Spirit from Intelligent Spirit, the real from the unreal. At times, Intelligent Spirit tends you toward errors, sins, and impiety; but Original Spirit objects to them.

Original Spirit drives you toward altruism, while Intelligent Spirit pulls you toward egoism.

Any thoughts or acts that do not twinge your Heart are reflections of Original Spirit; on the other hand, any thoughts or acts that prickle your Heart are influences of Intelligent Spirit.

The human Heart comprises Original Spirit and Intelligent Spirit. Sometimes they remain profoundly mystic, but other moments they prefer manifesting. They oscillate between spiritual and corporal activities. These are the two options to select. It should be clear that the Superior Conscience of DAO is totally different from the Inferior Conscience of profane. Similarly, the unreal body and the real body are of different natures.

.   What does it mean by the real body? How about the unreal body? Beside this unreal body, there exists a real one. What is that real body? It is the Double-Body. That body is everlasting like God; it is eternal, immortal, and immutable. Once this real body is perfected, you gain immortality, evade karmic cycle, and perpetually enjoy the Facility of Immortals in the Nirvana. That means you become a Real Man.

Your MASTER sees people that usually mistakenly think that through esoteric practice they can immortalize their profane body (human body) into the real body. How foolish! How silly! Due to such misunderstanding, they keep committing sins and errors, and sinking forever in the karmic ocean. Corporal body is heavy, sully, and fetid. Why do you cling to it avidly? Covered by a corporal body, the spark of Divine Light is like being crashed under the weight of a giant mountain and can only be liberated from that paramount burden when you are disincarnated. Never do esoteric practitioners who achieve self-dematerialization carry their carnal body for long time. With such a heavy shell never could they complete the journey around the world, even if they ride on racing horses from the date of their birth until their death. On the other hand, freed from the corporal sheath, they can traverse the four oceans in a single wink.

Divine souls rejoice tremendously after being rid of the loaned body. Those who are still under karmic burdens must follow Celestial Law to reincarnate in another body to expiate their karma. Immortals and Buddha are divine souls in the past who had incarnated their sparks of Divine Light in loaned bodies to self-perfect and attain enlightenment. They united Quintessence, Energy, and Spirit to fabricate the Double-Body. Only after obtaining the Double-Body could they establish their celestial standards and ranks. Otherwise, a spark of Divine Light is merely a tiny parcel of light, though it is profoundly mystic and able to participate in the Omniscience.

THE SEVEN EMOTIONS

Here I discuss on the seven emotions: JOY, ANGER, LOVE, HATRED, SORROW, PLEASURE, and ANXIETY.

Via the seven emotions and the six sensual attractions, humans squander their Spirit and exhaust their vital Energy. These demons push humans toward the pond of fire, the mount of swords, the profound cave, and the bottomless abyss.

JOY, ANGER, LOVE, and HATRED belong to common baseness and manifest without brakes or norms in human beings.

When desire is completely satisfied, JOY explodes. On the other hand, if desire remains offended and dissatisfied, sadness and grief dominate, leading to ANGER. These excesses quickly exhaust the vital energy of the Five Primordial Elements and the Three Treasures in humans.

Regarding LOVE and HATRED, when sensual tendency and carnal pleasure are satisfied, people are attracted to each other and fall in LOVE. On the other hand, if these desires are opposed, jealousy and envy dominate, leading to HATRED. These excesses quickly squander human Quintessence, Energy, and Spirit.

Regarding SORROW, PLEASURE, and ANXIETY, they are also among the deleterious emotions. If they are not promptly eliminated, they would constantly trouble you and pull you down into the baseness and ignorance.

Being human, you should maintain your noble will. Do not let the seven emotions subjugate you, nor allow the six sensual attractions to enslave you. Be firm and decisive in mastering them. Should you be weakling, these terrible servants would dominate you. Then no matter what their demands are, do you always have to satisfy them?

Besides the seven emotions and the six sensual attractions, the three meridians and the nine openings in a body are also adverse to human beings.

The three meridians locate at top, middle, and low energy centers of the body. These three demons block the three vital gateways, impeding the communication between Energy and Spirit along with the circulation of QIAN ($\equiv$) and K'UN ($\equiv\equiv$). As of those nine phantoms, they guard the nine body openings, hindering the communion between Pre-Genesis and Post-Genesis energies. Because of them, the human soul is exiled indefinitely in this corporal world.

Thus, esoteric practitioners should eradicate all these obstacles, so as for the vital energy to flow through the three meridians and the nine openings of his body to sublimate and communicate with the Universe.

This task is analogous to the balloon inflation. The balloon quickly deflates when there are leaks. Even tiny and imperceptible pores at needle-point size can leak air out and deflate the balloon. Never can such balloon be inflated. Where are those leaks in human being? What are they? They are nothing else than eyes, ears, nose, tongue, body, thought, the openings of the genital and excretory organs, as well as love, hatred, anger, and ignorance. If you do not block these leaks, you would keep pumping vital energy in and it keeps leaking out. Children! Pay good attention to these escapes. Esoteric practice requires such vigilance. Note that esoteric practitioners should avoid flaring up. Anger has no good. Anger may be justified only when it expresses a sense of justice, and not due to bad temperament.

Poem:

Eliminate the seven emotions and six sensual attractions,

Strain your souls day and night;

Eradicate the seven emotions to preserve the divine nature,

Forge yourself toward "Absolute EMPTINESS".

Once the three meridians and the nine openings are muzzled,

Practice esoteric exercises to unblock the nine energy centers;

Unite Spirit and Energy to attain enlightenment,

Fraternize the Yin and Yang to forge into Immortals.

I bless you all. I ascend.

The 16th day of the 9th month of Bính Tý year (1936)

MAINTAIN THE HEART AND PRESERVE THE NATURE

CAO-DAI SUPREME GOD

Poem:

CAO-DAI commands the return of predestined souls

By preaching the Saintly Doctrine via spiritic emission.

SUPERIOR people preserve their pure hearts and nature,

GOD offers them the unique chance for salvation and ascension.

Your MASTER. I am very pleased to descend in your séance to expose the Saintly Speech, shedding light on your noble origin, and encouraging you to return to your natural nature so as to be compatible with the atmosphere of the superior heavens. That is the secret of transforming profane into saint. (*I'm smiling...*)

Poem:

Maintain your heart and preserve your nature to attain Buddha's nature,[162]

Practice esoteric exercises to develop your virtuous wisdom,

Self-perfect unceasingly to penetrate the miraculous enigma,

Self-cultivate decisively to achieve the Universal Triad[163].

Children! It is so blessed if you can grasp the DAO within you. From the Antiquity till present, Saints and Sages have dispensed innumerable teachings to enlighten the world and save mankind. But humans do not strive to penetrate the profound spirituality of those

---

[162] In Buddhist texts, 'Như-Lai' means the perfect Wisdom, i.e., the Buddha Nature.

[163] The Universal Triad of Heaven-Earth-Man.

doctrines. As a result, their corporal nature degrades faster and faster, their spiritual nature degenerates further and further, and their moral nature deteriorates more and more. Due to such regression, humans depart from the saintly source of blessing, and spontaneously get caught in the six paths of metempsychosis. I feel so deeply compassionate. I cannot phlegmatically sit and view my children gathering in crowds or sinking *en masse* in the river of ignorance and the ocean of grief. Alas! Cyclones of sobbing and tides of mourning strike and echo in my heart! Therefore, I have to leave the Jade Palace and manifest in this world to preach the Saintly Doctrine so as to save living creatures in this Era of Annihilation.

In this world there are three distinguished categories of people: on top are the superior ones, at the base are the inferior ones, and between these two, the median people forming the middle class of common laymen.

Superior people are Sages. They maintain the pure and good heart that God conferred to them. Guided by this vigilant heart, they have deep compassion; even without being taught, never do they deviate from Divine Laws. Next is the middle class, comprising common laymen in society whose divine nature is somehow degraded. But a good education can easily and promptly restore their original nature. Only the inferior people, being stuck in deep ignorance, pose a stressful problem for the society. However, if they are willing to learn the Saintly Teaching and persistently practice it, they can manage to develop the pure heart and enlightened mind.

God creates humans and programs in them his own nature to guide them on the path to perfection, so that they can progress on the ladder of evolution. Unfortunately, they are gradually infected by material matters, launching further and further in the vicious cycle of karma, being denatured and departed from the path of God.

What is that nature? It is the original cause that engenders mankind. Therefore, the spiritual origin of humans is a principle.

That principle, omniscient and omnipotent, is distributed by God to everybody. Thus, that principle is nature. In God, it is principle. In humans, it is nature. Principle and nature are therefore identical. That is why God and humans can intimately communicate and interact with each other. Due to such communion, as man plans something, and even long before he takes action, God already knows it.

Originating from the same principle and the same energy, humans and God are linked together by indestructible bonds. Should humans nurture their divine nature until illumination, they would have no difficulty in communicating with God. Yet, though humans, the most advanced beings of all creatures, possess the divine nature, which is the most precious treasure, why do not they strive to forge and purify it? Why do they leave it further and further sullied and obscured? Alas! How naive they are! Kings NGHIÊU[164] and THUÁN[165], and even IMMORTALS, SAINTS, BUDDHA were all human beings in the past.

Lesson in verse:

The divine mechanism is profoundly mystic,

And the natural nature is essentially spiritual;

Rare people try to penetrate them,

So as to strain and illumine their heart.

You should clearly understand the vicissitudes of corporal worlds,

You should think leniently and generously to help save others.

You should deeply and thoroughly research human origins,

To realize that all humans identically possess the divine nature.

All beings come from the same furnace of Creator,

They share the mixture of pure and impure constituents.

That is why good and bad coexist,

---

[164] King NGHIÊU, or YAO (尧), 2356 – 2255 BC, was a legendary Chinese ruler.

[165] King THUÁN, or YU THE GREAT (大禹), 2200 - 2100 BC, was a legendary ruler in ancient China, famed for his introduction of flood control, inaugurating dynastic rule in China by founding the Xia Dynasty, and for his upright moral character.

Good or bad is due to their adapted habits.

Ignorance and ignobleness are created by humans,

These imprison people in the six paths of metempsychosis.

It is so, because these people do not forge

And purify their natural nature to restore its divine origin.

Natural nature is pure and brilliant like the full moon,

Natural nature is the divine body that God bestows.

Natural nature is not wicked,

Natural nature is omniscient and you should really look for it.

Fraternize your heart and nature with that of the Universe,

To communicate with all creatures in the world.

Natural nature is like a footpath,

Unfrequented, it would be filled up with brambles.

Natural nature flows like water,

Smoothly it develops toward perfection.

Natural nature is the faculty of knowledge and discernment,

That everyone should purify and activate.

It gets you back to your original noblesse,

To enjoy the great blessing and divine favor.

Those who maintain their nature intact,

Achieve perspicacity and absolute emptiness.

Never do dignified men part from their heart and nature,

They always guard their heart upright and trustfully;

Your spiritual heart is very sacred,

Do not bury it under the six sensual attractions and seven emotions.

Keep purifying your heart until illumination,

Favor good deeds and avoid wrongdoings;

Day and night, keep perfecting your nature,

Like a precious pearl needs polishing to shine up.

Your good heart is also miraculous and intelligent,

Maintain it to penetrate the celestial mechanism.

Do not let it ramble or degrade,

As to prevent flood, you should build the dykes in advance.

Those who lose their heart also end their spiritual life,

As the most precious part in humans is the HEART.

Losing it, humans are degraded to animal level,

Sages and Saints are those who maintain their good heart.

Your heart can be forged or distorted,

Your heart is subject to your own effort;

Your heart should be intact and purely conserved,

If it is corrupt or sullied, you have nothing left.

Kings NGHIÊU and THUẤN maintained their peoples' heart that way,

They do not differ from you at all;

Thus, becoming Saints and Sages is not difficult!

Conserving heart and preserving nature, you are named Buddha and Immortals.

Poem:

Immortal or profane, it all depends on the heart,

Impure heart yields Demon and Mara,

Pure heart generates Saint and Sage,

Vulgar men are those who corrupt their heart.

I bless you all. I ascend.

The 22nd day of the 9th month of Bính Tý year (1936)

CONTEMPLATION AND MEDITATION

CAO-DAI SUPREME GOD

Your MASTER. I greet you all.

Here I explain CONTEMPLATION AND MEDITATION.[166]

Poem:

Contemplate to seek the truth so as to enlighten the mind,

Practice esoteric exercises to create the Saintly Fetus;

Meditate to concentrate Spirit so as to activate intuition,

Communicate with the Universe to regain Buddha Nature.

It is crucial that esoteric practitioners learn a contemplation method to unravel the profound and imponderable principles that the Creator organizes and harmonizes the spiritual world, so as to penetrate the origin of life.

Without meditation and contemplation, how could one discover the Secret of Genesis? Therefore, anyone – esoteric-practicing or not – who wants to acquire a deep understanding of the Universe and its origin, has no choice but contemplation.

Moreover, being born human you should explore your origin. For instance, where does mankind come from? Why do humans exist? Why are they born to die? Why do they die to revive? Why do they evolve perpetually in the reincarnation cycle of the

---

[166] Original Vietnamese term '*Tham thiền nhập định*'. Note that the term 'meditation' correlates with 'nhập định' and 'contemplation' is 'tham thiền' due to their meanings as follows. According to Random House Webster's Dictionary (1993), to meditate is 1) to engage in contemplation, 2) to plan, intend; whereas to contemplate is 1) to observe thoughtfully, 2) to consider thoroughly, 3) to intend, 4) to consider deliberately.

Creator? Why should they enter this nasty world and get lost in the ocean of suffering and river of ignorance, to endure a tough life filled with grief that oppresses the soul and deprives the body, to sob for morning melancholy and evening sorrow, to lament on present complaints and future tears? With these questions in mind, if you have not made any effort in conducting a thorough research, deep consideration and analysis so as to gain spiritual intuition, would you have any other method? Indeed, this only method is called "CONTEMPLATION".

Without contemplation, how can you develop intuitive intelligence to penetrate the profoundly mystic principle of the absolute emptiness? But contemplation is a very difficult method. First, you should concentrate your mind in a noble and pure thought. Then based on that pure and illuminating thought you should think deeply and study thoroughly to let your enlightened mind[167] be spontaneously activated and your intuition naturally developed. At that moment the Truth is exposed clearly and fully.

Humans intrinsically possess the divine nature that God bestows upon their incarnation. Coming to this temporal world, they need a carnal body to experience life, so as to gradually become expert and continuously make progress on the evolution toward wisdom and virtues.

The corporal world is known as the ocean of suffering, the river of ignorance. But it is also a school for all creatures. Thanks to this school, all beings can develop their intelligence, enlighten their spirit, and escalate the evolution ladder.

Being human, you should constantly learn, study, and inquire. The insatiable curiosity opens the door to Wisdom that lets you discern good from bad, right from wrong so as to avoid errors and sins. Without learning and questioning, your spark of divine light becomes obscure, and you suffer from ignorance and ignobleness.

Whatever exposed in this world is useful and interesting lesson for humans. No matter whether it is pretty or ugly, good or bad, right or wrong, everything can serve as a good lesson. Things that are right, good, noble can be used as models for your spiritual

---

[167] Original Vietnamese term '*huệ tâm*' literally means 'enlightened mind'.

straining; those that are wrong, bad, brutal can serve as a mirror to improve your virtues. Today's erroneous steps are lessons to prevent future stumbling. Nothing in the world is useless! Useful or useless merely depends on whether you know or not know how to make use of it.

Though esoteric practitioners do not study deeply or research literally, they still know clearly and accurately every principle of life. It is so because through meditation and contemplation, their spiritual intuition is spontaneously activated and their enlightened mind is naturally developed. Hence, they can perceive much faster and that is why they know everything without learning.

Knowing everything without learning is because the manifestation of instinct and conscience in the discerning mind evokes the mechanism to develop intuition and acquire knowledge with clarity and accuracy.

Therefore, esoteric practitioners should exercise contemplation. Via contemplation they can reach the imponderable principle of Creation, penetrate the original essence of absolute emptiness, so as to ascertain that worldly life is merely a universal delusion. All beings displayed everywhere on the surface of the Earth have to be soon decomposed and transformed like water bubbles, melting dew, dispersing fog, dissipating smoke, flying clouds. So, life is unstable and impermanent; in fact, it is just a daydream, lasting for an even shorter time than that required to boil the yellow millet or that of the butterfly metamorphosis. Thus, it is said: *"Everything displayed in this world is unreal"*. Knowing so, humans are stoically determined to renounce the illusionary passions, willfully search for the Truth so as to evade from this world of ignorance and suffering.

But in order to prepare for effective contemplation, you should fully meditate. The goal of meditation is to assure the indispensable serenity and tranquility of your heart and mind, to eliminate all physical exigencies or mental troubles from the seven emotions and six sensual attractions that disturb your soul and body day and night. Then you should confine your thoughts into your brain. Do not let them ramble on bad and nonsensical paths. Instead, try to gradually strain your mind toward the perfect purity and illumination. You should also maintain your thoughts in such noble and perfectly pure state. Do not allow any exterior events to interfere with and disturb your mind. Once achieving such stage, you then introspect to see without viewing, to hear without listening, and to know without comprehending, i.e., nothing in this world can catch your attention.

In such a meditative state, the contemplation will yield extraordinary effects. It is so because during contemplation, your profound thought and serene reflection penetrate the subject of interest, while the senses and organs in your body gradually relax, to let your soul (the original spirit) detach from the carnal sheath and follow your thought to profoundly listen to the natural nature.

Some contemplation practitioners show symptoms of mental insanity or foolishness. It is because they contemplate without fully meditating to prepare for the serenity of their mind, prior to launching in excessive thinking and consideration that shake up their spirit. In such case, they just need to rest correctly in the calmness to promptly revert to the normal state.

I bless you all. I ascend.

The 22nd day of the 9th month of Bính Tý year (1936)

PRACTICE ESOTERIC EXERCISES

NAM PHƯƠNG GIÁO CHỦ
THE FOUNDER OF CAODAISM AT THE SOUTH

Poem:

Harmonize the South with the North[168] to elucidate DAO,

Purify your soul to escape from suffering and grief.

This miraculous method is taught to liberate from the three inferior worlds,[169]

---

[168] The Spiritual and Temporal, respectively.
[169] The world of humans, animals, and hungry ghosts.

It aims to return to the absolute emptiness and create the Saintly Body.

Here I discuss "PRACTICING ESOTERIC EXERCISES".

The esoteric method comprises spiritual traditions by which practitioners gain spiritual enlightenment so as to attain deliverance and ascension. It is so regrettable for those ascetics who observe vegetarianism but ignore the esoteric practice.

But why do I enforce esoteric disciples to strictly observe the five precepts? It is because the esoteric practice is not easy. Should you violate observances and precepts, never could you achieve deliverance.

Plant-based diets benefit the soul, whereas animal-based foods nourish the body. If animal-based dieters practice esoteric exercises, their souls are heavy and sullied by the post-genesis energy, and can barely escape from the middle world.

In addition, lust is the most critical issue for esoteric practitioners. I already emphasized that a drop of sperm is a mass of quintessence and spirit. Therefore, a leaked drop of your sperm sufficiently causes a great loss to your perisprit (double-body). Moreover, the number of such drops corresponds to the number of "sparks of Divine Light". When you die, they all come to the karma tower to request the restitution of their divine body. (*I'm smiling* ...) Children! You should keep in mind that they are "Divine body", not "human body"!

In the human body there are seven essential substances: the pure Yang, Quintessence, Energy, Spirit, bone, blood, and flesh.

Here I explain the pure Yang.

Human life is possible because the Yang energy circulates throughout the body to maintain the vital source of corporal substances. When this circulation stops, the person immediately exhales his last breath. Hence, esoteric practitioners should use respiration to converge the Yang energy into their body so as to be more robust and activate the circulation throughout the body to eliminate the impure, heavy, and toxic substances. Such exercises explain the esoteric practitioner's vigor and longevity. In addition, esoteric disciples also need this pure Yang to create their astral body. They must use respiration to absorb the vital energy into their true body. Regarding Quintessence, Energy, and Spirit, together they form an essential mechanism in human being. Only when Quintessence, Energy, and Spirit exist, humans can formulate the "true DAO".

Spirit is the master of human body, i.e., the spark of Divine Light bestowed by God. Energy is the supremely imponderable energy of the absolute emptiness that assures human health and happiness. In order to trace the origin of Spirit and Energy, there is no other method but penetrating the profoundly mystic mechanism of Genesis. This mystic mechanism is therefore the esoteric traditions that I bequeathed and you have practiced so far.

I explain the seven envelopes of human soul:

If a human soul from the Paradise or Nirvana wants to come into this inferior world, i.e., the 7th world, it has to traverse the six spiritual worlds of the superior atmosphere. Descending from one world to another, the soul has to conform to the Natural Law of Creation; thus, it adopts from each of these worlds a specific set of substances to cover the soul. The lower world the soul gets into, the denser and more obscure envelopes it has to bear. Arriving at this world of desires and passions, human soul needs one more layer -- the heavy and impure corporal body. But also thanks to the corporal body containing the full set of Three Treasures and Five Primordial Elements, awakened people can forge and strain themselves to attain the complete dematerialization and return to his original position. So far, I have discussed the progression or regression of a soul according to the edification and destruction law of Creation. Nowadays, in the era of Grand Amnesty, I manifest Myself to spread the true esoteric tradition to save all beings. It means I open a shortcut through which your immortal state or golden body can directly get back to ME, bypassing the spiritual worlds of the superior atmosphere, so that you can strip the seven envelopes that cover your soul all at once.

Ascension.

The 19th day of the 8th month of Bính Tý year (1936)

THE THREE STAGES AND THE NINE INITIATIONS
JADE EMPEROR SUPREME GOD

Poem:

The JADE brilliantly radiates to illumine all creatures,

The EMPEROR of the Universe manifests to save them;

HE preaches the SUPREME Esotericism to this world,

And bestows GOD'S favor in this Saintly Scripture.

Your MASTER. I greet you all.

You are exempted from ceremonials. Sit down in meditation.

Lesson in Verse:

I manifest in the Third Era to re-initiate the DAO.

By uniting the Three Ancient Religions

Into the Saintly Doctrine of Fraternity and Peace,

To establish the universal harmony and revivify the golden esotericism.

I reverse the Cosmic Wheel rotation,

To save all beings from the vicious cycle of reincarnation,

So that they can regain their ancient celestial position,

After abolishing the four sufferings[170] and detaching all karmic links.

On the river of ignorance the Ark of Salvation is waiting,

With the blessing water to wash off part of your sins.

Should you wish to become Buddha, Saints, and Immortals,

---

[170] The four sufferings are birth, ailments, decrepitude, and death.

I transmit to you the true esoteric traditions,

To remove the obscurity of your profane characters,

So that you can persevere on the radiant path,

And absorb the pure atmospheric energy of the superior worlds,

To create the golden body for your lightning ascension.

Two aspects to consider are Good and Bad,

Two paths to select are Death and Life.

Those who piously self-perfect will be sanctified,

Those who do not self-correct will suffer cruel vicissitudes.

Self-perfection could be achieved by either the spiral or the shortcut;

Those who take the shortcut will acquire the celestial mechanism.

Accomplishing self-perfection, they win the celestial banner,

And receive Divine Order to return to heaven in their saintly relics.

Those taking the spiral should remove the seven envelopes of the soul,

To wash off their profane nature by expiating all sins;

They progress little by little with the evolutionary rhythm,

During which the three profane consciences are cleared up.[171]

CAODAISM in the Third Era brings enlightenment

To those who, disenchanted of life, seek the true method of dematerialization.

The Grand Cycle of Esotericism reveals the Way of the Pre-Genesis,

To forge the soul and create the double-body for the spiritual ascension.

---

[171] The three profane consciences are the past, the future, and the present one.

You should know the method of heart in the Nine Initiations,

And scrupulously exercise them in accord with the rules of self-perfection.

You should live a life with appropriate disciplines,

To first off, dissipate the veil of ignorance.

To become Immortals and Buddha, you must know the miraculous mechanism,

You must meditate and contemplate to gain enlightenment;

Especially you should nurture Energy and conserve Quintessence,

If you expend Quintessence and exhaust Energy, the Spirit no longer exists.

In the FIRST INITIATION you should accomplish self-perfection,

To build the foundation for Energy-Spirit alliance,

Also to abolish all grief and maintain the emptiness of heart,

Once the seven emotions and six passions are shut, serenity emerges.

Develop the Conscience of DAO in serenity and quietude,

Nurture the Saintly Fetus in accord with the mystic laws;

Day and night, capture the primordial energy of life,

To harmonize soul and body, to unite mercury and lead.[172]

In the SECOND INITIATION, miracles manifest;

As the five carnal senses are shut, the Four Ancestors return home.[173]

---

[172] Mercury and lead, symbolizing the Post-Genesis Yang and Yin, respectively.

[173] 'the Four Ancestors return home' alludes to the convergence of the four original sources of vital energy. In reference to the Grand Cycle of Esoteric Teaching, chapter The Cross of Three Purities, section The Five Elements, these four original sources of vital energy are the four Primordial Elements: Metal, Water, Wood, and Fire corresponding to the four cardinals: South,

The Yin and Yang concertedly rise and fall,

And the Three Treasures rhythmically harmonize and sublime.

Activate the nine corporal energy centers to elaborate the golden pill,

Operate the Five Elements to circulate the micro-cosmos,

Tranquilly nurture the true soul,

To mystically fortify it until maturation.

In the THIRD INITIATION, the Post-Genesis ceases to descend,

"**THE FIRST STAGE**" is achieved, and your name appears in the Jade Board.

Your effort in extracting the pure from the impure

Has resulted in the formation of the magic pill of Immortality.

In the FOURTH INITIATION, the celestial mechanism is revealed,

And you evade the four sufferings of this world.

Converge all inside and outside thoughts,

Forge and purify them so that the Saintly Fetus becomes lighter.

In the FIFTH INITIATION, you penetrate the miraculous mechanism,

In deep contemplation you seek the origin,

In ecstasy your soul ascends to the Sojourn of Immortals,

To receive further profoundly mystic teaching of heart.

In the SIXTH INITIATION you are unperturbed by the three corporal consciences,

Your spiritual heart attains its original serenity;

Worldly dust no longer can sully or affect it,

North, East, and West that converge into the fifth element Earth at the center.

This **SECOND STAGE** of magic pill achieves the order of Immortals and Saints.

The SEVENTH INITIATION is the method for the energy of life,

To forge your true spirit into its original state;

On the sacred mountain the golden lotus blooms up,

It is so delightful after taking off the seven envelopes of the soul.

In the EIGHTH INITIATION the pure and noble virtues impregnate you,

At this stage you attain the order of *Kim Tiên*;[174]

Being absolutely empty, no posterior nor anterior,

You do not sense nor bear worldly grief.

Use the fire of LI ($\overline{\overline{}}$) to forge the gold of K'AN ($\overline{\overline{}}$),

Separate the Yin and the Yang in equal amount;

Though your soul is still sheltered in the body,

It no longer attaches to any worldly matters.

In the NINTH INITIATION you reach the blissful Thunder Voice;[175]

You freely traverse everywhere in the universe,

To play chess and enjoy saintly drinks at the lotus throne,

To receive the immortal peach in the harmonious realm of emptiness.

The mystic science of Immortals and Buddha is unfathomable,

Its spiritual power participates in the omnipotence.

What a marvelous and incommensurable facility!

Such leisure of going with the wind and appreciating the

---

[174] '*Kim Tiên*' literally means '*the Golden Immortal*'.

[175] Thunder Voice, alluding to the Sojourn of Buddha.

moon is inconceivable.

Here I briefly trace the "MIDDLE WAY",

The Doctrine of Impartiality and Harmony founded by Confucius.

Impartiality is the origin of humanity,

Not biased nor inclined, it is the center for all convergences.

Impartiality means not leaning toward right or left,

Impartiality means not varying more or less.

Impartiality is the middle way, straight, and flat,

Yet, everything strives to reach such equilibrium.

Do not tend toward the extremes of all-or-nothing,

Live a normal life to enhance your good nature,

As well as your instincts and conscience;

Develop your intuitive intelligence by diligently practicing the DAO.

Harmonize the Yin and Yang to augment the pure and eliminate the impure,

They combine into all living beings.

The Yin and Yang energies oppose and unite with one another,

They harmoniously transform to engender all creatures.

Never should esoteric practitioners deviate from the saintly teaching,

Instead, they should serve as proofs for such instructions.

First of all, they must prepare for self-correction,

To purify their body and pacify their soul.

Properly cleanse well in and out,

To achieve a pure and calm conscience.

Such serenity provokes the alliance of Spirit and Energy,

As QIAN (☰) elevates and K'UN (☷) precipitates,

dragon rises and tiger falls.[176]

The method of NINE INITIATIONS is based on the Purities,

By which you evade reincarnation and end all karmic links.

Absolutely free from such perpetual cycle,

You become Immortals and Buddha right on earth.

Poem:

Earthy world has exiled innumerable souls,

Who are submerged under the tide of passion;

Heavy karmic links perpetuate them in reincarnation,

To be wise, exploit circumstances to achieve spiritual progress.

I bless you all. I ascend.

The 18th day of the 9th month of Bính Tý year (1936)

NURTURE THE SOUL AND BODY

CAO-DAI BODHISATTVA

Poem:

Contemplate on Impartiality to penetrate the unfathomable infinity,

And attain the lotus throne of Nine Initiations in celestial hierarchy;

Meditate on Buddha-Nature to illumine your conscience,

And apply great bravery to your practice of the profoundly mystic DAO.

---

[176] *Heaven and Earth*, combined with *dragon and tiger* allude to the Pre-Genesis and the Post-Genesis pairs of Yang-Yin, respectively.

Your MASTER. I greet you all.

Poem:

> I nurture all beings until maturity;
>
> Enlightened people preserve their divine soul,
>
> And comply with celestial laws to grasp the DAO;
>
> I order them the miraculous esoteric method.

Here I briefly discuss "NURTURE SOUL AND BODY".

I founded the Saintly Doctrine in Vietnam right in the last era of the evolutionary cycle. Children! The walls of your dungeons are about to collapse; the grand ordeal is approaching. How can I sit back and nonchalantly watch my children sinking in the abyss of this total degeneracy? Thus, never mind challenges and hardships, I open the Way of Salvation to save you from this imminent catastrophe.

You should know that DAO comprises three eras forming the eternal cycle of the Universe. First is the SUPERIOR ERA. It is the "Era of Creation", in which the entire Universe was edified. Humans in this era were innocent, candid, simple, and good. They observed the laws of Nature, living in piety and fraternity. Absorbing the energy of the Natural Nature, together they enjoyed the blessed happiness and bathed in the favor of DAO. That is why the Age of High Antiquity was named the "AGE OF SUPERIOR VIRTUES", and the Superior Era, the "ERA OF SAINTLINESS".

Next comes the MIDDLE ERA, in which the human heart was altered, acquiring profane customs, adopting bad habits, and gradually deviating from their Divine Nature. Relying in their corporal power, they oppressed and exterminated each other in slaughter; the weak was crashed under the power of the strong, whose notions of humanity, fraternity, and dignity were completely absent. That is why the Middle Age was named the AGE OF SUPERIOR FORCE, and the Middle Era, the "ERA OF FIGHT".

Then arrives the INFERIOR ERA, in which the struggle for life reaches the culmination of violence, brutality, and ferocity. Disdaining muscular force, humans exercise their brains in devilish cunning, evil tricks, confusing impasses, and horrible traps to cause extraordinary terror and dissolution. Nevertheless, this struggle is also a natural selection: the more the competition is intensified, the more the progress is accelerated. But as rivalries become uncontrollable, atrocities elevate further and further, leading to total destruction. That is why this current time is named the AGE of LIFE ENDING, and the Inferior Era, the "ERA OF ANNIHILATION".

But after anarchy is restoration of order; thus, decadence precedes revivification. The Era of Annihilation is followed by the Era of Preservation, in which piety and fraternity are restored in the human heart to prepare for the return of the epoch like the Antiquity. That is why this Era is also called the "ERA OF RESTORATION".

Hence, mankind in this era is about to return to the Primordial Unity of the Grand Cosmic Revolution. Now it is time to reach this destination again, because the end of the last era of the Genesis has completed the full cycle of one hundred twenty nine thousand and six hundred years.[177] Therefore, a new Genesis is coming.

Children! I have come and tended my hands to save you. You should cling to my Saintly Doctrine, and persevere in forging your true nature until it becomes purely positive so as to avoid the coming vicissitudes. Children, keep that in mind!

Moreover, self-cultivation is the unique method of deliverance from this horrible world of grief. Thus, dignified people should constantly aspire toward spirituality to forge their moral conduct. You should know that in order to purify your true spirit, you must maintain your body healthy and strong. To fortify the soul, it is necessary to nurture the body. Therefore, you should not advance the spiritual at the expense of the temporal, nor care about the body while disregarding the soul. Body and soul must intimately rely on each other. Self-cultivation methods should not mutilate or sacrifice the body, since only a strong and healthy body can accommodate a penetrating soul.

Here I briefly explain how to "NURTURE THE SOUL".

---

[177] 129,600 years

BUDDHISM emphasizes "ABSOLUTE EMPTINESS OF MIND" to nurture the soul and spirit. Thus, disciples practice meditation to predispose their conscience to tranquility.

TAOISM focuses on "SERENITY IN MIND" to live according to the rhythm of Nature. Disciples keep concentrating and contemplating until they reach the spontaneity or illumination; they decisively maintain their conscience detached from worldly matters that stir up the seven emotions and the six sensual attractions leading to erroneous acts.

CONFUCIANISM preaches "PRESERVATION OF CONSCIENCE AND MAINTENANCE OF NATURE". It recommends peaceful meditation to conserve and maintain the good heart that naturally aspires toward virtues and the superior sense of balance and moderation.

Therefore, if you like to nurture your soul to perfection, you should not trouble your heart nor let your mind ramble around; instead, you should always maintain them in their natural, serene, and tranquil state.

Besides, nothing in human beings is as precious and essential as the CONSCIENCE. If this CONSCIENCE is lost or abdicated, what else in humans is worthy? In such deprivation, humans no longer differ from ants, insects, crickets, or even worms! Such life is worse than death; such existence resembles null. Alas! What a profound agony!

Now that I preach the Saintly Doctrine, you must bear it in mind, and try your best to preserve your conscience and correct your heart. In order to have a pure, light, and serene soul, day and night you must strain your conscience until it is absolutely empty, with no jealousy, hatred, envy, sorrow, inquietude, or fear of anything. To nurture and promote the noble thoughts, you must control your desires and passions whose explosion prompts you to the erroneous acts.

In addition, you should also discern the essential from the subordinate, so as to advance the former and drop the latter, as well as prevent the master to be abdicated by its servants. Otherwise, in your distraction, the accessories take over and suppress the major part, causing deep trouble. That major part is the **CONSCIENCE**, and its accessories, EYES and EARS.

The conscience is the SAINT-ESPRIT that God bestows to you, whereas eyes and ears ironically are its worst ENEMIES. Thus, if you let your eyes and ears stir up your desires and bury your conscience under the mountain of the "five turbidities"[178], alas! it would be extremely hard to disinter and lift your conscience up.

Therefore, as humans, you should unceasingly master your conscience, abolish sensational thoughts, erroneous acts, envy, jealousy, and rivalry, in order to maintain tranquility of your mind. That is the most precious treasure in this world. Do not let your soul be tempted or intoxicated by worldly riches and honors. Do not covet or bury your divine nature with corporal beauty and sweet scents.

In addition, esoteric practitioners must refrain from consuming some food items in their daily meals. It is true that palatable foods nourish your body. But what if they ruin your soul? For example, intake of the five fragrant herbs[179] can weaken your soul; why do you not refrain from consuming them?

Also, if esoteric practitioners involve in the four worldly dungeons: beauty, money, alcohol, and vanity, alas! they would not have any hope to be salvaged.

BEAUTY bewitches the soul,

MONEY distracts the mind,

ALCOHOL destroys the magic pill[180],

VANITY ruins the relic[181].

But above all, ANGER is the most detrimental factor. Even you have practiced meditation for a dozen years, a single blaze of anger is sufficient to completely burn and melt your interior magic pill into plain water.

---

[178] The five corporal senses: Vision, Hearing, Smell, Taste, and Touch.

[179] The five fragrant vegetables: onion, shallot, garlic, chives, and leek.

[180] the DAO interiorly elaborated

[181] the astral body

Even ordinary items such as tobacco and betel are also harmful to your magic pill. Therefore, you should pay attention and be vigilant.

Long Poem:

The three eras of Cosmic Revolution is about to complete,

Earth, Heaven, mankind, and all beings are bound to this mechanism.

It is time for harsh vicissitudes to happen,

And for the Ark of Salvation to receive the pious souls.

Buddha and Immortals select candidates,

Prompting superior spirits toward ascension.

Persevere in establishing the spiritual foundation,

Make it firm, strong, and immutable over the time.

What does it mean by "self-cultivation"?

It means like a blind one, groping around in dark night.

Do not complain even in hardship,

Keep your soul pure and serene.

Self-cultivation is like an addiction

Of a passionate lover, or a diligent moneymaker.

Step by step, carefully escalate the ladder,

Day and night, forge and strengthen your soul.

Do not be influenced by people's disdain,

As you should practice self-forgetting.

Do not pay attention to rumors,

Persevere in self-cultivation despite hardships and challenges.

Pretend to be an idiot,

With the eyes of a blind and the ears of a deaf.

Profane life tastes so bitter and sour,

Whereas that of Immortals is sweet and noble.

Self-cultivation means inspiring to the real bliss,

Ignore all conflicts, instead of aggravating them.

To escape from suffering and reincarnation,

Willfully purify your divine soul.

It is much easier to plan from your childhood

To discipline and guard your soul day and night.

Then your story would be encrypted in book and stone slab.

But children! Without the key can you open the celestial gate?

Here is the magic key that I am going to give,

Yet I only pass it to those with willful spirit.

For self-cultivation you should seek

To find the true way, profound and high.

Nowadays, the Spiritual Way is widely open,

It unifies the Three Ancient Doctrines to revivify Cao-Dai Great Way.

But be careful! There are countless traps!

Mistaken them, you will get caught.

The DAO of God is unfathomable,

Gauging it with your knowledge is like emptying the ocean with an oyster shell.

This is the period of universal vicissitudes,

That is why I come to save the pious souls.

I am Lord of the Universe,

Yet, I cannot modify the Celestial Law.

Perceiving that you have committed countless sins,

With Paternal Love I manifest Myself to guide and save you.

As a divine favor has still remained in the Orient,

Immortals and Buddha descend to preach the Saintly Doctrine.

Spiritual and Temporal, which one is better?

Never should willful and dignified men be deprived of self-cultivation!

Diligently and continuously practice esoteric exercises,

To develop the virtues of resignation and tolerance, fraternity and harmony.

Simultaneously self-perfect body and soul,

Flourish the Yang and diminish the Yin to achieve ascension.

Do not commit errors or sins to avoid repentance,

Maintain serenity in mind to reap the work for credit.

Fraternize Spirit and Energy,

Introspect so that Dragon rises and Tiger falls[182].

Forget and forgive everything else,

Concentrate in spiritual exercises to expiate past sins.

Being initiates in the esoteric way,

You should demonstrate exceptional virtues and conduct.

Perfect the nature and conscience by following good examples,

Amplify wisdom and intelligence to understand your role.

Nurture body and soul wisely,

Observe hygiene rules on food restrictions and abstinences.

Maintain serenity and quietude of mind,

To exert the Creator's power and circulate the Yang energy.

Condense energy at the lower elixir field,

To ally mercury with lead so as to conceive the Divine Fetus.[183]

---

[182] Dragon and Tiger allude to the Post-Genesis Yang-Yin pair.

[183] Mercury and Lead represent the Post-Genesis Yang-Yin pair.

In order to conform to the hygienic style of Immortals,

Nurture body and soul to serenity and perfection.

Establish the crown in Heaven and the censor in Earth[184],

Build the Octagonal Furnace to access the emptiness of heart.

Poem:

The emptiness of heart is achieved with your CONSCIENCE,

Conscience awakened, you do not err in aberrations.

Erring in aberrations, you hardly have an escape,

Adopting brutal habits, you put bestiality on hold!

Holding the Divine Justice, the Creator is absolutely fair,

In rewarding the good and punishing the bad;

Unfailing balance, even for infinitesimal deviation,

Yet people are not afraid, despite horrible scourges.

Scourges seem not to terrify mankind,

People show indifference toward saintly advice. (*I'm smiling…*)

They ignore wisdom and virtues,

But discuss fervently on beauty and money.

I bless you all. I ascend.

---

[184] 'Heaven' symbolizes human head crown and 'Earth', the low elixir field under the navel.

The 23rd day of the 9th month of Bính Tý year (1936)

THE UNIVERSE
CAO-DAI SUPREME GOD

Poem:

CAO-DAI perceives the world in decadence,

Leaving Jade Palace, I come to save all beings.

From the SUPERIOR World where eternal tranquility exists,

GOD the Savior descends in this catastrophic era.

Your MASTER. I greet you all.

Competition, fighting, and annihilation are favored in this current world of delusion and vanity. Mankind, frenzied and bursting with delirious instincts and passions, is whirling in the turbulent ocean of grief. I cannot turn my back on such a sad spectacle.

Poem:

Humans effervesce with bitter deceptions and prickly disillusions;

Immortals and Buddha frown in perceiving such destructive scourges.

People unceasingly tie to perilous catastrophes,

And suffer from calamities of the grand tribulation.

Here I give some elucidation on THE UNIVERSE (discussing some worlds in the Invisible).

Poem:

In this immense Universe,

There exist Invisible Worlds full of serene sojourns.

The Creator laid out miraculous laws,

To establish a world of Virtue and Wisdom.

Children! Why is it called VŨ-TRỤ (the Universe)? How do you perceive it?

The entire space forms VŨ (UNI). The extremity of this space is called TRỤ (VERSE). VŨ encompasses the four cardinal points, as well as the upward and downward directions. TRỤ also signifies the past and present. Thus, the term VŨ-TRỤ (UNIVERSE) encompasses both space and time.

Prior to the manifestation of the Supreme Being, that space was an amorphous and infinite nebula, because it was in the Primordial Chaos.

That space is the Non-Being or the Absolute Emptiness. In this Absolute Emptiness is the miraculous PRINCIPLE of the Natural Nature, along with its antagonist twin, the ENERGY of the Adapted (Naturalized) Nature. Such PRINCIPLE and ENERGY are respectively the Yang and the Yin in the Primordial Chaos. They united and crystallized slowly in infinite time to form a splendid globe of light. At the determined time and date, this massive ball of light exploded with an extraordinary detonation that shook up the space. A Divine Light popped out from this explosion, unceasingly swirling and waltzing in space, projecting around it a dazzling halo whose rays continuingly illuminate the entire Cosmos. That Divine Light is the Supreme Being of the Universe, emerging from the Absolute Emptiness (the Non-Being).

Since then, the Universe has had the Supreme Being, perfectly good, omniscient, omnipotent, immutable, and capable of transforming in infinite forms. The Absolute Master of the Universe sovereigns and commands the Genesis, applying the Yin-Yang mechanism to separate the pure from the impure and condense the Energy of the Primordial Nebula (the Non-Being) to engender all creatures.

That Yin-Yang mechanism functions without respite, without interruption, to assure the life and perpetuity of all beings, and maintain Heaven-Earth.

Scattering in the immense Universe are innumerable spheres: pure and impure, superior and inferior, bright and obscure. Obeying the pre-established order and harmony of the Celestial Mechanism, all these spheres move around here and there, ascend and descend continuously and perpetually.

Pure and light spheres surpass others in altitude to reach the superior atmosphere. Thus, the earth on which you reside, though material, visible, and impure, belongs to the middle level. Below it are much heavier and more obscure planets. These blasted worlds sink deeply in the abyss of the Universe and hence, collapse in the heavily negative atmosphere, darkness, sorrow, suffering, and grief. They are the exile for condemned souls who commit sins during their lives on earth.

In these inferior worlds, the condemned souls become more and more ignorant, confused, and obscure. Alas! What a misery! I can barely describe all the horrors in these worlds where sinful souls have to expiate their sins.

What are those worlds? They are the netherworlds, referred as Avici[185] or Hades in Buddhism.

Though netherworlds are the inferior worlds of exile, where condemned souls undergo horrible perdition, it is still a much favorable place than those for scrawny demons. Why is that?

It is because if a person fully expends his purely positive energy, he must become totally negative and must die. After death he must become a phantom or demon, incapable of joining and resting in any habitable globes, including the netherworlds of exile.

Being denied from all dwelling worlds, phantoms or demons can only shelter on the wind or cloud to wait for the day of their complete disintegration.

Demons cannot immigrate to any worlds because they completely exhaust their purely positive energy. Condemned souls,

---

[185] Avici (sankrit) is the most inferior world of darkness. The lowest and the worst of the eight hot hells, according to the Buddhist theory, the hells of no intermission of suffering. Hell of uninterrupted suffering, in which suffering, death, and painful rebirth are continuous until the retribution for the sufferer's evil karma is exhausted, at which time that being will be reborn in a higher planet of existence. Those who are born in this hell always suffer from the heat of fire.

though sinful, still retain part of their positive energy that authorizes their admission to the netherworlds for expiation. As long as part of the positive energy still remains, one day they would be able to return to the earth. Therefore, expiation and suffering in the netherworlds are still much enviable than demoniac fate.

Regarding the worlds a little superior, they are the transitional worlds for less sinful souls. Once delivered from corporal bodies, they come there for a lapse of repose while waiting for their next reincarnation.

Children! Read the following to gain deeper understanding.

Lesson in Verse

All earths and heavens in the Universe

Are commanded by the UNIQUE AND ABSOLUTE GOD.

Up above, HE governs the Thirty-Six Heavens

Where Buddha, Immortals, and Saints piously submit to His Law.

His omniscience and omnipotence are infinite,

His wisdom and favor are immutable and eternal.

Down below, HE sovereigns the Seventy-Two Earths

Where rewards or punishments are to educate humans.

Human planet is material, impure, and crude,

Where the souls suffer innumerable trials,

Where nothing is durable or stable,

And human lifetime is brief like a flash of light.

Such a planet is incomparable to the superior worlds,

Where immortal souls rest peacefully and eternally.

Then how can you escape from fatal vicissitudes?

You get blessed if you strive toward Wisdom and Virtue.

Endure all miseries and hardships in current life,

Afterwards you no longer deplore any grief or complaints.

This perishable world is created

As the school of evolution for all beings.

Try to do good and avoid bad,

So that your soul can elevate to the superior worlds.

But such stay is just a brief vacation,

Your soul should return to this earth to earn more spiritual credit.

You will pass the Superior Worlds one after the other,

The higher you reach the purer and lighter you become.

Depending on your work credit on this earth,

GOD and Buddha will fairly reward you after life.

The divine balance weighs your merits and sins

With an accurate and unfailing precision.

Children! I confine you in this world,

Where expiation law is executed without error.

The entire Universe is in My hands

You have no escape whatsoever.

Be wise by seeking and following the God-Way,

Forge your soul to penetrate the Genesis of Creation.

Humans have a true double-body,

Nurture it to self-perfect gradually.

Do not let it be sullied or corrupted,

So that your celestial rank remains.

Let ME discuss briefly the esoteric teaching,

So that humans learn the profoundly mystic DAO.

It is the method to strain the astral body,

That defies both space and time.

Why do demons and ghosts exist?

They are souls that commit lots of sins.

After life they become wandering souls or scrawny demons,

Having no refuge, they suffer from horrors of non-identity.

The human body is half positive and half negative,

Pure and impure, where DAO functions unceasingly.

Forge and strain your soul day and night,

To illumine and purify the Three Treasures.

Also perfect your corporal body,

Purify and replenish it with DAO.

Gradually eliminate the negative energy,

With the pure positive energy you will return to Heaven.

Those who still sink in ignorance,

Fill their souls with negative energy.

They exhaust their divine spirit,

As the positive energy wanes, they hardly survive.

Their soul and body detach from each other,

Because their divine energy is dissipated in impiety.

These dark souls become wandering demons

Or naughty ghosts to play tricks in human world.

They abuse impure mediums to dupe people,

Or name themselves Deities and Saints to receive offerings.

They demand naughty and malicious inquiries,

That superstitious people stupidly execute without thinking.

They terrify humans with their hideous outbreak,

And dwell on clouds or wind to avoid adversities.

Why do they not reincarnate?

Impossible, because they completely lost their Buddha body!

Without position or grade,

They do not have any shelter to avoid scourges.

Losing their purely positive energy,

They have to bear tons of cruel trials.

I bless you all. I ascend.

_____

The 25th day of the 9th month of Bính Tý year (1936)

THE 68th PLANET

CAO-DAI IMMORTAL
Poem:

CAO-DAI is the absolutely high and pure nature of the Emptiness,

Where the names of elected disciples are listed on the Celestial Board,

And where the miraculous remedy dissipates worldly delusion.

Whoever, losing the DAO within, die in the blaze of the Hades… (*I'm smiling*...)

Your MASTER. I greet you all. Sit down and listen.

You should self-cultivate in such a way that makes your soul pure, intuitive, and clairvoyant; then it is not hard for you to attain the sacred standards of Deities or Immortals.

Here I discuss "the 68th Earth", your planet, which is coming to its end.

I cannot turn my back to let you collapse in the vicissitudes of this agonizing world. So, I manifest Myself to save you by directing the Divine Ark to guide you to the Sojourn of Immortals.

Your planet is about to fall into decrepitude. It is predestined in the Celestial Book, and I scheduled for its due time and date. But it is also a pleasure to see all living beings progress to a much elevated level of evolution, because at the destruction of this planet, human souls will evolve onto the 67th Earth, the site predetermined by the profoundly mystic DAO.

This is the last time I come to guide you to a purer and lighter world, while the impious, rebellious, and sinful people will be dissipated into wind and dust. Children, you must come to the end. Those of you, who follow the God-Way, who persevere in self-cultivation, who practice piety and universal love, would be picked up by Buddha and Immortals. On the other hand, those who are brutal and passionate in worldly matters will hardly be secured in these last days.

How would the annihilation of this world happen? Do you know it?

One day those who have acquired wisdom and virtue, and observed vegetarianism to maintain a pure soul in a sane body, gradually get used to the Pre-Genesis energy; then at the regeneration of the pure Yang, they will be able to spontaneously assimilate and live at ease in such environment. The impious ones, who fully live in the environment of Post-Genesis energy, will not be able to conform to the rising of the Pre-Genesis energy at the day of Yin extermination and Yang regeneration; consequently, they will perish soul and body.

Now the Universe is touching its term of Periodic Revolution. I come to transfer you onto a more serene world, where you will rest peacefully and seek the mechanism of spiritual deliverance so as to penetrate the Sojourn of Immortals. Children! Do not despise these words as vulgar superstition. One day they will all come true.

Poem:

Supreme Being manifests in this world in the Inferior Era,

And tends His hands to guide humans back on the right track.

Who among you penetrate the miraculous mechanism?

Knowing it, why are you still dozing in the idleness?

Ascension.

The 25th day of the 9th month of Bính Tý year (1936)

THE PARADISE AND THE HADES

CAO-DAI SUPREME GOD

Your MASTER. I greet you all.

Here I discuss the chapter on PARADISE and HADES.

How do you conceive PARADISE and HADES? Children! A pure, clear, good, and pious conscience is Paradise; an impure, obscure, bad, brutal, and impious conscience is Hades. Thus, Paradise or Hades all depends on your "CONSCIENCE".

Normally you conceive PARADISE as an extremely fine, splendid, enjoyable sojourn in the nebulous realm of the infinity; whereas HADES, as an underground furnace.

It is very foolish to believe HADES is underground. In the core of the Earth, there is just fire. To the four cardinals of the Globe, there is wind, rain, hot, and cold. Moreover, this universe comprises innumerable earths: the pure and light worlds elevate on top to benefit from the positive energy and become very limpid and radiant, while the impure ones sink in depth to absorb the negative energy and become very obscure and heavy.

Hence, if you transgress the Celestial Law or commit serious crimes against mankind, your soul will be condemned on those blasted planets, surrounded by the miserably negative atmosphere, to expiate your sins in such grievous suffering that tears your heart and prickles your mind. It is cause-and-effect, karmic expiation, reaping of what you sowed in the past; it is the consequences of your own actions and thoughts that follow you to punish you. Nothing like strangulation, body sawing, or other tortures exist, as you imagine in the so-called the Ten Penitentiaries of King of the Hades.

Regarding the pious souls, they are authorized to dwell in a superior world or mingle with live people on earth to accomplish the work of piety so as to pay off their past karma; they can also further study to advance toward the realm of wisdom. Moreover, after quitting the profane body, the soul is also detached to refuge in the Cosmic Intermediary, waiting for the day to report to the Tribunal of Divine Justice and account for karma to be expiated in the next reincarnation; those who accumulate significant merits will be authorized to get back to receive the beatitude that I reward them.

Long Poem:

Unveil the ignorance that obscures human mind,

To discover the Spirit of Truth and unite with nature.

The profoundly mystic DAO is widely preached to humans,

To dissipate routine superstition and to establish Caodaism.

Human credulity is so surprising,

As people blindly rush into beliefs without thinking.

Due to such deep ignorance,

They are unaware that the Imperial DAO is within their heart.

Human errors are innumerable,

As superstition and treacheries are invented to lure people;

Mediums, charlatans, and sorcerers dupe the world,

By self-personating as Deities and Saints,

And by evoking the impure spirits to utter devilish lies,

That corrupt customs and ruin traditions in the human world.

Fanatic people swallow those lies with no doubt,

And stupidly perform superstitious cults to demons.

Fortune or misfortune, it is you who create,

God or Satan is inside you; right or wrong is within your heart.

Unveil those dark clouds that hide the full moon,

Clairvoyant disciples must seek the Spirit of Truth.

Think over and over on every aspect,

Before deciding whether it should be adored or despised.

Seek the Path of Enlightenment and avoid that of Ignorance,

Do not overload your Faith with ridiculous and congesting cults.

Instead, thoroughly introspect about your origin,

From where you come, and how you are in such transmutation.

Certainly there must be a First Cause,

The origin for the Genesis of the universe.

Vigilantly support your belief with full clarity,

And converge it to God Light.

God is the Spiritual Father of all beings,

It is sufficient to faithfully adore Him.

I bless you all. Ascension.

The 20th day of the 9th month of Bính Tý year (1936)

REVIVIFICATION OF THE GREAT WAY AND REVELATION OF CAO-DAI – METHOD OF WORSHIP

CAO-DAI SUPREME GOD

CAO-DAI, the topmost Spiritual Temple that few people search for;

It is in your spiritual heart where Spirit and Energy converge.

Once this Yin-Yang pair unites at the head crown,

SUPREME BEING is attained as the dragon rises and tiger falls.[186]

(*I'm smiling...*) The current life is full of horrible vicissitudes and trials. Scourges and catastrophes take turns to happen without interruption until the day when the Universe begins its next cycle. Humans are still unable to penetrate the mechanism of Genesis; but they have to move on to a new era. Alas! What a distress! This world is going to suffer from panic metamorphosis!

I manifest in this séance, to expose saintly words so as to wake humans up from their delusional reveries of yellow millet.[187]

Poem:

DAO[188], immense and invisible, animates all beings;

DAO creates Heaven and Earth, through which it operates;

DAO, once revealed to mankind, pacifies this world.

DAO is for humans to attain Celestial Dignity.

DAO is profoundly mystic, but perceptible in physical manifestations. DAO is both dynamic and static, to assure the perpetuity of all beings and animation of the Universe. From its unique "PRINCIPLE" and "ENERGY", DAO engenders an infinite variety of creatures. DAO sometimes conceals, sometimes reveals, and continuously transforms. What an omnipotent mechanism!

DAO dispenses life as well as death. But life or death are merely the products of a spiritual heart. DAO is within every being, yet people seek it outside. It is very simple, yet they search for complications. In addition, never does DAO leave humans, only people often leave DAO; and those who leave DAO can be barely alive. DAO is invisible and formless, non-odorous and voiceless.

---

[186] The rise and fall of the Yang-Yin pair, i.e., the harmony of fire and water energies.

[187] An allusion saying human life is like a very brief dream whose lapse is even shorter than the time required for boiling the yellow millet.

[188] 'the WAY', the SPIRITUAL UNITY.

People usually do not know where to look for it, because it comes and goes incessantly and without respite.

Here I briefly explain how the profoundly mystic DAO manifests in the material world.

Why is the GREAT WAY revivified as CAO-DAI manifests?

The revivification of DAO is due to my Universal Love and Mercy. Perceiving that the end of the cosmic revolution cycle is close to its pre-destined time, I am not content to let my children massively perish, body and soul, in the land of mourning and the ocean of grieving. Thus, I manifest in this world to restore the true teaching so as to transform corrupted humanity into the saintly society of Kings NGHIÊU and THUẤN[189]. I expose DAO and its Virtue to you so that humans learn to comply with the Celestial Law, quit evil, do good, discipline their envy, and leave their erroneous paths.

Essentially, DAO is exposed to save human soul from delusion and suffering. For this reason, DAO is disseminated everywhere to wake up the entire mankind.

As DAO is immutable, imponderable, and imperceptible to human senses, how to establish the religion?

The visible part of the Divine Mechanism must be exposed to clearly point out to humans its natural principle. Therefore, the way I establish this true teaching is nothing else than applying the determined traditions of the Ancient Doctrines to restore their essentials and unifying them into a harmonious syncretism.

The Three Ancient Doctrines: CONFUCIANISM, BUDDHISM, TAOISM, being preached long time ago, fell in decrepitude. Their traditions were modified, lost, and deviated from

---

[189] The peaceful and happy time under Kings Thuấn and Nghiêu in Ancient China. King NGHIÊU, or YAO (尧), 2356 – 2255 BC, was a legendary Chinese ruler. King THUẤN, or YU THE GREAT (大禹), 2200 - 2100 BC, was a legendary ruler in ancient China, famed for his introduction of flood control, inaugurating dynastic rule in China by founding the Xia Dynasty, and for his upright moral character.

the miraculous Celestial Mechanism. Consequently, numerous people practice these teachings without success.

Also due to deviation from the true teaching, these Three Doctrines have fallen further and further into decadence and corruption. The path of Truth is deserted and the way of Justice is abandoned. Little by little, bindweeds choke the former and brambles cover the latter. Consequently, mankind is unavoidably tied to the karmic cycle of the four sufferings, and endlessly moored in this world of exile. Humans gradually exhaust their source of DAO and Virtue, neglecting spiritual values to pursue the delusion of corporal senses and thus, inventing false rites, nice ritual music, and attractive appearances. They no longer aspire toward high morality and the profoundly mystic sense of DAO. They all confine to perceptible ideas, visible images, palpable forms, and audible sounds. Human envies exacerbate and push them toward crimes and sins. Due to their emotions and sensual attractions, they regress to animal or reincarnate in the six paths of transmigration[190].

The THREE ANCIENT DOCTRINES were denatured because

1) BUDDHISM, the ZEN Way, since the epoch of THẦN-TÚ[191], has invented superstition to dupe humans. It preaches the doctrine, competes for disciples, but only to push them into obscure and erroneous abysses. They do not study the mystic sense in ancient scriptures and oracles to seek the Truth; they meditate without composing their mind; they contemplate without concentrating their spirit.

2) CONFUCIANISM, after the epoch of MẠNH-TỬ[192], has drifted further and further toward the erroneous side. No longer do the

---

[190] The six miserable paths that sentient beings revolve in the cycle of birth and death, life after life. These are paths of hell-dwellers, hungry ghosts, animals, titanic demons or asuras, human beings and celestial beings.

[191] Yuquan Shen-Hsiu (玉泉神秀, 606?-706) was founder of the Northern School Zen Buddhism, concurrently with Hui-Neng (惠能) who founded the Southern School. Hui-Neng has been traditionally viewed as the Sixth and Last Patriarch of Zen Buddhism.

[192] Mencius (孟子; 372 – 289 BC) was a Chinese philosopher who is the most famous Confucian after Confucius himself.

disciples care about the God-Way, nor do they penetrate the Celestial Mechanism. They study the doctrine just to prove their intelligence and brilliance, to seek wealth and fame, to egoistically elevate at the expense of others. No longer do they study for self-correction, or for penetration into the profound secret of nature, the origin of all creatures.

To study is essentially to strain and develop human mind into the perfect morality and perfect knowledge of this world. If one studies because of honor and power, he identifies himself to the low-minded vulgar men, who do not aspire toward the precious and profound Celestial Mechanism, especially toward the sacred mission that GOD entrusts in everyone.

Human beings have two duties: one is divine mission, and the other, human title. The divine mission is the natural function that God attributes to each person, while the human title is the profane role that humans confer to humans.

Dignified men should always forge their characters into perfection, and purify their spirit so as to accomplish their divine mission. Once fulfilling the divine mission, they have no trouble accomplishing human titles. But oftentimes, people in this world embrace the twig and abandon the root. They devote themselves to the pursuit of human title, instead of caring for divine mission. What a pack of fogyish Confucians[193]!

3) TAOISM is extremely profound and mystic. It is so mysterious that only the superior-minded men could penetrate its source; ordinary men remain impermeable to this unfathomable mystery. That is why, with little or no understanding of either dogmas or principles, decadent Taoists invent extravagant exercises, indecipherable formulas that further corrupt human traditions and spread superstitions everywhere. Some of these are incantations to Deities of wind or rain, exorcism, devilish strategies that denature the saintly doctrine into idolatry or heresy. What a detriment!

Nowadays, I come to unify the Three Ancient Doctrines into a majestic temple, an everlasting shelter for mankind to escape from horrible scourges and suffering. Though these Three Ancient Temples are in ruin, with Infinite Mercy, I collect from them the

---

[193] false literates, or cracked scholars.

reusable materials and discard the debris. I retrieve intact pillars, crossbars, posts, slats, tiles, bricks, and remove broken or termite-damaged ones. I straighten up bent or curved sticks, and only discard the unfixable ones. With such materials, I edify the Temple of the GREAT WAY for mankind to venerate and practice self-cultivation. That is the Temple I establish in this Era.

Why did these Three Ancient Doctrines collapse? It is because their foundations were unstable and inconsistent. Built on sand dunes, no wonder they were naturally obliterated from wind gusts and/or tornados. Nowadays, I did instruct you to establish a solid and stable foundation, before building the majestic Temple of CAO-DAI GREAT WAY. Thus, this saintly doctrine will definitely last longer than the three previous ones.

METHOD OF WORKSHIP

Here I briefly explain the Cult of CAO-DAI GREAT WAY.

Why did I instruct you to worship "the DIVINE EYE", and not the images or statues like those in other religions? Children! You should understand that GOD is PRINCIPLE. This PRINCIPLE animates and encompasses the entire Universe. I am not human and do not utilize a corporal body that is visible to you. Therefore, worshipping the Divine Eye is worshipping ME.

Why does the Divine Eye symbolize your MASTER? I have taught: "Eye is master of the Mind, and the two sources of Light; Light is Spirit; Spirit is GOD; GOD is ME". EYE is the DIVINE HEART or CONSCIENCE in humans. That Conscience is the Creator, i.e., the SPIRIT, and SPIRIT is the Principle of the Absolute Emptiness. This immutable, eternal, and absolute Principle is GOD.

When an initiate transmutes Quintessence into Energy, Energy into Spirit, Spirit into Infinity, and Infinity into Absolute Emptiness, he opens up the Mystic Sight[194].

What is that Unique Mystic Sight? It is the Divine Eye. In humans, it is located in the Nirvana Chamber[195], gathering the entire

---

[194] The Unique Mystic Sight is the spiritual sense with which humans communicate with invisible worlds.

pure Yang energy of DAO. Human eyes are corporal and serve as the Yin-Yang pair. In analogy, the Supreme Being is God Eye whereas the two sources of light, the Sun and Moon, constantly lighting up the entire universe in the eternal rhythm of day-and-night, keeping the mechanism of Creation in its endless operation.

Poem:

Comprehend the miraculous DAO through the esoteric method,

To forge into Immortals and Buddha via the two eyes,

Where the promoter of the Yin-Yang pair resides,

To unify Spirit and Energy in the head crown.

Here I explain the LAMP OF ABSOLUTE EMPTINESS.

Before the creation of Heaven-Earth, the Energy of the Absolute Emptiness encompassed and illumined the entire Universe. It is the Center of the Universe, i.e., DAO. This DAO then engenders the Supreme Being[196] that, in turn, creates the Dyad. The Dyad comprises the Yang and Yin (dynamic and static). Then the Yin-Yang pair engenders all creatures.

The lamp that you place at the center of the altar symbolizes the Light of Conscience. Immortals and Buddha transmit esoteric traditions through it; and you attain spiritual enlightenment also through it. It is the Divine Light, exactly at the center, never flickering, never shaking, and illumines the entire Cosmos. While the Sun and Moon have day-and-night cycle, the Divine Light is always bright, immutable and eternal. Thanks to it, humans and all other beings are created, reproduced, and alive in joy and peace. Thanks to it, Heaven-Earth are illumined and perpetuated. Thanks to it, the initiates can transcend from profane into Immortals and Buddha. Should it shift to the left, it becomes satanic; to the right, diabolic;

---

[195] Nirvana Chamber, i.e., the ni-wan (the mud-pill) center, is the Crown Chakra of Hindu Yogic systems, and is connected to the Big Dipper and the hypothalamus gland.

[196] the +Infinity, the Monad

exactly at the center, it is the True DAO. Children! Try to grasp this principle. It is in your heart. A calm, serene, and pure heart is the Imponderable Nature of DAO; on the other hand, a conscience that flickers under the influence of devil and adopts wickedness and brutality is the diabolism. Children! There is nothing else than that.

As for the TWO CUPS OF WATER, they symbolize the Yin-Yang pair (static and dynamic). The Yin-Yang pair forms the static and dynamic promoter of Heaven-Earth; they are Quintessence and Spirit in humans. Without Quintessence and Spirit, how can esoteric practitioners forge their saintly fetus? Without the Yin-Yang pair, how can Heaven-Earth engender all beings? Without male and female, how can all beings reproduce and multiply? Thus, the Yin and Yang constitute the prodigious static-dynamic mechanism of Creation. The Yin-Yang pair also manifests as the Sun and Moon, represented by the PAIR OF LAMPs on the altar (the Dyad). That is why esoteric practitioners who succeed in introspection attain DAO via their eyes.

The CENSER on the altar symbolizes the Pre-Genesis creation of the Spiritual Crown, forming the Five Primordial Energies and the Five Primordial Elements. Below it, the Post-Genesis SANDALWOOD BURNER symbolizes the settlement of the Temporal Hearth, engendering the Five Spiritual Senses and the Five Virtues. In analogy, on top in the human head is the Crown, and below the navel in the elixir field is the Hearth.

Regarding FLOWERS, FRUITS, and TEA, they symbolize your Three Treasures[197]. As soon as you can harmoniously unify the Three Treasures, you attain spiritual enlightenment.

Long Poem:

From the Absolute Non-Being emerges the Supreme Being

That is the Unique Globe of Divine Light,

Immaterial, invisible, intangible,

Omnipotent, omniscient, prodigious, and miraculous.

---

[197] Fruits on the altar symbolize Quintessence; Flowers, Energy; and Tea, Spirit in human.

It is the Absolute Master of the Universe,

Who creates and sovereigns all Heaven-Earth,

Who nurtures and perpetuates in peace and joy

All humans and other beings, soul and body.

Willful people who adore DAO and Virtue

Should valiantly research the Principle of Creation,

To comprehend the miraculous Mechanism of Genesis,

So as to conserve their soul and body permanently.

The Universe encompasses all Heaven-Earth,

Where the Mechanism of Genesis functions in all directions,

So as to separate Hades from Paradise;

Humans are unable to unveil such profound secret.

DAO is sometimes concealed, sometimes revealed,

Immortals and Buddha transmit it to save humans.

It clearly instructs the method of deliverance;

Observing it, humans get back to their divine origin.

This method is to avoid the karmic cycle of four sufferings,

To lead humans to spiritual enlightenment.

It utilizes perceptible symbols and visible forms,

To reveal the nature of the profoundly mystic DAO.

Man is called a Micro-Cosmos

Identical to GOD, the Macro-Cosmos.

Whatever GOD possesses,

Humans can find it within them.

Carrying diverse bodies throughout the evolution,

Clairvoyant people should persevere in self-cultivation.

Regenerate what is degraded,

Return to the divine origin with an immaculate soul.

Buddhists meditate and contemplate to seek the Truth,

To nurture Spirit, Energy, and Quintessence,

To revolve the mystic wheel without respite,

To activate the Yin-Yang pair, animating wind and cloud.

Taoists maintain serenity in mind,

To render the heart empty and imperturbable.

If flickering, the mind is flooded with a storm of thoughts,

That overturns the pure and impure like a fiery torrent!

Pious disciples should preserve the pure Conscience

From the half Yin half Yang corporal body.

Meditate to revolve the mystic cycle diligently,

Let the Yin in and the Yang out[198] is the circulating way.

Eliminating the Yin, you attain enlightenment,

As the Yin ends, the pure Yang is sustained.

In such perfect purity you penetrate the Paradise

To become Immortal or Buddha, fleeing from the incarnation cycle.

Deprived of the pure Yang, you become Demon and Mara.

Comprising both Yang and Yin, you are human.

Absorbing the primordial energy of life, you conserve the Divine Soul

And nurture your body to longevity.

Children! Try to understand this brief instruction,

As I cannot unduly reveal the Secret of Creation.

Follow the path of enlightenment to achieve self-liberation,

Observe the rhythm of GOD to exert self-deliverance.

---

[198] Vietnamese original '*xuất huyền nhập tẩn*' literally means exporting the Yang and importing the Yin; in esoteric practice it is the complete cycle of energy circulation in human body.

DAO is imperceptible, and intangible,

DAO is quiet, natural, and immutable,

DAO circulates throughout spiritual and temporal worlds,

DAO is the key to the unfathomable Genesis.

DAO is neither high nor low,

DAO does not dazzle people with miracles,

DAO is absolutely true and perfectly right,

Its omnipotence and omniscience is the Immortality Pill.

DAO animates and nurtures all beings,

DAO dispenses both life and death.

Contemplate it thoroughly and comprehend it deeply,

To be able to sketch a rough draft of the Temporal Genesis.

Cao Dai credo is clear and straightforward,

It assumes the visible to exemplify the invisible.

The Divine Altar serves as a map,

For humans to trace the norms of their self-cultivation.

Though the Altar is merely an object in the visible world,

It exposes the same principles as those in the invisible one.

Esoteric disciples should observe these principles,

Considering them the norms in their quest for Celestial Mechanism.

Why are you instructed to adore the DIVINE EYE?

The Divine Eye is the origin of all creatures.

It symbolizes the Absolute and Unique Being,

The SUPREME GOD who creates all beings.

In His care, all breeds and strains of creatures

Exist, multiply, and perpetuate.

As the Cosmic Revolution reaches the end of the Inferior Era,

The DIVINE FATHER establishes a way to save all beings.

Pious disciples should organize their internal altar.

The Eye is taught to govern the spiritual heart,

And the heart is the Master of the Mystic World,

The immutable and eternal source of Wisdom.

Keep in mind: "Eye is Master of the twin light,

"Light is Spirit, and Spirit is GOD".

It is so miraculous, so astounding

That GOD and man do not differ!

GOD is the absolutely mystic Principle,

It is the Spirit reflecting throughout the Cosmos.

In humans, it is the original nature of the soul,

That is immaterial, immutable, and eternal.

This esoteric method transforms humans from start to end,

Enlighten them by unlocking the Mystic Sight,

With clairvoyance they penetrate the absolute emptiness.

Via the Mystic Sight they communicate with invisible worlds.

To access to the original Buddha nature,

Shine the nine energy centers like brilliant pearls.

To gain telepathy, the psychic power,

Reverse the light from carnal eyes into the Nirvana Chamber.

To penetrate DAO in your heart,

Eliminate the six sense objects, i.e., the six robbers;

To free the mind from all passions,

Stop the flow of thoughts, and absolutely quiet the mind.

Attaining DAO of Non-Being,

You gain clairvoyance through the Spiritual Eye.

This Eye is Spirit of the pure Yang,

Accomplishing it you become everlasting.

Consider the arrangement of the Divine Altar,

Where the visible demonstrates the invisible,

And the Three Ancient Doctrines are revivified,

To emphasize spiritual enlightenment and righteous impartiality.

Languages are incapable of thoroughly exposing DAO,

As it is impossible to describe the Mechanism of Creation!

Everyone possesses Buddha-Nature,

Seeking it, one will discover Paradise inside.

The most miraculous mechanism of DAO

Is the Yin-Yang alliance to create Immortals and Buddha.

It is the dynamic-static promoter

That yields the Immortality from the Yin-Yang balance.

Heaven, Earth, Man share the same principle and constituents,

In humans it is the alliance of Spirit and Energy.

Like hard and soft, male and female marrying with each other,

Extracting the pure from the impure, you attain Oneness.

The Five Incense Sticks symbolize the Five Elements,

That orient toward the four cardinal points.

The Pair of Lamps represents the Yin-Yang pair,

Which is also the Sun and Moon light in day and night.

These two light sources keep following their cycle,

They take turn to illumine everywhere.

They brighten the Universe without respite,

In humans they are nothing else than the two eyes.

Eye belongs to Fire element, LI ($\equiv$) trigram, the Spirit site,

Introspect to sufficiently collect one pound;

Unite Spirit and Energy to create the miraculous pill,

Diffused, this pill becomes Energy; condensed, the Double-body.

Quintessence, Energy, and Spirit are all in humans,

Flowers, Fruits, and Tea symbolize them.

Incense Censer and Sandalwood Burner on the Altar,

Represent the Pre-Genesis Crown and the Post-Genesis Hearth.

Ascension.

PART III
(THE SUPPLEMENTAL PART)

Proof of Sanctification

This is the name list of practitioners who had received the Esoteric Teaching leagued to the branch of "Vô Vi Tam Thanh"[199], achieved spiritual enlightenment, and manifested in spiritual séances from Bính Dần year (1926) to Canh Dần year (1950).

000

The 15th day of the 8th month of Bính Tý year (1936)

SÉANCE TO PUBLISH THE SCRIPTURE OF
THE GRAND CYCLE OF ESOTERIC TEACHING

I

Awakened, I piously practiced the miraculous method;
Dematerialized, I regained the Eternal Sojourn;
Strictly following the path of Immortals and Buddha,
I sheltered in their Mercy to avoid worldly tribulations.

GIÁC-BỬU NƯƠNG NƯƠNG. I greet all coreligionists of both sexes.

---

[199] "Vô Vi Tam Thanh" is literally means the Three Purities of the Pre-Genesis.

Long Poem:

Disenchanted by this world? - Seek the method of deliverance

To evade the exile of the worldly net.

Consider the revolving mechanism of Creation,

You find human lifetime is very brief!

Do not let worldly appeals fascinate you,

Since fame and wealth are baits for demons.

In this world, morning sorrow precedes evening grief,

Try your best to evade this mourning globe.

Forge yourself to be example of Wisdom and Virtue,

Remove worldly dust and step on the bright way.

Human life is as ephemeral as water bubbles,

Do not stick to this port of ignorance with little peace or joy.

Leaving Paternal Home, have you ever wished to come back?

Being smart creatures, why do you lean toward the abyss of Satan?

Previously I had been also a host of this world,

With all emotions, desires, and passions.

Then, being awakened, I renounced them all;

Day and night I persevered in self-perfection.

Recognizing the stinky taste of life,

I was no longer interested in any worldly competition!

I learned and practiced universal love and mercy,

And maintained my heart in serenity and purity.

To prepare the Immortality Pill and Magic Potion,

I persistently purified soul and body until perfection.

This world is a pond of blood and a mountain of swords,

Like boiling oil or fiery blaze spreading calamities

everywhere.

It would be better to dust off worldly matters,

Flee from the karmic cycle with absolute emptiness of mind.

Stop fishing the moon on seafloor,

Colors and tones, forms and shapes are all worldly delusion!

The Sojourn of Immortals is inexpressibly peaceful,

While this world is full of suffering, worries, and deceptions.

As long as you are secured from chilliness and hunger,

And can take care of your spouse and children,

You should stop attaching to this world;

Otherwise, you keep transmigrating into animals to pull cart or plow. (*I'm smiling ...*)

Poem:

The phoenix cart heads to the Séance of Immortals,

To greet the Congress of the Three Purities in evolving the mystic DAO.

This precious Scripture condenses Wisdom and Virtue of all times,

Certainly it brings peace and joy to mankind.

Good-bye to all coreligionists of both sexes.

Ascension.

The 2nd day of the 9th month of Bính Tý year (1936)

II

Poem:

The Jade Palace bell reverberates to wake humans up;

Achieving enlightenment they penetrate the Sojourn of Immortals,

Where prodigious amenities are beyond imagination;

Under CAO-DAI roof they shelter from worldly tribulations.

BẠCH-BỬU TIÊN NƯƠNG. I greet all devotees.

Poem:

Thanks to my absolute faith I achieved enlightenment.

Day and night I diligently exercised self-correction.

Persevering in the four daily esoteric practices,

I made a firm resolution to evade this illusionary world.

Long Poem:

Since birth till death,

Humans suffer from countless grief.

Never have they had a moment of inner peace,

As inquietude occupied their mind throughout the lifetime.

Alas! The mechanism of Creation evolves cyclic vicissitudes,

Tying humans and other beings to their endless Karma.

This reality is so lamentable!

Karmic debts keep accumulating and burdening;

It buries human souls in the darkness with no hope or joy,

And involves them in endless expiations and reincarnations.

This world is really an ocean of grief,

In which the entire mankind plunges and drowns.

I silently complained to God

About human fate filled with scourges and suffering.

Intuitively I was self-motivated to seek the Path of Light,

So as to escape from the worldly dungeons.

Willfully I devoted myself to esoteric practice,

And renounced all worldly pleasures.

Disentangling the spool of thread in my heart,

I ended all karmic links and exterminated the inferior self.

Disenchanted by this temporal life,

I turned away from vanity and avoided all wrongdoings.

Faithfully I follow the DIVINE MASTER;

Thanks to it, my soul could regain the Paradise.

The DIVINE MASTER shone my ignorance into enlightenment,

Delivered me from the karma, and returned me to the origin.

It is great sorrow to perceive humans in this world,

Who bear all grief because of ignorance.

They count the months and years of practice,

Instead of their conscientious effort in self-cultivation

To cleanse themselves from inside out,

So as to be example of Wisdom and Virtue.

It is challenging to achieve the "Absolute Emptiness",

But everyone should strive to acquire it gradually.

The corporal body is so heavy,

It suppresses the soul like a massive mountain.

Poem:

What is there in the Fairyland?

There is Wisdom, Virtue, and Mercy,

There are spiritual treasures and miraculous prodigies,

There are perfect Spirits that regain the Unity.

DAO is the top treasure, do you know it?

DAO and Virtue circulate throughout the universe,

DAO is so precious that you should always seek;

DAO is the only thing you should never disregard!

Self-perfection is a process of filtering silver from lead,

It is rare that the precious Jade is exposed!

Take the comments of Immortals,

Do not mix pure gold with gold-plated metals.

Good-bye all devotees. I leave.

The 14th/15th day of the 11th month of Kỷ Sửu year (1950)

III

CAO-DAI FOUNDER

Poem:

The SUPREME BEING is absolutely fair in rewarding and penalizing.

HE mystically guides those who believe and adore the DAO,

HE also bequeaths the Bible of Heart, revealing the brilliant jade

To those who persevere in spiritual exercises.

Your MASTER. I greet all children of both sexes.

I exempt you from ceremonials. Maintain the quietude of mind and listen.

The doctrine of your MASTER seems difficult; yet, it is actually very simple. Hard or easy depends merely on whether the disciple can grasp the essential point. I often guide and teach the pious souls who adore the DAO and venerate the Master, who faithfully observe the rules and measures, who strictly practice self-perfection so as to transform others, and who reject worldly fame as well as egoist interests.

I note that the majority of my disciples still erroneously engage in vicious discussions on whether Immortal or Buddha is superior to the other. I am going to clarify it here:

In this Inferior Era, it is I who sovereign the Universal Congress of the Three Teachings of Buddha, Saints, and Immortals. Therefore, the DAO that I bestow will forge the initiates having Buddhist virtues into Buddha, and those having Immortal virtues into Immortals. There are also people who achieve the Saint or Sage ranks, or even reincarnate to enjoy worldly fame and wealth. That is why the DAO of your Master is named the Great Way to the Primordial Origin or the Universal Religion.

In this séance I gracefully confer on LƯU the rank of "HẬU BÁT TIÊN" with the Celestial Title "BÍCH-VÂN TIÊN CÔ"; she replaces "HÀ TIÊN CÔ" who is promoted to a superior rank.

Continue your séance. I settle on the Altar.

THE SÉANCE CONTINUED:

Poem:

I surf on the blue water that reflects radiant light,

And fly everywhere on top of a pearly cloud.

It is the Immortal Pill that saved me from the world of calamities;

Studying the Bible of Heart, I accede to the Celestial Destiny.

The Cosmic Wheel keeps revolving and generating fatal vicissitudes,

The four seasons and the eight climates infallibly pursuit their cycle.

Penetrate HÀ-ĐỒ [200] to gain the Immortal Pill,

Attain the Spiritual Unity is the DAO essential.

Diligently practice esoteric exercises in the present life,

Achieve enlightenment to join the League of "Flying Dragons"[201],

Leisurely visit angelic mounts, and bathe in divine benediction,

Explore saintly caves, and illumine in our MASTER's Wisdom.

Keep in mind our MASTER's words,

Self-perfect to attain the Absolute Emptiness,

Strain the heart to become immune to all worldly sullies,

End the profane thoughts to gain the six supernatural powers.

BÍCH-VÂN TIÊN CÔ. Greetings to all brothers, sisters, and coreligionists in this séance.

After paying off my karmic debts and regaining the celestial position, I usually spend my leisure time to explore angelic mounts and saintly caves. Now I see clearly that the corporal world is much obscure, glacial, asphyxiating, and infecting. In contrast, the spiritual world is where Wisdom and Virtue permanently reign, where rare herbs and exotic flowers flourish, where the pure, serene, calm, and delightful atmosphere revolves throughout the four seasons. People

---

[200] 'HÀ ĐỒ' refers to the Pre-Genesis Eight-Trigram plan
[201] the Paradise

in the spiritual world have no sign of aging, despite their multi-millennium longevity; and other beings never change their appearance, despite their thousand-year existence. Indeed, *"Immortals cannot reside in the profane world, and sentient beings hardly approach the Immortal realm"*.

Human life in the corporal world is as ephemeral as morning dew on a grass blade, or as snow on a mountain top. All disappear in a blink. Yet, few people grasp this startling point and reflect to seek a self-correcting method so as to evade from such delusional life that blossoms in the morning and fades in the evening. Instead, they keep competing for wealth, power, fame, and pride, ruining their souls in the path toward death.

I was blessed to receive our MASTER's Teaching early in my lifetime. Due to my absolute faith and my infallible loyalty, I attained the Celestial Title. Indeed, that is an invaluable reward after the ascetic life full of prickly setbacks, bitter deceptions, deep suffering and profound humiliation.

Poem:

Self-perfection starts with hardships to end at bliss,

With forbearance and perseverance, the ascetic passes all trials;

From bitter to prickly, and finally to sweet,

Stay tuned with esoteric practice until the last breath.

Long Poem:

In the caress of a cool breeze and fine moon,

I rode on a cloud to wander around my cave.

Suddenly the Divine Order came,

Commanding me to descend in this séance.

I compose this long poem,

To commemorate my Celestial Investiture.

CAO-DAI Founder, Senior Immortal,

Preaches the Great Way to bless all beings.

HE bequeaths the method to restore light from dark,

Also transmits the mystic vestige in the bible of heart,

For humans to recall their celestial origin,

And seek the method of self-sanctification,

So as to enjoy the bliss of Wisdom and Virtue,

And rid of all profanity with inspiring poetry and blessing wine.

With His exceptional benediction and tolerance,

HE even humiliates Himself to pamper all beings,

As long as they understand and step in the right path,

As long as they quit reveries and start self-correcting.

It is now the end of the Inferior Era,

Vicissitudes transit the universe into a new cycle.

The Mechanism of Creation cannot be duly exposed,

It is so blessed to receive the DAO of God in this Third Era.

Strive to self-perfect in preparing for the Contest of Flowery Dragons,[202]

Lagging behind, you would bog in this corporal exile for millennia.

Though all profanes suffer from the universal tribulation,

Buddha and Immortals protect those persevering in self-cultivation.

Ascension.

---

[202] alluding to the General Judgment.

"CHIÉU-MINH"
THE SÉANCE OF CHỢ-LỚN

The 23rd day of the 7th month of Tân Ty year (1941)

I

CAO-DAI FOUNDER

Poem:

CAO-DAI canonizes the successful disciples,

Whose names are inscribed in the Celestial List of Dragons;

They have conserved His pure and immutable teaching,

And it is HE who summons them back to the Nirvana.

Your MASTER greets you all.

I manifest in this world to found the Great Way,[203] primarily for the original men, who incarnate and mingle with laymen to undergo all trials, vicissitudes, calamities, and suffering of human conditions. This experience is to prepare them for their upcoming mission of guiding all beings back to the spiritual nature. You are fortunate to gain access to My Teaching. Hold your pure and infallible faith. Never give up. Follow piously the examples of Immortals and persevere in My Teaching until your last day. In the case of TRỌNG, he is also an original man, taking My Order to incarnate in this world. As he well fulfilled his secular and spiritual duties, I summoned him back to the original post.

Poem:

Valiantly persevering in esoteric practice,

---

[203] The Universal Religion

Disciples of Tam Thanh[204] are enlightened.

Braving through the karmic cycle in this world,

They rally erroneous beings back on the right track.

Thus, under the Celestial Law, I confer TRỌNG to the rank of ĐẠI-GIÁC CHƠN TIÊN. I authorize him to descend into today's séance to have a direct talk to you. I settle on the Altar.

THE SÉANCE CONTINUED

ĐẠI GIÁC CHƠN TIÊN. I greet all coreligionists in this séance.

Poem:

Upon receiving the Celestial Decree from our MASTER,

I headed up toward the West to regain the Sojourn of Immortals.

Honoring the Saintly Speech of the Divine Father,

Immortals and Buddha joyfully welcome me to the Nirvana.

Replicate Poem:

I accomplished my missions in all my incarnations,

And fulfilled all my vows and pledges.

I maintained my conscience pure like gold and firm like rock,

I progressed in esoteric practice like the growing cedar or pine tree.

I studied the Mystic Science by imitating the Creator's way,

I worked out the Spiritual Exercises by observing the Master's method.

Now as my spiritual and temporal work are well accomplished,

I blissfully receive the Divine Investiture.

---

[204] The Three Purities

Lesson in Verse:

Receiving the Celestial Decree,

I was half-asleep half-awakened,

Our MASTER unblocked the Nirvana Chamber of my head crown,

To deliver me from this world, and bring me back to Jade Palace.

In front of our MASTER I received the Divine Investiture,

And then participated in the Peach Banquet of Immortals.

I enjoy the leisure and facility of the Eternal Sojourn,

Where phoenix bow and cranes dance to welcome me.

Pure and noble pleasures charm me morning and afternoon,

Leisurely trips entertain me with grandiose scenes.

Golden lotus blossoms to support the heels

In my visit to Tử Phủ, Động Đình[205], and everywhere.

Morning on Fairy Island and evening in West Kingdom,[206]

Everywhere nature exhales irresistibly sweet-scented fragrance.

Visualizing such prodigies of the Nirvana,

Awakened people should hurry to find the return.

Recall the times our MASTER sent me for mission in this world,

To organize séances preaching the Universal Salvation.

Since then the miraculous mechanism had been established,

Then one by one our MASTER summoned back the original men.

At Trước Lý[207] esoteric vestiges have been employed

---

[205] 'Tử Phủ, Động Đình' refers to the Blue Cave of the Supreme Master of DAO, and Động Đình Lake of the Great Immortal Li Tai-Pei (李白).
[206] The West Kingdom is the House of Saints and Immortals.

To select the most pious disciples;

It is the profoundly mystic site,

Where Cao-Dai reigns and teaches the DAO.

This institution temporarily exists and will be removed,

Once our MASTER's Doctrine penetrates the human heart.

Our MASTER's method is designed as follows:

Esotericism and Exotericism are the two cycles of the DAO.

Provided that you know the Esoteric Teaching,

I will transmit to you the original doctrine,

And delineate the method to transform profane into Saint.

Receiving it, you should valiantly practice it day and night.

For all the details that were previously taught,

Always conserve and strictly follow them.

Self-perfection requires perseverance and diligence,

ĐƯỜNG TĂNG[208] attained it after myriad of bitter and prickly trials.

I frequently received support from our MASTER,

Who gave lots of advice and encouragement in my debut.

Many times trials completely boggled me,

And rendered me like a lamp in gust or a flag in storm.

But I decisively held up my infallible faith,

Thanks to our MASTER's frequent reminders.

As an absolutely faithful servant of God,

Never did I fail under the temptations of wealth and fame.

---

[207] '*Trước Lý*' is one of Chiếu Minh invocation sites.

[208] Xuanzang (玄奘; c. 602 – 664), was a Chinese Buddhist monk, scholar, traveler, and translator who described the interaction between China and India in the early Tang dynasty. He became famous for his seventeen-year overland journey to India, which is recorded in detail in the classic Chinese text *Great Tang Records on the Western Regions*.

After willfully devoting my life to the Saintly Doctrine,

I was able to get hold of the Sacred Banner on my last day.

Though regretting the coreligionists' affection,

I headed up Westward to regain the Sojourn of Immortals.

Bát Nhã Ark[209] was waiting,

Steering the Mystic Sight I headed up to Jade Palace.

What a delight in this Westward trip!

Accomplishing the mission, I was rewarded in the Celestial Court.

Poem:

Here is the blessing wine of the West Kingdom,

Let us drink for our friendship and fraternity.

Saint and profane are now separated,

But the miraculous DAO will later radiate in history.

I depart. Ascension.

---

[209] It refers to the Perfect Wisdom.

The 30th day of the 10th month of Đinh Sửu year (1937)

II

CAO-DAI SENIOR IMMORTAL

Your MASTER greets His children of both sexes.

Today, due to your sincerity as well as under the Merit Codes, I gracefully confer LÀNH[210] to the rank of NGỌC VÂN TIÊN NƯƠNG[211].

Poem:

The IMMACULATE JADE radiates at Đào-Nguyên Cave,[212]

This Noble CLOUD enjoys the Delight of Paradise,

Her ANGELIC Nature regains the ancient post,

Sheltering in the grace of the Divine Mother.

Children! Enter in deep meditation and continue the séance. I authorize this nominated disciple to descend in the séance. I settle on the Altar.

THE SÉANCE CONTINUED

Poem:

Since the day I returned to the Jade Palace,

I have enjoyed the delight of Paradise.

---

[210] Vietnamese term 'LÀNH' literally means good, or intact; and theologically it means free of sin or IMMACULATE.

[211] Vietnamese term 'NGỌC VÂN' literally means 'JADE CLOUD'.

[212] Vietnamese term 'cõi Động Đào Nguyên' literally means the PEACH-TREE CAVE, referring to the Celestial Kingdom or the Paradise where the Divine Mother reigns.

Who knows Saint and profane co-exist?

Shelter in the DAO to self-perfect body and soul.

NGỌC-VÂN TIÊN NƯƠNG. I greet the Elder Sister and all coreligionists of both sexes. Our MASTER authorizes me to come in this séance for a direct talk to you.

Long Poem:

It is deplorable for those who confuse spiritual and temporal values,

And it is delightful for those who renounce profanity.

Life in this world is like a misty cloud,

Appearing and disappearing, yet spiritual values are everlasting.

Shelter in the DAO to gain the Divine Investiture,

Cumulate virtues to support the self-perfection.

Like a carp waiting for the metamorphosis into a dragon,

You will succeed after persevering in your lifelong asceticism.

Vietnam is blessed in this Universal Amnesty,

To directly access to the Esoteric Teaching!

Sisters and brothers! As you already know Cao-Dai,

Hasten up in the self-perfection to regain the Paradise.

Have absolute faith in God and renounce the profane world,

Strictly follow the teaching and observe perseverance-forbearance,

Practice spiritual exercises diligently day and night,

Bathe in Divine Benediction to gain peace in your everyday life.

Like a boat sailing swiftly downstream,

You will cross the karmic ocean to reach the Paradise;

That is due to your effort in self-perfection,

To be on time in the return to the Nirvana.

This is my first manifestation in séance. As the medium's spirit is weak, I cannot discuss further. I will continue later. Good-bye.

Ascension.

The 30th day of the 5th month of Đinh Sửu year (1937)

III

CAO-DAI SENIOR IMMORTAL

DAO is very difficult to escalate. You should maintain a valiant and infallible faith to overcome the trials that assail you in all facets of life. With respect to esoteric exercises, you should strictly follow the Traditions taught by your MASTER in order to discover the miraculous effect of the DAO.

Poem:

In the LIMPID POND Castle she enjoys the serenity,

And gets in and out of the PALACE at her convenience.

Your MASTER gracefully conferred this title

To the JADE MAID who has practiced the method of mystic sight.

DIÊU-CUNG NGỌC NỮ [213]. That is the Celestial Title of QUÍT. She has not well accomplished in esoteric practice. Though I conferred this title to her, she still needs to continue earning more credit for her spiritual achievement.

I authorize QUÍT to descend in this séance. I settle on the Altar.

THE SÉANCE CONTINUED

I would like to greet Elder Brothers, Elder and Younger Sisters.

How blissful! Under the Order of our MASTER, I manifest in this séance to bring up some important issues. When I was in this world, I devoted myself to the esoteric practice in my very early age because of my predestined nature. Unfortunately, my religious life was so short. Thanks to the Grand Amnesty, our MASTER brought me back to the Celestial Realm. Since then, it is so hard for me to continue self-perfection with only the soul. Hence, while sheltering in your corporal sheath, try to take advantage of that apparatus to advance as much as possible on the process of self-perfection. Otherwise, you will regret the imperfection of your soul after death, as I do.

Poem:

The LIMPID POND PALACE is about to open the Peach Festival,

Its JADE radiates brilliant white rays toward the Vietnam sky.

As male and female youngsters still attach to this profane world,

I manifest with my humble words to wake them up.

---

[213] Vietnamese term 'DIÊU CUNG NGỌC NỮ'; DIÊU CUNG refers to the Palace of Limpid Pond where the Divine Mother reigns; NGỌC NỮ literally means the Jade Maid

Long Poem:

With His Infinite Mercy and Universal Love,

God spreads good seeds on the five continents in this globe.

Cao-Dai saves the world and brings mankind back to the Origin,

Embark in Bát Nhã Ark[214] to avoid the grand tribulation.

It is deplorable that humans withstand bitter trials,

And embrace sorrow in the worldly net.

Day and night, mourning tears wet their shirts,

As karmic links tie them up from head to toes.

Ignorance induces hatred and discord,

Few people discern radiant paths from the dark ones.

Blinded by the delusion of the four dungeons,

Humans squander spirit and energy, obscuring their conscience.

Enslaved to the seven emotions and the six passions,

They cultivate bad seeds in their spirit;

Yielding to evil cunning and diabolic tricks,

They gear toward sensual love, resulting in further karmic debts!

Nothing is real in this world of illusion,

Where human hearts are torn by death and separation.

Whoever contemplates deeply on this issue,

Should seek the illuminating path to return to the origin.

The method of deliverance is within the esoteric teaching,

Clairvoyant people should find in it the means to self-perfect.

Reach and accede to the serene and invisible realm,

---

[214] It refers to the Perfect Wisdom

To flee from vicissitudes and enjoy the eternal facility.

Step on golden lotus to escalate the nine ranks of Celestial Hierarchy,

Ride on blissful cloud to fly over blue mountains.

Appreciate fairy birds chirping on branches,

Magical trees lining up in seven rows of intensely green color,

Flowers with exquisite fragrances blooming at Động Đào[215],

And listen to celestial music to rejuvenate your spirit.

Knowing you are free from the world of ignorance,

You absorb the Divine Benediction and enjoy the Eternal Facility.

My coreligionists! Please contemplate this.

Ascension.

---

[215] The Peach-Tree Cave where the Divine Mother reigns.

"CHIẾU-MINH"
THE SÉANCE OF THẢO-LƯ

The 30th night/1st day of the 11th month of Mậu-Dần year (1938).

I

JADE EMPEROR SUPREME GOD

Poem:

The Divine JADE radiates and lights up the Vietnam sky,

As the EMPEROR of DAO proclaims His disciple's achievements.

SUPERIOR men receive and practice esoteric teaching,

GOD summons them back to the Paradise for the Celestial Investiture.

Your MASTER greets you all.

At this mystic time I radiate spiritual energy to accelerate your self-perfection. I bless you all.

Ascetics wait for their spiritual enlightenment, just as farmers do for the blooming and fructification of their plants. Knowing it, you should persevere in the self-perfection and never be discouraged by challenges or trials, as they pertain to the evolutionary mechanism. Notice and understand it to appease yourself.

In this séance, I proclaim NIỆM to be: "GIÁC-MINH KIM TIÊN". You continue the séance. I settle on the Altar.

THE SÉANCE CONTINUED:

Poem:

AWAKENING leads to the discovery of the Spirit of Truth,

ENLIGHTENMENT results in the revelation of mystic mechanism,

The GOLDEN fetus is created from the introspection,

The IMMORTAL body is required for the return to the origin.[216]

GIÁC-MINH KIM TIÊN greets all coreligionists.

After such a long separation,

I am so glad to be back with you.

Myriad prodigies in the Paradise delight me;

But our friendship urges me to return,

To encourage you on the steep path of self-perfection.

Rhyming Prose:

Under the serene sky of the Paradise, hundreds of flowers are blooming,

Here are the radiant lotus thrones; there, the brilliant castles.

Sitting in meditation on a square of braided reed, I nurture Spiritual Peace by counting the beads.

Suddenly, I recall the world of anguish where vicissitudes periodically recur,

Profoundly touched, I descend in this séance to warn and wake humans up.

Employing melodious poetry and tuneful proses, I delineate the Eternal Verities,

---

[216] In this poem, AWAKENING means GIÁC; ENLIGHTENMENT, MINH; GOLDEN, KIM; and IMMORTAL, TIÊN.

To disenchant people from repugnant illusions of this corporal world,

And serve the Golden Bridge across the Silver River to offer access to the Paradise.[217]

Original men! Thoroughly contemplate and decisively self-perfect to prepare for the Grand Day.

The Contest of Flowery Dragons[218] is to select Saints and Sages,

Perceiving clearly the karmic mechanism, superior men should hasten to expiate sins and return to the spiritual realm.

This perilous world perpetuates in the cycle of morning grief and evening mourning; never could it be comparable to the serenity of the Nirvana.

Esoteric science is the mystic study of the Imponderable and Semi-Imponderable; only can the absolutely pure mind discern golden chips from vile pebbles.

Caodaism assures the salvation to the Việt people; its Bác Nhã Ark[219] is fishing the immaculate souls.

Day and night, sharpen your Sword of Wisdom to rupture all karmic links,

The Celestial Gate will open at your will, and the culmination of Wisdom[220] will assure you the blissful days in Buddha land.

---

[217] It alludes to the very rare occasion that should not be missed out, based on the Chinese and Vietnamese folk tale of *the Weaver Girl and the Cowherd* in Heaven. As their love was not allowed, they were banished to opposite sides of the Silver River (symbolizing the Milky Way). On the 7th day of the 7th lunar month every year, a flock of magpies would form a bridge to reunite the lovers for just a single day.

[218] The Final Judgment.

[219] The perfect Wisdom.

[220] Vietnamese terms 'non Khứu lãnh' means the Vulture peak, a hill near Rajagriha in northeast India, which was one of the many retreats given to the Buddha for the use of the Sangha. In the context of the poem, it alludes to the culmination of Wisdom.

Ascetics should take advantage of trials and challenges to self-correct. Strive to grasp this mystic sense and be cautious. Phlegmatically overcoming difficulties or grievous situations means mastering over profane nature. Do not consider challenges as hardships; but do requite evil with good. Those are the qualities of great people or dignified men.

I bless all coreligionists. Ascension.

The 6th night of the 3rd month of Ất-Hợi year (1935)

II

CAO-DAI SUPREME GOD

Your MASTER.

Poem:

I transmit the Esoteric Method to recover the original men,

And to bless and guide all male and female children.

After hundred millennia of worldly exile, strive to return to the origin,

By willfully persevering and preserving this esoteric teaching.

Children! The Great Way has been opened. But the right track and the tortuous ones are intermingling, as it is predetermined by the Creator. Persevere and willfully hold up your pure and vigilant faith to steadily advance in the God-Way.

Tonight I authorize HỦYNH to manifest in this séance. You should resume the séance at midnight.

Long Poem:

With his valiant perseverance in self-perfection,

I blessed and guided him back when he left the world.

His outstanding conscience is like gold among pebbles,

HUỲNH now receives My Decree to return to the Paternal Home.

Children! Consider this divine confirmation,

Strive to self-deliver from ignorance and profane nature.

I am the Creator, holding the Divine Balance,

I highly reward your effort to persist in self-forging.

Children! Keep cultivating the Four Sources of Gratitude,[221]

To get back to the Immortal Realm for the Celestial Investiture.

I bless you all. Ascension.

THE SÉANCE CONTINUED

Poem:

Do people really know each other?

Yes, when they practice the absolute emptiness of Cao-Dai.

Thanks to it, the virtuous emperors assure the perpetuity of their dynasty,

Without it, even the original men perpetuate in the worldly exile.

---

[221] The Four Sources of Gratitude or Four Grand Debts toward (1) Heaven-Earth, (2) parents and teachers, (3) spiritual friends, and (4) sentient beings.

THIÊN MÔN ĐẾ QUÂN. I am NGUYỄN-VĂN-HÙYNH, returning to greet coreligionists, in particular, NIỆM, HỒNG, and my children. Listen to me.

  Since the day our MASTER summoned me back to the Jade Palace, the more I enjoy the Sojourn of Immortals, the more I feel desperate for this world of exile. In the Jade Palace, after expressing my solemn adoration to GOD FATHER, I was granted to resume my post at the Celestial Gate. Today, in the occasion of the one-hundredth day of my farewell, I descend in this séance to greet all coreligionists.

Rhyming Prose:

Heaven opens the Golden Way and Earth creates the world.

The DAO is established in this Third Era,

To build the Universal Fraternity,

And transmit the Esoteric Tradition to the best seeds of mankind,

Who can discern life from death, and good from evil.

Diligently self-cultivate and unceasingly aspire toward perfection,

Get away from carnal exigencies and illusionary vanity.

In the Nirvana you will enjoy the eternal facility and mercy,

Free from the three tormenting exiles[222] in the vicious karmic cycle.

Make up your mind to persevere in self-cultivation,

Wake up from your reveries to pilot the ark,

Leading it straight toward Paradise.

DAO teaches disciples to self-perfect and perfect others,

It specifies clearly their roles in this union.

Unfortunately, schism and discord tear off this fraternity,

---

[222] The three realms of woes or the three miserable world are the hells, the world of hungry ghosts, and the world of animals

In which jealousy, envy, and ambition lead to antagonism.

Dear coreligionists! Be advised to decisively eradicate anger

For the Original Spirit to circulate thoroughly;

Also minimize thoughts and worries

For the Energy to come in and out smoothly.

Once your true spirit sublimes from its mystic chamber[223],

You can perceive all errors or imperfection in the profane world.

Our MASTER has clearly taught us the perfect tranquility,

Who among you could penetrate it?

It is true that DAO cannot be exposed as a concrete science,

But it could be outlined as rules and codes.

Perfect tranquility should unite with the absolute emptiness,

This profound doctrine emphasizes the serenity of mind.

Contemplating on the meaning of life,

You live in this world but should not attach to it.

The corporal body is a means to create the double-body,

And elaborate the true spirit via esoteric practice.

Persevere in those daily sessions of spiritual work,

Once attaining enlightenment, you can travel to other worlds.

Good-bye coreligionists! I return to the CELESTIAL GATE,

Leaving right-wrong discussion to humans in this dusty world!

Ascension.

---

[223] The Nirvana chamber in the head crown.

The 6th night of the 3rd month of Ất-Hợi year (1935)

III

CAO-DAI SUPREME GOD

Your MASTER greets all children of both sexes. In this séance, I bestow HUY to the Rank of Immortals, celestial title "HUỆ-MẠNG KIM-TIÊN", and authorize him to manifest in this séance. Continue your séance. I ascend.

THE SÉANCE CONTINUED

Poem:

HUỆ-MẠNG KIM-TIÊN is my Celestial Title,

This is my third manifestation in your séance.

After accomplishing a pious life, I return to the Paradise.

My worldly name was BÙI QUANG HUY.

Greetings to all coreligionists. The DAO at present relies on your existence in this world to accomplish our MASTER's goals.

Long Poem:

Disciples of the Doctrine of Immortals

Should follow the past examples of Saints and Sages.

Practitioners of esoteric methods

Should diligently fulfill the four daily sessions of meditation.

This Saintly Doctrine comprises all strategies for self-perfection,

It tames the tiger inside and puts brakes on the dragon outside.[224]

---

[224] The tiger and dragon allude to the Yin and Yang, respectively.

It is definitely the mystic science of spiritual cultivation;

Achieving it, you will gain the omniscience.

This Esoteric Tradition covers all levels from low to high,

It filters the pure from the impure to elevate you toward the absolute emptiness.

But keep in mind whatever you achieve

Cannot be unduly expressed or discussed.

Self-cultivate like CHƠN-VÕ in the ÂN Dynasty,

Who sacrificed himself for the sake of others.

Not only did he save animals,

But also he applied mystic science to transform adversities.

He is really an example of dignified ascetic,

Who leave imprints in human hearts from past till present.

Regarding the word "absolute emptiness",

Seek "the absolute emptiness" in your heart.

Our VENERABLE MASTER keeps teaching us

Fall or rise depends solely on our Conscience.

The miraculous DAO is summarized in "quietude",

Perfectly "quiet" your mind to shine the true spirit.

Should your mind quivers unceasingly,[225]

Your conscience is continuously occupied and your spirit cannot shine.

It is like the infestation of the Monkey Genie in the Celestial Empyrean,[226]

---

[225] Original Vietnamese text: '*Nếu tu sớm Sở chiều Tần*' alluding to a case of inconsistency, like a man who adores the King of SỞ in the morning and switches to the King of TẦN in the evening.

[226] In the tale about the trip toward the West Heaven, i.e., toward the Sojourn of Immortals.

A situation that is so hard to resume the order.

Such muddle obstructs the Nirvana Chamber,

Confining the soul in the astray concupiscence of the five elements.

Persevere in esoteric practice throughout your life,

Once you attain enlightenment we will reunite.

I advise all of you to cheerfully live in fraternity and vigilantly accomplish your duties. As your names have been posted in the Registry of Immortals, Demons and Mara challenge you with all sorts of trials. To commemorate my Celestial Investiture, let us fraternally share blessing wine together.

Poem:

Our MASTER has posted your names in the Registry of Immortals,

Maintain your pure conscience and never let it vacillate,

Also keep your spirit immaculate,

Pay much attention to speech karma.

Ascension.

"THE SÉANCE OF CHIẾU-MINH"
TRƯỚC TIẾT TÀNG THƠ

The 14th night/15th day of the 5th month of Kỹ-Mão year (1939)

I

CAO-DAI IMMORTAL. I greet you all.

I exempt you from ceremonials. Listen:

I mystically guide those who are humble, who recognize and correct their mistakes, who are not egotistical, who hold up the DAO and faithfully conserve the esoteric tradition that is only mouth-to-ears, heart-to-heart transmitted to prevent it from adulteration or degeneration. Such preservation results in the following: First, mankind can access the original DAO; second, you can bathe in divine benediction. Nothing is worthier than that.

Long Poem:

I sovereign the noble and profound DAO,

And reward those who diligently preserve its Original Traditions.

Be determined in conserving the God Way,

Obey the Celestial Order and observe the Divine Teaching.

Strain yourselves to become honest and upright,

Never boast your virtues nor brag your competences.

Follow the examples taught in Cao-Dai doctrine,

Keep your conscience serene and abolish all vain arguments.

Day by day focus on ending all karmic links,

Fully accomplish spiritual and secular duties.

Practice esoteric exercises and amass credits of piety,

Be the most virtuous disciples.

Participate in religious activities while preserving esoteric traditions,

Never alter or adulterate the original traditions of the mystic DAO.

Scrupulously observe the five precepts and the three refuges,

Never dispute fame or wealth.

Today a disciple regains his throne of lotus,

His name, MINH-HUẤN, is nominated in the Celestial Investiture.

Nothing is more valuable than divine benediction,

I authorize him to descend in your séance.

Today I bestow to MINH-HUẤN the Celestial Title of ĐẠO-ĐỨC KIM TIÊN. Children! Try to grasp its sense and implications.

Ascension.

THE SÉANCE CONTINUED

Poem:

I gained WISDOM by strictly preserving the esoteric traditions,

I accumulated VIRTUE by keeping intact the Original Nature.

I maintained my conscience immutable like GOLD,

I now regain my lotus throne in the Sojourn of IMMORTAL.

ĐẠO-ĐỨC KIM TIÊN. At this time being and under our MASTER's Order, I come to greet all coreligionists, and discuss some aspects of Wisdom and Virtue.

Since the day I received the Decree to return to the Nirvana and report to our MASTER, I have realized that the Celestial Law is perfectly impartial and distributes rewards and penalties with an absolute justice. Coreligionists! You should understand that disciples of the Grand Cycle who scrupulously observe the esoteric traditions will be mystically guided by Divine MASTER, and at the point of their death they receive His Celestial Decree to regain their ancient throne. Those who follow their own impetus, acting against the Natural Laws, seeking quarrels or disputes, mistaking the wrong to be right, and disregarding God's Will, will hardly get any decent results. But even if they maintain a sterile asceticism throughout their lifetime, at death their original spirit evades their body without the Celestial Decree and could not regain their original throne. By then, it is too late for the repentance! They have to submit to the Creator's law of reward or expiation. Coreligionists! Follow strictly what you are taught so as to live accordingly with the Natural Nature. Never listen to anyone else but our MASTER's Instructions, to avoid swaying the DAO from its sacred goal, because the esoteric teaching that our MASTER transmits to us primarily aims to salvage the original men, not the progressive ones. That is the selection mechanism. If you disregard our MASTER's selection, with your free will you may recruit progressive men and they will cause you much trouble and harsh trials; they also exploit the Saintly Doctrine and blaspheme it. Thus, from now on, you should be cautious about admitting disciples so as not to thwart our MASTER's Will and later, not to regret it bitterly.

Poem:

Weigh carefully your spiritual and secular behaviors,

So as to become dignified disciples!

You would rather refuge under a tranquil sacred banner

Than wave an immense megalomania of ambition.

God the Creator has traced a radiant path,

Your karmic vehicle should avoid the tortuous tracks.

Either glad or sad, do not gossip it;

Either good or bad, do not comment it.

I greet all coreligionists. Ascension.

The 23rd of the 9th month of Tân Ty year (1941)

II

CAO-DAI FOUNDER

CAO-DAI FOUNDER blesses those who make great efforts,

And bestows them the title and throne in the Celestial Noblesse.

HE instructs all disciples to strictly preserve the Saintly Teaching,

So as to receive His Sacred Order to be back to the Paradise.

Your MASTER. I greet you all.

This time, I manifest in the séance to proclaim the Celestial Investiture to VINH. Children! Meditate in deep quietude to capture the divine emission.

THE SÉANCE CONTINUED

Poem:

My SAINT-ESPRIT delightedly evades from the corporal world,

And blissfully refuges in the Paternal Home;

Thanks to my persistent esoteric practice,

I was able to expiate most of my karma.

LINH-BỬU CHƠN NHƠN. Greetings to all coreligionists.

Today our MASTER authorizes me to manifest in your séance to share the blessing with you.

Lesson in Verse:

At the end of the Cosmic Cycle, DAO is reopened to save the world,

It is the periodic salvation for the original men.

By means of the Esoteric Teaching, our MASTER spreads His net,

To fish the enlightened and sieve the ignorant.

Everyone knows Caodaism by its name,

Yet rare people expertise in its esoteric traditions;

Absorbed in the conquest of fame and vanity,

Humans obscure their conscience with powers and profits.

I myself was also lost part of my lifetime,

Thanks to our MASTER, I was awakened from such reveries,

And able to discern right from wrong,

As well as the Path of Buddha from those of Mara.

Then I sought the method of deliverance,

Under our MASTER's feet, I strictly observe the integral asceticism.

Indeed, while being imprisoned in the carnal shell,

No one could avoid committing errors and sins.

Thanks to the firm and absolute faith to CAO-DAI,

I self-armored in our MASTER's Esotericism.

Despite myriad bitter or prickly trials,

I persevered in the abrupt path toward our MASTER.

Now as I paid off my karmic debts,'

And no longer worried about the fatal vicissitudes of this world,

In the quietude of the Paradise,

I attend the morning Celestial Court and perform the evening meditation.

Thanks to the years of perseverance in practicing esoteric exercises,

And the spiritual determination until my last breath,

Our MASTER mystically guided and blessed me,

And delivered me from the ocean of karma.

As my karmic debts are paid off,

I leave traces of my ascetic life in the Séance of Trước Tiết Tàng Thơ.

Coreligionists! Piously adore and preserve our MASTER's cults,

To win His Infinite Benediction in the future.

Persevere in the spiritual work,

Within several years completely purify your soul and body.

One day you will reach the Sacred Goal,

And escalate the God-Way while holding the Sacred Banner.

Manifesting in this séance to retrace my pious life,

I would advise you to strictly and patiently follow our MASTER,

The more you practice the miraculous DAO, the more you discover its profound implications,

The higher you elevate in the Celestial Hierarchy, the deeper you identify to the Universal Conscience.

Ascension.

The 5th of the 8th month of Đinh Sửu year (1937)

III

CAO-DAI SUPREME GOD

Your MASTER. I greet all disciples of both sexes.

In this séance I bestow to CHIÊM the Celestial Title "ĐẠO-NGẠN[227] CHƠN QUÂN". Continue the séance. I ascend.

THE SÉANCE CONTINUED

Poem:

The miraculous doctrine is preached to save mankind,

But even the superior people hardly reach the PORT of WISDOM.

Discern clearly the real from the unreal,

Revere God and Divine Beings, your name will be posted in the Celestial List.

ĐẠO-NGẠN CHƠN QUÂN. Greetings to all great brothers, sisters, and coreligionists who reunite in this séance to celebrate my Celestial Investiture.

Poem:

Here is something we should remind each other:

The universal chess game is so confounded!

Day and night, forge yourself in the path of Wisdom and Virtue,

And disclose the cultivation method to save mankind.

---

[227] 'ĐẠO NGẠN' literally means the PORT of WISDOM or of DAO.

Lesson in Verse:

Metempsychosis is so horrible to consider!

Devilish traps and malicious tricks are set everywhere.

Caught in such fatal vicissitudes of this world,

Humans have no way to avoid grief and bitterness.

Karmic debts are contracted and expiated,

This world is indeed an immense delusion!

Passionately lost in such reveries,

I did not realize that I had gone through eighty-one incarnations.

Considering it, I burst into tears,

Many times I had to bear unimaginable trials to expiate my sins.

What a misery! I kept diving into this illusionary world,

And even being incarcerated in a variety of animal bodies.

Due to ignorance, I committed so many errors and sins,

I changed from animal bodies to humans and vice versa.

Frequently laughs intermingled with sobbing,

What an impassable sort of expiation!

Once upon a time, I had resided in the quietude of the Paradise,

Violating the Celestial Codes I had been exiled in this purgatory.

Inadvertently committing such errors,

I had to pay for them in my incarnations since then.

And I sank further and further in the corporal world,

Being passionate of fame and wealth;

I repeatedly risked my life under the gusts of arrows or gunshots,

Being exhausted by fatigue, chilliness, and starvation.

Yet in some lifetimes, I also devoted myself to servicing humans,

Opening my heart and arms to the salvation of all peoples.

Though three times I renounced the secular life,

Being lost in the labyrinth of the six paths of metempsychosis,

I was unable to regain my original throne.

Since I have been just recently delivered from the corporal world, my spiritual energy is still weak. I will continue the discussion later.

Ascension.

"CHIÉU-MINH"
THE SÉANCE OF PHÚ-LÂM

The 5th day of the 9th month of Mậu Tý year (1948)

I

CAO-DAI SUPREME GOD

Your MASTER. I greet all children of both sexes.

In this séance I grant your fervent wishes to nominate MƯỜI into the Order of Immortals with the Celestial Title of "THANH-HƯ[228] ĐẠO NHƠN". Continue the séance. I settle on the Altar.

THE SÉANCE CONTINUED

Poem:

Cultivate the SERENITY of your heart with the essential DAO,

Captivate the energy of the EMPTINESS to nurture your Golden Body.

Attaining the spiritual enlightenment you will shine like the South Superstar,

Accomplishing your karmic expiation you will evade the corporal world.

Replicate Poem:

The corporal world is the ardent furnace producing endless chains of grief,

Persevere in self-cultivation to regain the Divine Origin.

---

[228] 'THANH HƯ' literally means SERENE EMPTINESS.

The Peach Banquet and the Angelic Cave are your Lotus Throne,

Where, in the morning and evening, you will attend the Celestial Court.

Replicate Poem:

In the Celestial Court you will adore the GREAT IMMORTAL,

CAO-DAI SUPREME GOD, for His elaboration to save the universe.

HE bestows the GREAT WAY throughout this world,

To fish the original men from the ocean of karma.

THANH HƯ ĐẠO NHƠN. I greet all coreligionists.

Long Poem:

Thanks to your wish for this fraternal meeting,

As you fervently prayed and supplicated our MASTER.

With the Infinite Mercy, HE authorizes me

To come to this séance to meet with you.

Neither the pen nor words could express our joy,

Let us greet each other by sipping a couple of wine chalices.

Everything in this world is impermanent,

Understanding it, you should focus on your self-cultivation.

Attaining the spiritual enlightenment, you will regain the serene realm,

Where you enjoy the eternal facility with angelic chess and saintly wine.

Avoid contracting further karmic debts from secular activities,

Refrain from the desires of acquiring fame and wealth.

Follow the examples of Saints and Sages,

Diligently self-cultivate the seeds of love and mercy,

With which Buddha and Immortals usually save humans,

Freeing them from the karmic cycle to return to the Celestial Kingdom.

This world is full of vicissitudes,

Nothing is permanent, because oceans can become continents.

Self-perfect to gradually move toward the Eternal Sojourn,

Cultivate Wisdom and Virtue to establish the Immortal standard.

Our Paternal Home is the Nirvana or the Paradise,

While this illusionary world is a port of ignorance or an exile.

I recall my incarnations in this corporal world,

Where I endured lots of harsh trials in my ascetic life;

Yet I was always content with my status as a devoting disciple,

Gradually I elevated the ladder of Immortals by repenting my sins.

Now that my sacred will and vows have been accomplished,

I would like to give you some advice, dear coreligionists,

Forge your souls as noble and pure as the apex of the pine or cedar trees.

Spiritually enlightened, we will certainly meet in the Peach Banquet.

Now it is time to separate from each other,

Though inconsolable, Immortal and profane belong to two distinctive realms.

Ascension.

The 4th day of the 11th month of Giáp Tuất year (1934)

II

CAO-DAI FOUNDER

Poem:

At the spiritual apex is the SUPREME BEING's throne,

From this Highest Tower[229], HE mystically saves the profane beings,

By founding and preaching the DAO in the corporal world,

To teach humans the method of fleeing from scourges and grief.

Children! Maintain the serenity and sincerity of your mind. I authorize NGỌC-THIÊN[230] TIÊN NƯƠNG to descend in the séance. I ascend.

Poem:

The precious JADE[231] has now been adored,

This HEAVENLY Secret cannot be unduly revealed;

Immortal and profane differ by the clairvoyant mind,

Link together in the self-perfection to catch up with the new Era.

NGỌC-THIÊN TIÊN NƯƠNG. I greet all brothers and sisters. Upon the Divine Order, I manifest in this séance to expose some truly honest words.

---

[229] The High Tower literally means Cao-Dai in the Vietnamese language.

[230] NGỌC THIÊN literally means the HEAVENLY JADE.

[231] the Saint-Esprit or the Universal Conscience.

RHYMING PROSE:

Receiving the Celestial Decree from the Ninth Heaven,

And ending my worldly life, I rode a crane to the Paternal Home;

Under our MASTER's feet, I received His blessing,

And regained my eternal post in servicing to the JADE EMPEROR.

Karmic debts, both positive and negative, were paid off,

The Saint-Esprit radiantly shone in me and elevated me to the Paradise.

Subserviently kneeling under our MASTER's Throne,

I submitted my work of piety to enter the Jade Palace.

It was our MASTER who had presided the predetermined selection,

In which I had been among the twenty disciples incarnated in Vietnam,

To undertake the common mission.

Then at the debut of the Cao-Dai preaching,

Realizing this illusionary world I sought the Spiritual Master,

And received the esoteric traditions archived from the Three Purities.

After diligently persevering in the esoteric practice,

I paid off my karmic debts and regained the Celestial Post.

Via the beaked basket, I leave some pious messages,

For the profane to understand the Natural Nature,

And hasten in the self-perfection to save their nine genealogical lineages,

Together with their seven ancestral levels, they will return to the Original Unity.

Only when I return to my celestial post, I realize the Infinite Celestial Mechanism. So, I would advise you to persevere in the esoteric practice, and hopefully we could soon gather under our MASTER's Throne. To reach this goal, you should expiate your karmic debts, pay them off until your last breath.

Ascension.

The 9th day of the 1st month of Tân Ty year (1941)

III

CAO-DAI SUPREME GOD

Poem:

CAO-DAI SUPREME GOD radiates His Divine Light,

To bless His children who attain the spiritual enlightenment;

Heaven-Earth approve their sincere will,

HE congratulates all of their glorifications.

Today is a blessed day. I, along with the Immortals and Buddha, manifest in your séance. I bless and authorize HỘI to descend and share her bliss with you. I settle on the Altar.

THE SÉANCE CONTINUED

Poem:

In the JADE Palace I enjoy the leisure,

While the TREASURE Saint-Esprit radiates everywhere;

From the Angelic Sojourn that God assigns me,

I ride a crane flying on cloud to ramble the corporal worlds.

NGỌC-BỬU[232] TIÊN NƯƠNG. I greet all coreligionists of both sexes. Today is a blessed day. Under our MASTER's Order, I come to share my joy with you. Since the day I received the esoteric tradition leagued by our MASTER, I have continuously maintained my serene conscience, and always upheld my sincere faith. Thoroughly, valiantly, diligently, and immutably, I performed the spiritual exercises in the four daily sessions without exaggeration or alteration. To reward my effort, our MASTER summoned me back to the Sojourn of Immortals where the eternal facility reigns.

Long Poem:

After paying off my karmic debts,

I regained the Paradise to kneel under our MASTER's Throne.

Bathed in the divine benediction,

I was assigned to a post in the Limpid Pond Palace[233].

Myriad prodigies and miracles charm me,

Celestial Symphony and Peach Banquet delight me.

I am perfectly satisfied of getting back to my original post,

To my Lotus Throne, Celestial Title, as well as all the privileges.

I am so delighted in the Sojourn of Immortals,

Definitely free of fatal vicissitudes in the corporal worlds.

Today I am very glad being authorized to descend in your séance,

And to fraternally share my joy with coreligionists.

I recall countless troubles of the corporal world,

Where karmic links tie humans up.

Self-perfection means cultivating the best spiritual seed,

---

[232] NGỌC BỬU literally means the JADE TREASURE or the PRECIOUS JADE.

[233] Diêu Đài or Diêu Trì Cung literally means the Limpid-Pond Palace, where the Divine Mother reigns.

Which can thrive only when it comes from a good fruit.

Our MASTER always guides and saves all beings,

Who wish to escape from the cycle of grief and regain their Original Nature.

Self-perfection aims to liberate the soul for its ascension.

And nothing in this corporal world is comparable to that!

It is so fortunate for those who receive the benediction of CAO-DAI,

As GOD MASTER manifests in this world to reveal the Celestial Mechanism.

HE bequeaths to each of His disciples the Esoteric Plan,

Following it, they self-perfect in the quietude of their cell for meditation and wait for the ascension time.

This esoteric tradition simultaneously purifies soul and body,

You should faithfully practice it and strictly follow the norms.

Piously conserve the quietude and peace of mind,

To prevent the rage from the karmic ocean that threatens your frailty.

Performing self-cultivation, you should observe the Celestial Law,

That assures the absolute and immutable Justice.

The richer wisdom you acquire, the nobler virtue you should establish,

As your richer wisdom induces Satan to tempt you with harsher trials.

Willful heroes! Do not be discouraged!

You are selected only when you win the contest of Wisdom and Virtue.

Challenges and trials are to distinguish the weak from the strong,

After several selections, your name will be posted on the list of Elects.

The day our MASTER approves your ascension,

You will quit the corporal worlds to return to the Sojourn of Immortals.

I am so glad for you, coreligionists,

As you comprehend the bible of heart our MASTER bestows.

You have received such an invaluable treasure,

Diligently practice it in the four daily sessions of meditation.

Enjoy the miraculous mechanism and the springtime,

I wish you the best in attaining the Celestial Rank.

I greet all coreligionists of both sexes. I leave the séance.

Ascension.

"CHIẾU-MINH"
THE SÉANCE OF LONG-ẨN

The 16th day of the 5th month of Đinh Sửu year (1937)

I

CAO-DAI SAVIOR

Poem:

CAO-DAI canonizes the Elects into the Celestial Hierarchy,

HE radiates the Saint-Esprit to guide and save mankind.

HE delivers humans from the perpetual cycle of grief,

By revealing the DAO in this Inferior Era.

Your MASTER. I greet you all.

Today, in commemoration of ĐỆ's One-Hundredth-Day, you reunite in this séance to celebrate and honor her success in creating the Aura of Light[234] and returning to her ancient post. Thus, I bestow to ĐỆ the Celestial Title "NGỌC-DIÊU[235] TIÊN NƯƠNG", and authorize her to manifest in this séance. Continue the séance. I settle on the Altar.

THE SÉANCE CONTINUED

Greetings to all brothers, sisters, and coreligionists.

---

[234] The Double-body, the Golden Body or Buddha Relic.

[235] NGỌC DIÊU literally means the JADE POND or the JADE in the LIMPID POND.

Poem:

My JADE is precious but not yet brilliantly sparkling,

In the LIMPID POND Palace I am tranquilly settling;

I enjoy so much the prodigies of the Paradise,

And refuge in our MASTER's mercy.

Replicate Poem:

Though being so glad to reside in the eternal realm,

I still miss the sisters in our communal house.

As you are in this world and I have regained my original post,

I am waiting for your return to the Paternal Home.

NGỌC-DIÊU TIÊN NƯƠNG. I am so blessed by our merciful MASTER. Not only did HE save but also promoted me to the Celestial Hierarchy. While alive, my work of credit and meditation was so mediocre. Now I regret in vain such indolence. Though being recruited into the eternal sojourn, I still need to continue the esoteric practice until thoroughly purifying the three souls. As for you, while being in the corporal world, please strive to persevere in your self-perfection to invigorate your original spirit so as to attain higher ranks in the Celestial Hierarchy.

In the past, my spiritual cultivation was not as good as yours. But, touched by my brief lifespan in this world, our MASTER mercifully guided and saved me. Today I compose a rhyming prose to commemorate my Celestial Investiture.

Rhyming Prose:

Thanks to my self-cultivation in the past lives,

I can catch up with the universal transition this time.

Being enlightened by the esoteric practice,

And mystically guided by our merciful MASTER,

I was able to evade the cycle of the four sufferings,

And embark on the salvation ark to return to the Paradise.

From my post I improvise while watching the pine and cedar trees,

In the excursions I leisurely enjoy the grandiose spectacles.

Recalling this corporal world, I am disheartened by its corrupt traditions;

Engaged in their struggles for life, humans do not realize the fatal vicissitudes,

As this world is just an immense expiation site,

And at death they have to let go of everything gained.

Hence, knowing the bitter remedy, you need to intake it,

To become supernatural, you should persevere in the esoteric practice.

Work accumulated month-after-month one day can turn into great success,

Self-cultivation in a single life can lead to the complete deliverance.

Dear coreligionists! Decisively persist in the spiritual practice,

Attaining enlightenment, you become Immortal.

Human life cycles between sorrow and happiness,

While in the DAO no one cares about competition.

Focus on fulfilling your secular duties,

Cultivate harmony, love, and honesty,

So as to set examples to our posterity,

On their way toward spiritual enlightenment.

Dear coreligionists! The corporal world is merely a delusion. It is the ocean of suffering, the fortress of grief, where dissolute souls have been exiled. This place consists of all kinds of toxic commodity, few are sweet and hearty, but many bitter and piquant, few straight lanes, but many tortuous roads. Thanks to your awareness, you decisively uphold your will and persist in the self-cultivation. You should consider fame and profit as negligible as a bird feather, whereas wealth and noblesse are as dispensable as morning dew or water bubble.

Few can live hundred years in this corporal world; but all is everlasting in the spiritual realm.

Ascension.

The 27th day of the 4th month of Bính Tuất year (1946)

||

GIÁC-MINH[236] KIM TIÊN

Poem:

The CLAIRVOYANCE guides humans away from the port of ignorance,

The brilliant Pearl[237] rallies them back to their original realm,

Where golden table, jade cups, and Divine Beings are awaiting,

And where their names are inscribed in the Registry of Immortals.

I greet all junior brothers and sisters.

Esoteric practitioners always wish to attain spiritual enlightenment the fastest way possible. But in fact, some could reach their objectives very soon, while others spend a lot of time without coming close to their goals. Fast or slow is determined by each individual's destiny and karma. Nevertheless, any disciple, who faithfully upholds a pure and infallible will, strictly observes the

---

[236] GIÁC MINH literally means ATTAINING CLAIRVOYANCE.
[237] The Saint-Esprit or the Conscience

rules, and diligently performs the esoteric exercises, will certainly attain spiritual enlightenment and have his/her name listed in the Registry of Immortals.

In this séance I, under our MASTER's Order, attest the commemoration of TRONG's One-Hundredth-Day, and nominate him "NGỘ-TÁNH[238] CHƠN NHƠN". Continue the séance. I leave.

THE SÉANCE CONTINUED

Poem:

Nothing is comparable to the PENETRATION of the DAO!

Strive to purify your NATURAL NATURE in this current life,

Detach the Saint-Esprit from your carnal body to regain the Sojourn of Immortals,

Pay off your karma to enjoy the Eternal Facility at the Peach Cave.

At the Peach Cave you will wait for the Contest of Dragons on cloud,[239]

To be assigned in the Nine Ranks of the Celestial Hierarchy;

Your work credit will direct you into the path of either Buddha or Immortals,

Your evolutionary level will lead you into the Three Stages of Divine Initiation.

NGỘ TÁNH CHƠN NHƠN. I greet all coreligionists of both sexes. Please sit down and exempt yourselves from ceremonials.

Once stripped out of the heavy and sullied body, I clearly realize that human life in this temporal world is such nonsense. This

---

[238] NGỘ TÁNH literally means THE PENETRATION OF THE NATURAL NATURE.

[239] the General Judgment

place is merely a purgatory where we pay off our karmic debts and rectify our errors. Impious people blindly wallow in the delusional attractions of this world; they unceasingly create more and more karma, and eternize themselves in the vicious cycle of incarnations and reincarnations. As for the pious ones, their Divine Soul quickly disillusions them of this world and aspires them toward the radiant path; they uphold the virtues, and purify their body and souls; these righteous people are blessed to receive the esoteric traditions to create their Aura of Light so as to evade from the karmic cycle, attain the spiritual enlightenment, and regain the Celestial Realm.

Poem:

I am full of gladness, sadness, as well as joy,

Glad of being able to penetrate the Sojourn of Immortals,

Sad of seeing my coreligionists suffering in the corporal world,

And joyful of anticipating our reunion in the Celestial Realm.

Long Poem:

Today I am blessed to receive the Celestial Title;

It is the result of multiple ascetic lives,

In my last incarnation I was fortunate to receive the esoteric traditions,

Scrupulously practicing them, I was able to regain my Celestial Post.

Deciding to be the SUPREME GOD's devoted servant,

I no longer cared about fame or vanity.

I withdrew from the noisy and sumptuous places,

I followed Buddha and Immortals' examples in publishing scriptures and books.

Temptations and trials challenged me in myriad forms and scenarios,

I overcame them with composure.

I persisted in the esoteric practice,

Achieving work credit and spiritual enlightenment, I accessed the Paradise.

In the tranquil serenity, lotuses greet me and chrysanthemums smile to me,

What a calm rejuvenation in the Sojourn of Immortals!

Floral scents are spreading everywhere,

And the spectacles are extremely splendid and serene.

Now settling in the Celestial Realm,

I feel pity for my former co-disciples,

Who are still struggling with trials,

And mingling in this world while humbly leading an ascetic life.

It is because of the Creator's predetermined plan,

As disciples, you should wait for the GOD MASTER's Order.

Though currently profane and saint are separated,

On the Final Day we all reunite at the origin.

People lament for separation and death,

Because they do not know the causes or reasons.

Esoteric practitioners can absolutely master their intelligent spirit,

And end the karmic cycle to leisurely enjoy the eternal peace of mind.

Brothers! Now you are waiting for the Order from the Ninth Heaven,

Revise your self-cultivation and be ready, as the Final Day is about to come.

Check your virtues, work credits, and spiritual achievement,

Accomplishing them, you will certainly return to the serene celestial realm.

As confidants I would tell you,

Persevere in self-perfection until the last day, to reunite with our MASTER.

We will meet each other in the Sojourn of Immortals,

And will share the Peach Banquet after the Contest of Dragons on cloud.

Poem:

This is an indigenous wine of Viet-Nam,

Not the angelic one from Buddha land;

Let us share it in this commemoration,

Before the separation of saint and profane.

Ascension.

The 15th day of the 4th month of Át Dậu year (1945)

III

CAO-DAI SUPREME GOD

Your MASTER greets you all.

Poem:

Bear the hardships in this ascetic life,

After that, you will leisurely enjoy the eternal facility;

Freed from the karmic cycle, you become everlasting,

Exiting the six paths of metempsychosis, you no longer reincarnate.

There is no sorrow or grief in the Sojourn of Immortals,

Nor come or leave in the Paternal Home.

I have entrusted to you the esoteric method,

Persevere in it to regain your original post.

I approve your petition and sincerity. Thus, I proclaim HÓA the Celestial Title of "NGỌC-HOA[240] TIÊN NƯƠNG". Continue the séance. I settle on the Altar.

THE SÉANCE CONTINUED

Poem:

The hidden JADE is in the marvelous mountain where the phoenix joyfully crows,

The Lotus FLOWER serves as the Golden Throne in the Nine Levels of the Celestial Noblesse,

With the spiritual enlightenment, I regained the original post,

Under CAO-DAI's shadow, I washed off my karmic debts.

Poem:

The karmic debts had tied me up in so many lifetimes,

I am glad being freed from those incarnations.

Keep in mind our MASTER's affection and our fraternal union,

Also the infallible Faith and strong will are essential on God-Way.

NGỌC HOA TIÊN NƯƠNG. Greetings to all coreligionists in this séance …

I was delivered from this corporal world solely due to our MASTER's mercy, because my self-cultivation was inadequate. Luckily, we are in the Grand Amnesty. Now I clearly realize that human life is just like fog and dew, appearing and disappearing

---

[240] NGỌC HOA literally means JADE FLOWER.

instantly; a hundred-year lifetime is like a dream, in which everything is delusional. Should you persist in self-cultivation to purify your soul and body, you are bathed in our MASTER's benediction, and will be able to return to the Paternal Home after evading the corporal world.

Lesson in Verse:

Receiving the Celestial Decree from the Ninth Heaven,

I left the corporal body to penetrate in the Celestial Realm.

Alas! The corporal world is full of fatal vicissitudes,

Where humans have to bear all kinds of grief and suffering.

I am now back to the Paternal Home,

In the Peach Cave I compose poems;

On the Angelic Mount I wander with leisure,

I attend the Celestial Court in the morning and meet friends in the evening.

After just one mediocre ascetic life,

Our MASTER mercifully granted me the amnesty to regain the ancient post.

The Paradise is filled with prodigies,

In the radiant light flowers display an infinite spectrum of colors and forms.

Looking back in the corporal exile, I am profoundly touched

By its spontaneous scourges, calamities, grief, and suffering;

A hundred-year lifetime flashes out like a dream,

As humans, you should deeply contemplate to penetrate the origin.

Coreligionists! You are predestined and wise,

Please firmly hold up your will of "self-perfection to guide others";

Practice the esoteric method to attain the Three Cycles of Divine Initiation,

Let us reunite at the Summit of Wisdom in the Peach Banquet.

It is commonly said that God above has a ubiquitous eye.

Being in this transitional period of the grand upheaval,

Should you still be tempted by fame and wealth,

You will get stuck in this mire for hundreds of years.

In the occasion of my Celestial Investiture,

I would fraternally advice you,

Willfully persevere in your esoteric practice,

To be bathed in divine benediction on your last day.

So long, my co-disciples! Ascension.

DIVINE INVESTITURE

MALE NOMINATION

Celestial Title	(Saint or Birth) Name
MINH KHAI KIM TIÊN	Phan Tấn Lộc
NHỨT BỔN CHƠN NHƠN	Nguyễn Thiên Thượng
MINH BỬU ĐẠO NHƠN	Minh Tạo
TAM BỬU CHƠN NHƠN	Minh Hào
GIÁC NGỘ CHƠN NHƠN	Nguyễn Văn Dõng
CHÁNH GIÁC CHƠN NHƠN	Minh Thêm
DIỆU GIÁC CHƠN NHƠN	Minh Cẩm
GIÁC NGẠN CHƠN NHƠN	Minh Song
GIÁC THIỆN CHƠN NHƠN	Phan Quan
TỪ MINH CHƠN NHƠN	Minh Ai
HUỆ PHÁP CHƠN NHƠN	Minh Giác
THANH BỬU ĐẠO NHƠN	Lê Minh Khương
CHƠN BỬU ĐẠO NHƠN	Minh Tiến
HẠNH BỬU ĐẠO NHƠN	Minh Khai
CHƠN MINH ĐẠO NHƠN	Minh Hương
HUỆ CHIẾU ĐẠO NHƠN	Minh Bẩy
QUÃNG PHÁP ĐẠO NHƠN	Nguyễn Văn Mùi
GIÁC BỬU CHƠN QUÂN	Minh Dậm
PHÁP BỬU CHƠN QUÂN	Minh Môn
BỬU GIÁM CHƠN QUÂN	Minh Xưa
BỬU ĐẢNH CHƠN QUÂN	Minh Se

LẠC THIỆN CHƠN QUÂN	Minh Kẹm
VĂN THIỆN CHƠN QUÂN	Nguyễn Văn Hanh
KHẢI NGỘ CHƠN QUÂN	Minh Thới
ÂU THIÊN QUÂN	Minh Inh
PHỔ ĐỨC THIÊN QUÂN	Trần Minh Lục
HẢI HUỆ CHƠN QUÂN	Hoàng Huy Hòa
THIÊN BẢO TƯỚNG QUÂN	Kiều Công Kiệm
CHƠN THANH SỨ GIẢ	Ngô Văn Tịnh
KIM PHAN ĐỒNG TỬ	Minh Huỳnh
LINH BỬU THIÊN ĐỒNG	Minh Lầu
PHÙ SỨ GIẢ	Nguyễn Đăng Khoa

FEMALE NOMINATION

Celestial Title	(Saint or Birth) Name
DIỆU BỬU NƯƠNG NƯƠNG	Trương Thị Sâm
NGỌC THANH TIÊN NƯƠNG	Minh Thanh
NGỌC ĐẢNH TIÊN NƯƠNG	Minh Cảnh
NGỌC BỔN TIÊN NƯƠNG	Minh Của
NGỌC ĐÔ TIÊN NỮ	Minh Thương
THANH THIÊN TIÊN NƯƠNG	Minh Ngài
DIỆU HẠNH TIÊN NƯƠNG	Phạm Thị Tất
NGỌC LINH TIÊN NỮ	Lương Thị An
NGỌC QUYỆN TIÊN NƯƠNG	Nguyễn Thị Đát
TỪ HUỆ TIÊN NƯƠNG	Minh Thình
NGỌC LIÊN TIÊN NƯƠNG	Minh Trâm

References

ĐẠI THỪA CHƠN GIÁO 2nd Edition, Chiếu Minh Séance, Canh Dần year (1950).

LE GRAND CYCLE DE L'ESOTERISME, the French translated version in the 2nd Edition of ĐẠI THỪA CHƠN GIÁO, Canh Dần year (1950).

LE VÉRITABLE ENSEIGNEMENT DU GRAND CYCLE CAODAISTE, the French translated version by Quách Hiệp Long, Quý Ty year (2013).

French-English Dictionary: http://www.larousse.com

English-English Dictionary:
        Thesaurus Online Dictionary: http://thesaurus.com
        Merriam-Webster Online Dictionary: http://www.merriam-webster.com

TUỆ QUANG BUDDHIST Multimedia Dictionary: http://www.phathoc.net/tu-dien-phat-hoc

Vietnamese-English Dictionary: http://www.lingvozone.com

Index

65143271R00193

Made in the USA
Lexington, KY
01 July 2017